Is Violence Inevitable in Africa?

African-Europe Group for Interdisciplinary Studies

VOLUME 1

Is Violence Inevitable in Africa?

Theories of Conflict and Approaches to Conflict Prevention

Edited by

Patrick Chabal
Ulf Engel
Anna-Maria Gentili

BRILL
LEIDEN • BOSTON
2005

This book is printed on acid-free paper.

Library of Congress Cataloging-in-Publication Data

A C.I.P. record for this book is available from the Library of Congress

ISSN 1574-6925
ISBN 90 04 14450 1

PRINTED IN THE NETHERLANDS

CONTENTS

PART TWO

MANAGING CONFLICT AND IMPLEMENTING
CONFLICT RESOLUTION IN AFRICA

PREFACE

This volume is an attempt to analyse the causes of conflict in Africa, to review the various approaches to conflict prevention or conflict resolution and to discuss some of the practical difficulties in ending violence. It brings together a wide range of scholars and practitioners, with specialist knowledge of a large number of African countries.

The study of conflict and conflict resolution has, over the years, resulted in the publication of a large volume of material, extending from NGO reports to theories of war. As a result, books on the subject often lack a clear focus. For this reason, the editors have been careful to ask the contributors to address the question in a way that would ensure not just that the chapters were complementary but that the book as a whole should be coherent.

The intention here is to provide, within a single volume, a survey of the various approaches to conflict in Africa, a systematic discussion of some of the root causes of violence, as well as case studies on the consequences of violence and the effects of conflict resolution. The book is in four parts. The Introduction develops a political analysis of violence in Africa. Part I discusses a variety of theories of conflict and outlines the main approaches to conflict resolution. Part II presents case studies of conflict management and resolution. The Conclusion reviews the literature and offers an original way forward.

The editors

INTRODUCTION

VIOLENCE, POWER AND RATIONALITY:
A POLITICAL ANALYSIS OF CONFLICT IN CONTEMPORARY AFRICA

Patrick Chabal

Conflict today seems to be a hallmark of African societies. Indeed, the continent now endures a greater degree of violence than at any time since independence. From large-scale regional conflicts (as in the Central African region) to intractable civil wars (as in Angola or Liberia), by way of genocide (as in Rwanda), warlordism (as in Sierra Leone) or seemingly generalized anomic criminal activity, African men and women have endured inordinate suffering. Not only is there nowadays more civil discord, more fighting, but there is also an extraordinary degree of strife in everyday life, ranging from the abuse dispensed by police and other authorities to the increasing use of religiously sanctioned or witchcraft driven brutality. Finally, there is now more death due to hunger (sometimes, as has happened in the Sudan, deliberately engineered) on the continent than at any time in the past few decades. Government neglect and callousness inflict untold damage upon the fabric of society and the lives of innumerable individuals. Why?

There are many possible ways of approaching this question—of which the best known, though not the most convincing, is the 'greed versus grievance' debate—discussed later in the book. I propose to limit my discussion to the two broader arguments. The first links violence with the social and political pangs of development: all societies have evolved in this way. It is enough to look at the history of Europe since the sixteenth century to establish that such is truly the way of historical 'progress'. The consolidation of the state and the transformation of society cannot be achieved without force. The second is to ask whether there are features of the modernization of the African continent that make it prone to a greater degree (and range) of violence than might 'historically' be expected. Are we, in other words, confronted with a situation in Africa that differs substantially in systemic terms from that experienced elsewhere in the world?

Of course, conflict is a multi-faceted process and not one amenable to simple explanation. From state-controlled warfare to psychological brutality, there is a wide range of social, economic, political and personal factors that can account for what is taken to be a single phenomenon. Equally, the question of cause and effect, and of possible motivation, invites careful consideration. The issue of why force is meted out, collectively or individually, is always intricate, even if its consequences are plain to behold. Seen as morally wrong, evil, socially disruptive and politically unsustainable, violence nevertheless forms part of the everyday (political and economic) calculus of life and, as such, deserves analysis, rather than mere (albeit sincere) condemnation.

I specifically want to examine here the relation between conflict and the practice of politics in contemporary Africa. What this means is that I am leaving aside other, equally significant, aspects of the phenomenon in question such as the sociological, economic, psychological, religious or the personal. Whilst, clearly, various aspects of violence are connected, in that they impinge on all the areas mentioned above, as well as on areas of individual and collective life that are not so easily explained by social science, it is useful to circumscribe one's enquiry analytically. Privileging the political, as I do, does not in any way imply that I neglect the link between all the above mentioned facets of the question, but only that I study violence by analysing the exercise of power on the continent. Thus, for instance, an explanation of the genocide in Rwanda would focus on the political configuration that made this appalling event possible. Clearly, however, any comprehensive study of genocide ought to delve as well into the individual and psychological causes of killing.

Concentrating attention on the connection between violence and power means analysing the ways in which it is politically meaningful and the political implications it may have. It is, inevitably, to limit one's focus on what may appear to be an excessively instrumental view. There are many instances where the political dimension of the phenomenon seems to be secondary to the personal, psychological or moral: witness the chopping off of hands in Sierra Leone. There are indeed serious questions to be asked about what has happened in that country in the past decade—not least whether the 'drug' of violence did not become an end in itself—but what concerns me here is what political significance these events may have had in the historical context of contemporary Sierra Leone. Others may, quite justifiably, want to argue that the psychic damage inflicted on young people in such conflicts is of greater overall moment than the more contingent political calculations involved. Yet, it cannot be denied that the calculus of power presides over the destiny of all communities, however wretched they may become.

Finally, an analysis of this type implies a study of the causalities that may be found between the two. As such, it brings about a search for conceptual and systemic generalizations, which could appear to be overdrawn. Often, crime, conflict, strife, coercion, brutality and war can be explained by means of proximate causes which, linked as they are to the particulars of the case, seem not to lend themselves to meaningful generalizations. Yet, it is the business of the social scientist to seek the connections between factors that may appear unrelated. The search for causality, or rationality, should thus not be construed as an attempt to simplify the events in question but merely as an effort to make sense of a more general pattern. Hence, to continue with the previous example, cutting off hands in Sierra Leone has political causes and consequences, even if the psychological aspects of these atrocities might, in the long run, turn out to be more important.

This chapter is in three parts. The first examines the nature of power in contemporary Africa. The second discusses the links between politics and violence. The third touches on the issues of rationality and modernity.[1]

Power

Politics in Africa is best understood as the exercise of patrimonial power. What this means in concrete terms is that, despite the formal political structures in place, power transits essentially through the informal sector. Or rather, it is in the interplay between the formal and the informal that power is exercised on the continent. This form of governance, often dubbed neo-patrimonialism, rests on well understood, if unequal, forms of political reciprocity which link patrons with their clients along vertical social lines. The operation of political institutions is thus very largely conditioned by the exercise of

---

[1] My argument draws in part from my last two books on African politics: *Power in Africa: an essay in political interpretation* (London: Macmillan, 1992 & 1994) and (with Jean-Pascal Daloz), *Africa Works: disorder as political instrument* (Oxford: James Currey, 1999).

personalized power. Politicians use official bodies for their own, patrimonial, purposes—regardless of the effect such behaviour may have on the institutional well being of the government. The logic of the political system, therefore, does not correspond to its Western equivalent. Bureaucrats, for example, are seen not primarily as the impartial servants of public service but as links in the patrimonial chain that connects patrons with their clients.

In a neo-patrimonial system, the quest for political legitimacy requires the fulfilment of particular obligations, which have nothing to do with the emergence of a public sphere transcending infranational identities. While most political leaders at independence were 'modern' rather than 'traditional' elites, the parameters of the neo-patrimonial system they put in place owed a great deal to principles of authority that go back to the pre-colonial past. Among those, the most significant had to do with a system of accountability in which the legitimacy of politicians was perceived by all (from top to bottom) to rest on their ability to provide for their own (most often ethnic) constituents. Consequently, in postcolonial Africa political representation has been seen to occur when patrons meet their obligations in respect of their clients.

Although such a neo-patrimonial system worked well in many countries after independence, it was inherently unstable. First, the postcolonial situation of relative economic well being—useful colonial assets and stable export prices—was shattered by the world economic crisis in the seventies. As revenues declined and debt increased, African patrons began to run out of means. In a situation where the search for resources became ever more difficult, political competition increased. Since in the African neo-patrimonial system access to governmental assets is paramount, the struggle for power intensified. Second, this political system was essentially inimical to economic development as it occurred in the West, or later in Asia. This is because it failed to foster, and in many ways totally undermined, economic growth, which is the prime basis for sustainable development. Because political legitimacy was based on the politicians' ability to feed the networks on which their position depended, they could scarcely defer consumption and expenditure for the longer-term purpose of 'national' economic growth. For this reason African states as well as entrepreneurs rarely invested in economically productive activities.

Such an analysis of the nature of power in Africa stresses the importance of historical and socio-political continuities and highlights the links to be found between the pre-colonial, colonial and contemporary exercise of power. In other words, it does not regard decolonisation as the 'radical' political break it is sometimes taken to be. Despite the admittedly massive differences between the political institutions inherited by the nationalists after decolonisation, there has been a quite remarkable convergence in the political evolution of independent Africa. In the first long decade (1960–75) after independence it seemed that the colonial legacy had enabled the establishment of working Western political institutions in Africa. Yet, the economic crisis unleashed in the 1970s by the sharp increase in oil prices revealed that this analysis of the patterns of authority on the continent had been superficial.

Put very simply, what that crisis made manifest is the extent to which nationalist euphoria had masked the continuities between the pre- and post-colonial eras. Contemporary politics on the continent had to be analysed in greater historical depth. What had in fact occurred is best described by what I call the Africanisation of politics—that is the process by which the new African rulers redesigned the political structures inherited at independence and redefined the parameters guiding political action. Although the modalities of such Africanisation differed substantially depending on the nature of the political system put in place after decolonisation, what is significant for political analysis are the evident similarities. Indeed, the widespread notion that the colonial heritage, as well as the vagaries of decolonisation, were decisive for the formation of the post-colonial political 'order' turned out to have been vastly exaggerated.

In retrospect, what is striking is that the Africanisation of politics had similar systemic effects everywhere. In essence, what took place amounted to the overlapping of two apparently discordant political logics. On the one hand, there was an ostensible strengthening of the political institutions as they emerged out of the decolonisation process— whether peaceful or violent. On the other, there developed a new political dispensation that was frequently at odds with the newly constructed formal structures. The supposed democratic and pluralist organs of political representation set up in most African countries at independence rapidly gave way to the one-party state—the unfolding of a single, not plural, political logic. Further down the line, the system evolved in such a way as to call into question the nature of power, and particularly the role of the state, as had been conceived by most political analysts.

This trend, which I call the informalisation of contemporary African politics, is best explained by reference to the notion of identity and the relation between the individual and his/her community. Western political systems rest on the assumption that citizens are discrete, autonomous and self-referential individuals who express electoral preferences according to overtly political criteria. The reality in Africa is different: the individual cannot be conceived outside of the community from which (s)he hails, however geographically distant (s)he may be from it. The political system thus operates according to criteria that embody this core 'communal' dimension. The individual is less the self-conscious citizen than someone whose behaviour accords to the multi-registered (and sometimes contradictory) logics that guide his/her place within the community. These belong essentially to the realm of the informal, meaning here only that they are not encompassed within the 'official' legal and constitutional order.

The manner in which power is understood and exercised helps to explain why politics in contemporary Africa diverges from that of the West. Briefly, the state in Africa is not much more than a relatively vacuous shell, useful insofar as it permits the control of the resources which it commands but politically feeble because it is neither institutionalised nor functionally differentiated from society. Similarly, there is no self-standing civil society because vertical ties remain markedly more significant than horizontal (professional or functional) links. Finally, African political elites behave according to the norms of political legitimation and representation inherent in the neo-patrimonial system. They use their official position to fulfil their unofficial obligations to their clients and to meet the clientelistic demands on which their power and standing as rulers rest.

Violence and Politics

Returning to the question as it was framed at the outset—whether conflict in Africa is merely the historical concomitant of present day 'development'—I wish here to suggest that the specific nature of the notion of power outlined above impinges on the degree and nature of violence on the continent. In other words, it is not just that the tensions inherent in Africa's political sedimentation are particularly conducive to force; it is that the present political systems are prone to produce more, rather than less, strife. The informalisation of politics is inimical to the type of institutionalisation that would make it possible for the formal structures of governance to contain force and exercise their (legal) monopoly over the socially necessary forms of coercion. Since the state in Africa south of the Sahara, with a few exceptions (most notably Botswana and South Africa), does not properly discharge its nominal formal responsibilities, there exists a vast socio-political space in which numerous acts of illicit violence occur.

The analysis of power, however, must go beyond the immediate notion that the state in Africa has been 'criminalized' or 'privatised', for this would presuppose that it had once been properly institutionalised. Since independence, power has always been exercised simultaneously at the formal (state) and informal (patrimonial) level. It is only the dereliction of the neo-patrimonial system, which has revealed the extent to which the connections between the two had begun to crumble. The lack of resources, on which the patron-client relations are constructed, has revealed the fiction that the state was institutionally functional. Instead, it has become more nakedly 'informal', and as a consequence it appears to have 'privatised' its criminal and coercive activities. In truth, what has changed is merely the ability of the state to maintain the proprieties of its formal role. Devoid of the means to realise its ambitions, the state (or what is left of it) in Africa is more dependent than ever on the power and resources of its key politicians, whose informal reach extends into the world of the 'criminal'.

The consequence of the demise of functional neo-patrimonial systems has been the use of disorder as political instrument. In brief, this refers to the process by which political actors in Africa seek to maximize their advantage from the state of confusion, uncertainty, and even violence, which characterizes most African polities. Although there are obviously vast differences between countries in this respect, I would argue that all African states share a generalized system of neo-patrimonialism and an acute degree of apparent disorder—as evidenced by a high level of governmental and administrative inefficiency, a lack of institutionalisation, a general disregard for the rules of formal political and economic sectors, and a universal resort to personal(ised) solutions to societal problems.

To understand politics in such a context is to understand the ways in which individuals, groups and communities seek to instrumentalise the resources they command within this general political economy of disorder. To speak of disorder is not, of course, to speak of irrationality.

It is merely to make explicit the observation that political action operates, rationally, but largely in the realm of the informal, uncodified
and un-policed—that is, in a world that is not ordered in the sense
in which we usually understand it in the West. In an ordered, institutionalised and regulated polity, political opportunities and resources
are defined explicitly and codified by legislation or precedent. In a
world of disorder there is a premium on both the vertical infra-insti-
tutional relations through which the 'business' of politics can be conducted and on the access to the means of maximizing the returns
that the 'domestication' of such disorder requires.

Since the structural dynamics of African political systems remain
essentially patrimonial, and since resources are steadily diminishing,
the political elites increasingly use disorder instrumentally. This is
conducive to conflict in two fundamental ways. The first is that instability and arbitrariness are natural breeding grounds for the use of
force. The second is that the threat or actual use of violence becomes
a vital expedient to generate revenue—directly through illicit appropriation or indirectly through the negotiation of funds/aid as the
price to pay for the ending of violence. In other words, the logical
outcome of the use of disorder as political instrument is the rule of
force, not of law.

The most notable development in the last decade in Africa has not
been the transition towards multi-party 'democracy' but, much more
disturbingly, the willingness of political actors to resort to ever-greater
violence. Indeed, the move to competitive party systems has frequently contributed to disturbance and civil strife (as, for instance,
in Kenya, Cameroon and Côte d'Ivoire—countries with apparently
'orderly' politics). Beyond the cases of electoral disharmony, however, loom much more serious abuses. I refer to two types of violence
in particular.

The first concerns the deliberate use by governments, or rather
the holders of state power, of severe and arbitrary acts of brutality
against their own population. Here the example of Sudan, employing
starvation as a political weapon, and of Rwanda and Burundi, indulging
in 'ethnic' genocide, come readily to mind. But these are only the
most severe cases. The consequences of the breakdown of Somalia,
the wars in the Horn of Africa, the conflicts in the Democratic Republic
of Congo, the savagery in Liberia, northern Uganda and Sierra Leone,
are all part of a pattern of deliberate force against civilians. Although
it is sometimes difficult to understand what the aims of such inten-

tional attacks against civilians can be, it would be wrong to suppose that their apparent 'barbarity' does not have a political purpose. The genocide in Rwanda and the appalling levels of brutality in Sierra Leone can, regrettably, be interpreted (in large measure at least) as a peculiarly vicious way of reaching certain political ends in a context where other methods seemed more onerous to warlords or other would-be politicians. The view that such violence is 'irrational' or 'atavistic' does not carry much conviction since it would still have to be explained why it should have broken out when and where it did.

The second turns around the less severe, but perhaps even more insidious, exploitation by political elites of the suffering endured by their populations as a result of strife, disorder, and (natural or man-made) calamity. This pattern, to be found in a large number of African countries, consists in failing to take action against, or frequently in fuelling, the causes of conflict and misery in order to extract foreign aid, which otherwise would not be forthcoming. The cases of Angola and Ethiopia are symptomatic of two slightly different scenarios. In the former, the state used the pretext of its war against UNITA to relinquish any responsibility for the well-being, or even the survival, of most of its own population. It merely encouraged the international community (UN agencies, NGOs, etc.) to take care of the 'problems' brought about by the wholesale, and quite deliberate, neglect of a majority of the country's people. In the latter, the government had long ignored international pressure to end its war with Eritrea but deliberately publicized the deteriorating plight of its population—due in no small part to the fact that the government devoted far too few resources to alleviate the effects of drought and starvation—in order to ensure that vital foreign aid was not cut off.

The model is a familiar one. Governments which are seemingly incapable, or unwilling, to ensure the most basic living conditions for their own people display the consequent suffering in order to generate outside assistance—the bulk of which (except directly received food aid) does little to alleviate the predicament of those most in need, and may even fuel further violence. Even where the situation is less drastic, there is today on the continent a greater range of abuse committed, directly or by stealth, by governments upon their own populations than there was in the decade after independence. Where scarcity and disorder prevail—which is almost everywhere—corruption, predation and other forms of exploitation are rife. And ordinary Africans can only hope to avoid such violence if they become the clients of powerful enough patrons within the political elite. In the end, the increasing breakdown of law and order makes it possible for a large array of 'private' violence of one type or another to thrive: from petty crime to wholesale racketeering or blackmail—not infrequently linked to, when not organized by, government circles.

Rationality and Modernity

The extent of violence experienced in Africa today raises the question of rationality in at least two ways. First, can such a degree of violence ultimately serve 'any' purpose? Second, are the types of particularly vicious conflicts currently witnessed in a number of countries evidence of 'irrational' behaviour or, to put it another way, evidence of the behaviour of 'irrational' people? The discussion of rationality is, obviously, a most delicate matter, dependent as it is on the reference grid from which the analysis proceeds. Here, I link the issue of rationality with that of modernity. Although these questions, if they were to be treated within a proper cultural, philosophical and psychological framework, would require much more attention than can be offered here, my main aim is more prosaic. I want only to examine the problem within the context of the evolution of politics in Africa.

The crux here is whether the type and range of conflict found on the continent can be explained in terms of power or whether there are other processes at work that would invalidate a political approach to the question. Anthropologists, economists, psychologists and students of religion, among others, sometimes doubt that a number of cases of individual and collective violence currently experienced can be reduced to simple political explanations. Events in Uganda, for example, where religion, politics and violence have so readily mixed, are a case in point. Can Alice Lakwena, the Lord's Resistance Army and the killing of scores of followers of a religious sect, all be explained in political or, even, rational terms? Is religion here solely instrumental? Does violence become an end in itself? Similarly, can one really explain the behaviour of the RUF in Sierra Leone purely in political terms? Is not the process of committing an atrocity itself the fuel that propels this brutality forward, in an endless orgy of maiming and killing?

There is no denying that a study of the individuals who engage in such acts of atrocity would reveal a number of conscious and unconscious motives, many of which have little connection to politics: psychoanalysis might well be enlightening. Equally, an analysis of the group dynamics of those who mobilize and act with such violence would show that much of what we know of sect psychology applies in those cases. Nevertheless, I want to suggest here that not only can such action not be divorced from the political context in contemporary Africa, but also that it is intimately connected with the current process of 'modernization' on the continent. In other words, this violence is not a resurgence of 'age-old' or 'atavistic' tendencies—as so many observers have suggested—but part of a process of severe change now convulsing Africa, even if such change brings about precious little 'development'.

The question may arise as to the usefulness of the notion of modernization in a situation where Africa appears ostensibly to 're-traditionalise'. My argument is, precisely, that the appearance of 'backwardness' is deceptive and that the events taking place, though expressed by means of apparently 'traditional' forms, such as the occult, ought in fact to be understood as part of a process of transformation. This should not be so surprising since, on reflection, it is obvious that modernization everywhere has always followed the path of existing social, cultural, and religious traditions. In other words, modernity is nothing but the 'transformation' of 'tradition', and as such can only be seen as an on-going process rather than a state of achievement. No society is modern *per se*, only more or less modern, and modern in different ways. Asia's modernization, for instance, of which Japan is perhaps emblematic, has travelled a very different road from that of Western Europe, even if the end product, at least in technological and economic terms, is relatively similar.

The same is happening in Africa. The notion that the continent, because it has hitherto failed to develop economically, is not in the process of modernization cannot withstand serious examination. Indeed, the fact that much of the current violence appears to be 'backward' should not distract us from the realization that it is in many different, and sometimes subterranean, ways part of a process of adjustment to a new, more globalised, world. Nowhere is this more apparent than in the behaviour of the young people involved in conflict. Among many others, studies on the 'rebels' in Sierra Leone, the

militia in Brazzaville, and the miners digging for diamonds in southern Congo/northern Angola, all point to interesting links between
the 'rationality' of their actions and their perception of modernity.
Cutting off limbs may appear to be 'primitive', and in some fundamental way it obviously is, but the model followed by those child soldiers and 'rebel fighters' is Rambo, not some ancient African god.
Such violence, therefore, must be understood as part of a process of
rapid change, in a globalised age, within a political context in which
youth in Africa is politically and economically disenfranchised, when
not entirely cast away, by the elites controlling the faltering neo-patrimonial system.

Similarly, the efflorescence of religious groups, or sects, is best
understood as a collective means by which those who are not part of
a functioning clientelistic network—a number increasing all the time,
for the reasons discussed in part one—can cope with the misery and
arbitrariness of the world in which they live. Whilst, again, the nature
of some religious groupings often harks back to 'traditional' beliefs,
many others, like Pentecostal Churches, are resolutely forward-looking and embrace modernity. All, however, offer relief and rationality
in a setting where modernization has not brought about any significant economic improvement. If, occasionally, one of those sects self-
destructs, as happened a few years ago in Uganda, it is not because
it is 'backward' but, on the contrary, because its set of beliefs is no
longer anchored in the rationality of accepted 'tradition'. In this
respect, then, it has more in common with similar movements found
in 'developed' countries such as the United States, where millennial
violence is not rare, than with African culture. Both are by-products
of an ill-digested globalised modernization.

Another area in which there are contradictory views concerns
witchcraft. On the one hand, it is seen as a 'leftover' from a traditional age and as such expected to abate with 'development'. On the
other, it is plainly thriving in Africa today. Again, the contradiction
is the result of a perspective which fails to understand that the continent is modernizing but that it is doing so in its 'own way'. Witchcraft
induces, as well as contains, violence. As such it serves distinct social
purposes. A closer analysis of its role today reveals that it has adapted
to the socio-economic changes brought about by modernization and
that it continues to bring about both control and resolution of conflict that find no other plausible conclusion. The phenomenon serves
at least three distinct aims, which all have political significance: heal-

ing, binding communities together, and social levelling. Since these are areas of social life that are not well served by present political arrangements in Africa, it is unlikely that witchcraft will wither in the foreseeable future. Here too, therefore, the rationality of 'traditional' belief can help ease the difficult transition to 'modernity', which the continent is presently suffering.

The question of conflict in Africa can easily be misunderstood, or misrepresented. The issue for interpretation is less that of degree than of genesis. Indeed, it matters a great deal how analysts explain what is going on today on the continent. If the current violence is seen merely as the historical by-product of the transformation of the countries concerned into developing nation-states, then what is happening will easily be dismissed as historically inevitable. If, on the other hand, it is viewed as the consequence of the Africans' atavistic nature, it will be brushed aside as culturally inevitable. Both approaches are ultimately reductive, for they fail to address the causes of the present disorder.

The task of the social scientist is to go beyond these clichés and to analyse what makes sense to the people concerned within their own historical, social, economic, political and cultural setting. For this reason I believe that an analysis stressing the rationality of the use of disorder as political instrument is enlightening, if not necessarily cheering. Although it would be simplistic to claim that all violence in Africa can be attributed to politically instrumental reasons, it is unwise to neglect the political roots of present processes. Indeed, a closer examination of many of the conflicts that so baffle outsiders reveals overt or covert motivations. For example, the Sudanese government can be seen to have spurred and supported many of the Northern and Eastern rebellions in Uganda. Similarly, Liberia's Charles Taylor is known to have backed the RUF in Sierra Leone since its inception. A number of countries have been involved in the conflicts that raged in the Democratic Republic of Congo. Finally, the development and tribulations of many newly formed sects in Africa can be explained in terms of the economic benefits, and hence political clout, they provide their founders and followers.

Of course, the forms that violence takes and the consequences for those who practice or suffer it are not solely to be understood in political terms. There is evidently a need for an economic, anthropological, cultural and, even, psychological approach to the phenomenon. Clearly too, the insights which these other disciplines bring to bear

on our comprehension of conflict are importantly relevant to political analysis. Indeed, as I have long argued, the analysis of politics in
contemporary Africa is impossible without a wide-ranging, or interdisciplinary, framework, making use of the insights provided by other
social or economic sciences. In sum, then, violence and conflict in
contemporary Africa are undoubtedly blighting the continent, but
they are still amenable to rational analysis. And there can be no successful conflict prevention, or resolution, unless the root causes of
violence are properly understood.

PART ONE

EXPLAINING CONFLICT AND UNDERSTANDING
CONFLICT PREVENTION IN AFRICA

CHAPTER ONE

ANGOLA AND THE THEORY OF WAR

Christopher Cramer

Contending Schools of Thought

Since the end of the Cold War a lid has been lifted on the study of conflict. It has become obvious that wars in developing countries cannot simply be written off because of geopolitical tensions and 'external causes'. Conflict has moved to the foreground of development studies, producing a profusion of projects and labels: students must pick their way through a thicket of 'civil wars', 'intra-state conflicts', 'new wars', 'complex humanitarian emergencies', 'resource wars' and so on. This chapter outlines some of the main contending theories on contemporary conflicts, and then applies them to the history of Angola. Two broad schemes will help to separate different theories on the etiology of war—though with the proviso that some explanations of conflict combine elements of alternative types of theory. The first scheme for categorizing theories of conflict comes from Eckstein (1980), who argued that all theories of conflict must differ after a fundamental 'branch point' in analytical perspective. One branch leads to 'contingency' theory and the other to 'inherency' theory.

Contingency theory holds that the normal state of social affairs is peaceful, but that extraordinary upheavals can provoke an affective, irrational outburst. The mechanism that would unleash such outbursts is the 'frustration-aggression nexus'—but this mechanism would only operate if there were a confluence of a range of facilitating, quasi-accidental, i.e. contingent, factors. Gurr's (1970) theory of relative deprivation as the origin of conflict is an example. If people feel a discrepancy between what they have and what they expect to be able to have, this will trigger the frustration-aggression nexus. But that nexus will only generate collective violence if there is a propitious combination of facilitating factors, including 'justification'—through ideology or a tradition of culturally learned violence—and 'balance' in the allocation of coercive capabilities between the state and others.

Inherency theory begins with an assumption that human society is naturally disposed to violence as much as towards peace, and that actual collective violence represents the outcome of a rational choice of violence as simply one option among a continuum of possible political actions. The possibility of violence is always present in the perpetual jockeying for power among interest groups—what trips the switch is the right mix of cost and benefit. Here, again, factors such as the coercive balance come into play, though in this type of theory they have a more centrally determining role given the underlying disposition to violence. Eckstein cited Tilly's (1978, e.g.) explanations for violence in early modern Europe as an instance of inherency theory.

Reference to relative deprivation suggests that development matters because it throws 'traditional' mores, and organization into disarray, generates expectations and hence ups the ante on relative deprivation, failing to produce the political institutions to cope with such frustration. Collective action theories—at least those close to Tilly's variant—stress the way that economic and social development reshapes the organization of power and the technology of violence. As states develop, they tend to make demands on subject populations who, naturally enough, either want a greater stake in central authority or resist these demands—at times with force. The emphasis, then, is on group dynamics and on how economic and technical change provokes realignments in the organization of power relations, with potential implications for violent conflict.

A second scheme for distinguishing between theories of violence is proposed by Tilly himself (2000). This divides them into theories of ideas, and behavioural and relational theories. 'Ideas people' stress beliefs, concepts, rules and values; 'behavioural people' stress the autonomy of motives, impulses and opportunities; and 'relational people' stress the role of transactions, as well as generally insisting that collective processes have irreducible properties distinct from individual propensities.

There are two additional points. First, in recent years the role of neo-classical economics has expanded in the social sciences. What both detractors and champions call 'economic imperialism' (Fine 2001) has also affected the study of conflict (see Hirshleifer 1994). Second, there is an enduring tension between types of evidence that are regarded as admissible, and there are enduring imperfections in all relevant evidence. Thus, many theories will stress the role of subjective factors: for example, relative deprivation highlights perception, and more recent studies emphasize that perceived inequality or grievance is as relevant as are objective conditions. On the other hand, some theories are only interested in 'objective' factors, often equated (rightly or wrongly) with quantifiable variables. These types of explanation are particularly scornful of 'narratives of grievance': i.e. just because someone tells you they are fighting to overcome injustice does not necessarily mean it *is* why they are fighting. It is fairly obvious that where we are faced with perceptions we are relying on extremely delicate judgements about the veracity, reliability and significance of qualitative information and about the appropriate sources of this information. But it is equally true that most statistical research into conflict is just as fraught with empirical fragility.[1]

New Wars

One common view is that contemporary wars are 'new wars'; they differ from those in developing countries before the end of the Cold War. There are varying interpretations of this concept. However, certain features of a new war perspective stand out. They are generally regarded as close relatives of other major phenomena associated with globalization. As the nation-state fades from view, so nationalism and grand political ideology fade from political 'discourse' and from the organization of armed conflict. Meanwhile, as privatization sweeps across the world, so too is war privatized. As Duffield puts it (2001: 13), "liberal peace and the new wars have blurred and dissolved conventional distinctions between peoples, armies and governments". One implication is that the way war is fought has changed. Kaldor (1999) captures this in the claim that the ratio of military to civilian deaths in war was inverted, from 8:1 early in the twentieth century to 1:8 by the century's end.

For some observers, new wars are characterized by an absence of politics altogether—they are simply acts of brutal aggression (de Soysa and Gleditsch, 1999). Money replaces politics and ideology as the motor of conflict. And the characters that play out these new wars are not the romantic figures of the Cold War but hard-nosed 'warlords', often manipulating the naïve interventions of aid agencies and humanitarians. Yet Duffield (2001) argues that new wars are simply not about liberal Western political ideology: indeed, he replaces the

---

[1] On these empirical problems see Cramer (2003) and Sambanis (2002).

idea of complex humanitarian emergencies by the term 'emerging political complexes', founded on profoundly illiberal forms of economic accumulation and organization of power.

Not everyone is convinced by the value of the concept (Kalyvas 2000). First, the new wars concept relies on a vague characterization of the world economy and on overblown claims about the extent and nature of globalization. Second, so-called new wars typically display many features associated with old ones while some of the attributes of newness are really well worn (Marchal and Messiant 2001).

Resource Scarcity

The argument that resource scarcity causes conflict has some rather dramatic proponents, e.g. in Kaplan's 'The Coming Anarchy' (1994). The most thorough advocate of the argument is Homer-Dixon (1999), who proposes that environmental degradation generates 'social scarcity' as people are forced off unviable farming land and swell the population of poor peri-urban areas and as elites manoeuvre to secure access to remaining assets. The social tensions arising from this predicament are akin to relative deprivation, and gain a particularly violent twist when crystallized around ethnic divisions.

Critics such as Gleditsch (1998) complain that there is more polemic than sound analysis in environmental conflict literature, that there is no consistent definition of what is meant by environmental conflict, that significant political and economic variables are neglected and downplayed in the literature, that there is selection bias, that directions of causality are confused, and that some models are too unwieldy to be tested effectively. Meanwhile, Fairhead (1997) argues that the environmental argument *depoliticizes* violent conflicts.

Resource Abundance

An alternative argument, to which we will return below, is that it is not scarcity but abundance in natural resources that 'causes' wars. One version of this argument goes something like this: natural resource abundance insulates rulers from their subjects and frees them from the tiresome challenge of raising revenue from the population and, as a consequence, having to account for this revenue by reciprocal initiatives such as providing a social and economic infrastructure. Resource wealth encourages leaders to pursue violence as a method of staying in power and attracts the attention of rivals. War then becomes the ultimate form of rent-seeking activity. There are basic and subtler versions of resource-centred analysis. Le Billon (2001) develops a sophisticated analysis of the spatial and economic distinctions among natural resources (e.g. distinguishing between 'point' and 'dispersed' production), relating these to varying propensities to influence the characteristics and causes of political and violent conflict.

The empirical evidence tying resource abundance or concentration to the incidence of violent conflict remains disputed. While Collier (2000a and b) finds that the concentration of primary commodity exports in GDP is a strong predictor of civil war others, such as Fearon and Laitin (2002), claim that there is no significant correlation. Meanwhile, di John (2002) points out that there is no clear pattern of resource rich countries dominating the distribution of 'complex humanitarian emergencies' in the early to mid-1990s. There is also a possible problem of spurious correlation, or of correlation failing to reproduce a direct causal link: for most contemporary wars have been fought in low-income countries and if the economic structure of many of them is dominated by primary commodities this does not mean resource concentration causes conflict.

Ethnicity

Some arguments emphasize cultural difference as the mainspring of violent conflict, e.g. ethnic difference in the former Yugoslavia or 'primordial' ethnic tension in Rwanda and elsewhere. Given the ascendancy of orthodox economics in the social sciences in recent years, and certainly in the study of violent conflict, it is worth illustrating how ethnicity is treated within the recent economic literature on war. Orthodox economists try to model war in order to predict it. Typically they begin with the fundamental axioms of neo-classical economics but then introduce quantifiable 'social variables'.[2] One example is the ethno-linguistic fragmentation index, measuring the probability of the next person you run into coming from a different ethnic group than yourself. Model builders can then argue about what 'score' best 'predicts' outbreaks of civil war.

This kind of approach is based on an assumption that the political significance of ethnicity is invariable, i.e. wherever a society's ethnic

---

[2] See Cramer (2002) for a critique of neo-classical economic theories of war.

fragmentation score is high there will be one kind of implication and wherever, across contexts, the score is low then another uniform implication will hold. The glue that binds together countries with equivalent scores like this is the collective action theory. Collier's version of the argument (2000a and b), for example, is that a high degree of ethnic fragmentation is unlikely to make for a high risk of civil war. This is because high ethnic diversity raises the costs of mobilizing support for rebellion, while an ethnic structure closer to polarization reduces mobilization costs. Aside from inconclusive empirical evidence at the multi-country statistical level, there is a further problem that it is not always straightforward to measure ethnic diversity, let alone to capture quantitatively the political significance of ethnic identity across a range of specific contexts. For example, there are competing assessments of the degree of ethnic diversity in Afghanistan: "a German treatment of the subject concludes that there are about 50 [ethnic groups], while a Russian study claims 200" (Schetter 2001).

Inequality

Another variable often associated with the origins of armed conflicts within societies is economic and social inequality. On the one hand, the argument is commonly made in more or less structuralist development terms—e.g. much of the study on wars in Central America highlights the role of the extreme inequality of income and/or assets in the origins of rebellion and war (see, for example, Booth 1991). On the other hand, orthodox economists nowadays tend to agree that inequality is bad for economic growth, and one of the reasons for this is that inequality causes political instability and even war, which in turn reduces investment (Alesina and Perotti 1996). Again, at the level of large datasets of cross-section data the evidence linking inequality with conflict is inconclusive (Cramer 2003).

However, two recent developments suggest a potentially more fruitful way of looking at the political significance of inequality. Where studies focusing on the Gini coefficient of land or income distribution find a distributional score across the whole of a society *vertically* arranged from the richest to the poorest, Stewart (2000) argues that the more appropriate analytical perspective is that of *horizontal* inequality. Horizontal inequality captures inequality across groups with common identities, e.g. ethnic, regional or religious communities, in terms of distribution of income, assets, educational opportunities, political positions, allocation of state subsidies, etc. Stewart claims that the significance of horizontal inequality lies in perceived inequality as much as in objective distributional characteristics.

In some ways this is close to Tilly's (1999) concept of durable 'categorical inequality'. Tilly focuses on pairings of categories—men/women, nationals/immigrants, blacks/whites, Hutus/Tutsis, and so on—that are bound together by relations of exploitation, by institutional ties that preserve unequal relations, and by mechanisms of 'opportunity hoarding' and adaptation. Although Tilly's analysis is chiefly concerned with why such categorical inequality is so durable and, therefore, in a way with why it does not lead more often to open conflict, the analysis offers some clues to further research and thinking about the sources of violent conflict. For example, where categories of inequality have paired blacks and whites in exploitative relations, the political implications appear to have varied with the type and degree of formal institutionalization of these relations (in South Africa, the USA, and Brazil). The chief difference between Tilly and Stewart is Tilly's closer focus on the particulars of the ties that bind groups together rather than just the outward forms expressing difference in access to resources and opportunities.

Greed versus Grievance

Recently, some of the differences in perspective between theories of contemporary conflicts have been grouped according to neat but arguably highly misleading distinctions between greed and grievance. The framework is mainly associated with Paul Collier, who as head of research at the World Bank was an influential commentator on these issues. His view is basically that greed is what causes war, not grievance. Rebel leaders may spout the rhetoric of righting wrongs and overturning injustice but this does not accurately address the causes and motivations behind collective violence.

Critics such as Cramer (2002), Gutierrez (2003), and Keen (2001) have pointed out that there are serious empirical and conceptual problems in this framework. The indirect variables or proxies chosen to quantify observations of greed and grievance are flawed and highly ambiguous. For example, both the preponderance of primary commodity exports in GDP and the level of educational attainment may reflect either greed (the prevalence of easily lootable commodities and the comparative advantage of violence for the poor) or grievance (frustration and anger at failed government policies). As with all the comments above, the empirical evidence for grand claims about the predictive success of models based on these variables is weak, affected by imperfect data and sample selection bias. However, there is a more fundamental issue. It may be that one group's greed will interact with another's grievance to produce conditions propitious for war; and it may be that greed and grievance are themselves internally related. In the latter case, evidence of 'greedy' behaviour—looting, predatory taxation, etc.—may well arise from grievance.

Do the Theories Fit the Angolan Case?

The characteristics of Angola's history of conflict offer both confirmation and a challenge to the various explanations for the causes of conflict outlined above. Angola's history also raises two further questions. One is from Buijtenhuis (2000): have wars changed or is it that we have changed the way we understand them? The other is whether it is possible to find a convincing general theory of war applicable to all wars, or whether instead every war is *sui generis*.

Is Angola's Conflict a 'New War'?

There is a yes and a no answer to this question. At one level the Angolan conflict, at least during the 1990s and up until it appeared to fizzle out with Jonas Savimbi's death in 2002, was a clear case of a new war. Conflict during this period seemed devoid of ideological difference. Both the MPLA and UNITA were reconciled to the rhetoric, at least, of capitalism and the market economy. And war in Angola thrived on links to international 'networks', both those woven around the trade in diamonds and those built up to sustain interests within the global oil sector.

Blurred distinctions between peoples, armies and governments are also a feature of war in Angola. There have been repeated reports of members of the government's armed forces selling weapons to UNITA officials. Global Witness's (2002) 'All the President's Men' report highlights evidence of extraordinary criss-crossing interests between private entrepreneurs and French and other national governments, between these interests and officials in the Angolan government, and between interests in the banking, oil and arms sectors. One example, which shows how these webs of accumulation not only fuelled the war in Angola but also fuelled mighty inefficiency in the war effort (and in fact shows a complete disregard either for military efficiency or for a political project to win the war) concerns the trade in obsolete arms. For at least some of the materiel piled up in the arms junkyards outside Luanda seem to be arms that were non-functioning even before they arrived in Angola, the worthless rejects left over after deals in which all players appear to have gained.

Angola's was also perhaps a new war, in that enormous numbers of non-combatants have died, been seriously injured, uprooted and traumatized in the course of the conflict. There are few estimates of the total numbers of war casualties; the UN, though, estimates that during fighting in 1992–94, one of the fiercest periods of the war, there were some 300,000 related deaths, including those in battle, from aerial bombardment, from starvation under siege, from landmines, and from disease and malnutrition caused by war.

At another level, though, Angola challenges the new war thesis and suggests an enduring continuity of conflict. The atrocities of war in the 1970s and 80s already had a very 'new war' feel. UNITA kidnapped thousands from the highlands and took them south to form an internal colony of forced labour (Birmingham 1992). UNITA rebels destroyed oxen, and ate or destroyed seed, they planted landmines on rural paths, all to bring the economy to its knees. The MPLA adopted similarly brutal policies against rural civilians, driving them from their homes to prevent UNITA from finding and cultivating any social base. Soldiers frequently looted food convoys. There was massive internal population displacement and civilian suffering. Angola's was a complex humanitarian emergency long before the term was coined.

The Cold War gave the conflict a nice ideological buff, and the rival nationalist movements developed an attachment to ideological models. However, Cold War ideology ran rather shallow through Angolan society—where the social preconditions for nationalism and for other twentieth century ideologies barely existed. Instead, the war in Angola has arguably always been, as it were, a war of position. What drove allegiance and commitment to conflict was a desperate struggle for social position, with expectations and resentments born chiefly out of the historical and material formation of social identities. Furthermore, within each of the three main movements involved in the anti-colonial war there was rivalry and conflict, in which political position or stance combined with competition over positions within the movement, leadership and privilege (Messiant 1998). Even the 'new war' phenomenon of warring parties co-operating and fighting simultaneously is not new: one well-known example involved UNITA collaborating with the Portuguese secret police, PIDE, during the anti-colonial war.

The MPLA's socialist ideology was for the most part a sham. Leaders and their friends led lifestyles wholly at odds with the ideological precepts and legal restrictions that affected most of the population. Private and public interests overlapped long before the end of the Cold War. The Marxist-Leninist MPLA encouraged joint oil exploration and production with international firms, especially with US firms whose government would not recognise the MPLA government. The combination of shortages of food and consumer goods, official fixed pricing, and oil money made for a fabulous parallel economy where, again, ideological, public and private distinctions blurred.

Angola's war has also always been associated with international links, both political and economic. Oil and diamond interests are only the most recent of major commodity causes related to the origins and course of violent conflict. The idea that something new called 'globalization' is causing the war is unconvincing. Angola's linkage to the world economy—and the way this relates to warfare—stretches back through the Cold War, the colonial period, and even to some 500 years of violent conflict. Duffield (2001) argues that new wars are tied to a shift in the nature of international capitalism: where once capitalism was expansionary and inclusive, now it is consolidating in core capitalist countries and exclusive of the rest of the world. Arguably, though, this is a misleading distinction to impose on Angola. From the early days of the slave trade right up to present day oil and diamond concerns, capitalism has taken a brutal interest in Angola. Capitalism itself has not been purely inclusive or exclusive at any moment in this history. Reno (2000: 231) argues that "the commercialization of diplomacy and strategic interests in relationships between non-African and African states is occasionally portrayed as a novel feature accompanying the expansion of the global economy", but in fact this is a very old practice, harking back to the mid-nineteenth century; and the MPLA government has shown a considerable capacity to "manipulate the conditions of their own bureaucratic weakness" (ibid.: 231f.).

Finally, in the early twenty-first century national states continue to be important in deciding the fate of Angola. The state in Angola itself remains the key to social position, political power and economic privilege. And other state interests influence war and society in Angola.

National state political concerns have affected the extent of UN intervention in Angola; and state interests and competition affect regulation of the diamond business and the closely linked markets for oil
and arms. As Reno (2000: 224–5) shows, US assistance to Angola goes
well beyond state-to-state diplomatic measures and includes use of
the Africa Growth and Opportunity Act, equity financing schemes run
by the Commerce Department, Treasury and Department of Transportation, commercial guarantees by the quasi-official Overseas Private
Investment Corporation (OPIC), and the Export-Import Bank, as well
as US influence in the World Bank's Multilateral Investment Guarantee
Agency (MIGA).

Is War in Angola Caused by Commodity Scarcity or Abundance?

It is *blindingly* obvious that high value commodities (oil and diamonds)
have had a massive effect on conflict in Angola and, though this is
less commonly acknowledged, that scarcity for most Angolans is critical to their involvement in the war. Control over the diamond fields
enabled UNITA to continue the war after Cold War patronage faded
away at the end of the 1980s. Meanwhile, oil revenue kept the MPLA
in power and the military machine turning over. Global Witness (2002)
shows how important the secretive nexus of deals and competition
involving the oil industry was to the government's ability to secure
a steady flow of arms, and hence a new lease on power, in the aftermath of the return to war after the 1992 elections. But do resources
determine outcomes alone? If so, why do countries with oil, diamonds,
etc., not experience the same kinds of conflict?

A more realistic analysis of Angolan conflict would examine the
direction of causality more closely and explore the social relations
that shape the role that commodities play in politics and in conflict.
First, oil and diamonds had little to do with the beginnings of the war
in Angola in the 1960s. Mineral production levels were still quite modest at that stage and political conflict, particularly the start of the
war of liberation, erupted as a result of various histories of urban tension, rural repression and rebellion (particularly the 1961 uprising in
the north-west), and proto-nationalist politics. In fact, in some ways
war and economic policy after independence created a new dependence on mineral resource exports. The economy had been under-
going significant structural change in the late colonial period, with
one of the most rapid manufacturing booms experienced anywhere

in Sub-Saharan Africa in the late 1960s and early 70s (Ferreira 2002: 253f.). All that changed after independence. "As war progressed, and the economy dramatically deteriorated, with sharp falls in agricultural and industrial production, oil output increased and oil revenue came to represent almost all of Angola's currency earning and the bulk of state income" (Messiant 1998: 154). So the direction of causality seems almost the reverse of that presumed by resource curse literature. Nonetheless, rapidly increasing oil revenues certainly allowed the MPLA to wage one of the most expensive wars in Africa, sustaining large armed forces and huge arms imports. Angolan military expenditure in 1999, for example, was equivalent to some 21 per cent of GDP.[3]

Second, commodities have played an important role in shaping political and violent conflict in Angola, and the specific properties and production requirements of these commodities—slaves, coffee, oil and diamonds over the past five centuries—have helped to define the particular characteristics of war. However, rather than beginning and ending with the commodity itself, it is important to explore the social relations that surrounded, were built up around and helped determine policy towards particular commodities. The true role of oil, for example, cannot be appreciated without seeing how the development of the oil industry has been entwined with the much older history of the formation of a Creole elite and slightly more recent emergence of so-called 'new *assimilados*' chiefly in Luanda. For these social groups were first encouraged to take leadership roles in Angolan society, and were then humiliated in the twentieth-century *Estado Novo* period of colonial rule when there was a huge influx of Portuguese settlers. Later still they formed the basis of MPLA rule and the evolution of a nomenclature intent on preserving social position, political power and immense wealth.

Similarly, in an earlier phase of conflict in Angola coffee played a key role (Angola being, by the early 1970s, the fourth largest coffee exporter in the world). Production was concentrated in the northwest, a region with a strong Bakongo history and identity, a history that tied many people in the region into the economy, language and society of the Belgian Congo and that was to affect the formation and politics of the FNLA (Frente Nacional de Libertação de Angola). Coffee

---

[3] See SIPRI website: <http://www.sipri.org>.

was critical too because the Portuguese colonial regime chose to organize coffee production partly through small-scale Bakongo farming
but also by encouraging huge land expropriation and settlement by
Portuguese immigrants and by corralling migrant labour from the
Ovimbundu highlands in the centre and south of the country to meet
labour demand on settler coffee plantations. A dispute between the
social groups involved in the coffee economy broke out in February
1961, triggered by a dispute over payment of wage arrears, resulting
in the most violent rural anti-colonial uprising in Africa.

Finally, more recently scarcity of resources and poverty in rural
areas have definitely helped to perpetuate warfare between the MPLA
and UNITA and to sustain military operations. However, these are not
the real culprits. And while it is clearly true that joining the military
is one of the only ways poor young men and boys, in particular, can
survive, it is not enough simply to state that the poor have a 'comparative advantage in violence' or a 'low opportunity cost of violence',
as neo-classical economists would have it. War and political conflict
have created scarcity, and have pushed people into military camps,
into towns, and resettlement villages and refugee camps where many
have joined up but many more appear to have been forced to join
militias. It is not merely a case of relative opportunity or the balance
of cost and benefit, for these suggest a large measure of rational calculation and choice. Rather, for most people it is a matter of coercion: of being press-ganged into the military or (for many girls and
women) prostitution by the MPLA and UNITA.

Is Angola's Conflict Caused by Ethnicity or Inequality?

Angola is a fantastically unequal society. War has aggravated inequality, as the income from thriving sectors such as oil, diamonds and
trade is concentrated in relatively few pockets, while immense numbers of people are driven to the very edge of starvation (and many
pushed beyond). Reliable distributional data is not available.[4] Social
indicators, to the extent that they exist, suggest horrendous levels
of poverty. One indicator produced by UNICEF estimates that as a

---

[4] One 1995 urban poverty study cited in Hodges (2001) found that monthly expenditure by the richest decile of urban households surveyed was twelve times more
than that of households in the poorest decile, compared with the ninefold difference
in equivalent spending found in a 1990 Luanda survey.

consequence of war the under-5s mortality rate is 292 per 1,000-two thirds higher than the Sub-Saharan African average (cited in Hodges 2001).

Meanwhile, ethnicity has certainly been a factor in the country's political history. Some commentators have emphasized ethnic division as the basis for the competing projects of the three (and later two) warring parties.[5] The FNLA, for example, never really escaped from a narrowly Bakongo base. Indeed, aside from the authoritarian leadership of Holden Roberto, this ethnic narrowness was one of the reasons why significant numbers—including Jonas Savimbi—left the movement. UNITA has often been associated with an Ovimbundu social support base, while the MPLA drew support from the Mbundu areas around Luanda as well as from *mestiços* in the capital.

However, in terms of causing, and sustaining, the conflict this is misleading. Inequality mattered in Angola in terms of the specific history of evolving and institutionalized disparities between groups rather than in terms of the vertical income range among individuals that is measured by the Gini coefficient. Ethnicity was not by itself a very powerful determinant of conflict, and conflict itself has not provided ethnic characteristics: there has been no ethnic cleansing, for example. Ethnic identity was not an evenly distributed source of mobilization. Apart from the Bakongo, "there did not exist in Angola in 1974 any strong ethnic tradition. One could not speak of the Mbundu or the Ovimbundu as 'corporate groups'" (Messiant 1998: 144). Economic expansion and structural change in the late colonial period, by provoking greater social differentiation had undermined the simplicity of the three great ethnic blocs in the country, and there was increasing diversification of interests within 'ethno-linguistic groups'. Moreover, as the war has provoked massive and ongoing population movement and urbanization, so people's collective identity has shifted and in the burgeoning cities there seems to be evidence that ethnicity matters less and less (Hodges 2001). Further, many Ovimbundu people have fled the fighting to seek refuge in government-held towns, and many Ovimbundu fight in the MPLA army. Pereira (1994) argues that evidence suggests quite strong cross-ethnic support for the MPLA in the 1992 elections.

---

[5] See, particularly, Marcum (1969).

Ethnic differences have mattered when they collide with material or ideological interests, including economic and religious denominational conflicts between, for example, Presbyterians, Methodists and Baptists.[6] Unequal social status, wealth and social, economic and political opportunities across groups with varying degrees and forms of collective identity were extremely important factors in the origins of war in Angola. This was all the more so because groups were not just separate but united in envy; they were often directly linked in political or economic terms. One example is coffee production, which bred resentments between dispossessed Bakongo peasants and Portuguese settlers, and between migrant Ovimbundu labourers and coffee farm owners. But the most dramatic and enduring source of political rivalry developed between the Luanda Creole, *assimilado* and *mestiço* society and 'black African' Angolans. From the earliest days of the anti-colonial struggle, issues of legitimate claims to 'Angolanness' and 'Africanness' were intensely divisive. Ultimately this, together with emerging differences in political objectives and encouragement from international interests who inevitably took sides, became the organizing principle around which contests for position in Angolan society developed. This is hardly surprising, given the long-standing association of the coastal Creoles not only with the benefits of monopoly in an early capitalist society but also with direct complicity in the slave trade and the raids on the Angolan hinterland, and given the colonial institutional system of privilege which operated according to Portuguese, *assimilado*, or indigenous identity coding. Thus, inequality does seem to have been a cause for discontent, but only if we see it in terms of Tilly's pairings of Creoles/black Africans, settlers/farmers, northern landowners/migrant coffee labourers, and if one notes that these pairings are fundamentally based on class rather than emerging out of free-floating or long entrenched 'identity politics'.

Conclusion

Each abstract theory or possible 'independent variable' appears at first to have solid historical content in the Angolan conflict. Yet the closer we get to that historical content, the more these theories and

---

[6] See Clarence-Smith (1987), Heimer (1979) and Birmingham (1992).

variables quiver like mirages and then evaporate. There are two conclusions from this, each requiring further exploration. One is that perhaps there can be no general theory of war. The other is that if a context-sensitive theory is possible, it may have to take account of one factor ignored by the current stock of theories. Despite the fact that war seems to exist outside history and specific modes of production, war is actually profoundly historical, and contemporary wars are rooted in the transition to capitalism.

In terms of the organizing methods for distinguishing between theoretical perspectives on conflict, there may be a case for an orderly eclecticism, i.e. an eclecticism that nonetheless gives priority to certain factors. The historical analysis outlined above, for example, suggests that individual behavioural impulses and choices do matter; and that ideas, beliefs, memories and traditions matter too; but that an effective explanation for the causes and characteristics of war in Angola can only be derived from a relational and social analysis. Similarly, the relative deprivation suffered by many Angolans was aggravated by colonial upheavals and institutionalized class and social identity differences; but there was not just an 'affective', irrational outburst of violent expression of frustration. Instead, relative deprivation occurred over a long period of time among social groups vying for power and position. They hoped to hoard opportunities and lay claim to particular structural places or levels in society, to be exploiters rather than exploited. There was purpose in this constantly renegotiated, conflict-ridden history, but this cannot be rationalized as self-interest or neo-classical economic theory.

Where some see greed, arguably primitive accumulation and brute survival are more appropriate characterizations. Some individuals (Angolan and non-Angolan) have been and continue to be extremely greedy in this conflict. What is more important, however, are the social relations formed over centuries and influenced by political and economic changes, which generate sources of power and wealth and threaten older sources of power or livelihood. Where some see choice, it might be better to stress coercion: press-ganging into the armed forces, the material pressure to survive, the imposition of historically institutionalized cultures of obedience, and so on. Where some would highlight the causal role of resources, this perspective emphasizes that of relations and power. Power in Angola, since the arrival of the Portuguese and the beginning of the slave trade, has depended on the interaction of local organizations of power and the manipulation of production and trade. Where some see scores of ethno-linguistic fragmentation or Gini coefficients, this perspective redirects analysis to policies, politics, history and culture. It is not a quantifiable score for ethnic fragmentation or income inequality that mechanically determines outcomes, but the specific historical relevance of ethnicity and class.

Bibliography

Selected Readings on Angola

Birmingham, D. (1992), *Frontline Nationalism in Angola and Mozambique*, London, James Currey.

Clarence-Smith, G. (1980), 'Class Structure and Class Struggles in Angola in the 1970s', *Journal of Southern African Studies*, vol. 7, no. 1, pp. 109–126.

Ferreira, M.E. (2002), 'Angola: Civil War and the Manufacturing Industry, 1975–1999', in Brauer, J. and J.P. Dunne (eds.), *Arming the South: the Economics of Military Expenditure, Arms Production and Arms Trade in Developing Countries*, Basingstoke, Palgrave.

Global Witness (2002), 'All the President's Men': the devastating story of oil and banking in Angola's privatized war, London: Global Witness.

Heimer, F.-W. (1979), *Der Entkolonisierungskonflikt in Angola*, Munich, Weltforum Verlag.

Hodges, T. (2001), *From Afro-Stalinism to Petro-Diamond Capitalism*, Oxford, James Currey.

Marcum, J., (1969), *The Angolan Revolution, vol. 1*, Boston, MIT Press.

Messiant, C. (1998), 'Angola: the challenge of statehood', in Birmingham, D. and P.M. Martin (eds.), *History of Central Africa: The Contemporary Years, since 1960*, Harlow, Longman.

Miller, J. (1988), *Way of Death: Merchant Capitalism and the Angola Slave Trade, 1730-1830*, London, James Currey.

Pereira, A. (1994), 'The Neglected Tragedy: The Return to War in Angola, 1992–93', *Journal of Modern African Studies*, vol. 32, no. 1, pp. 1–28.

Reno, W. (2000), 'The real (war) economy of Angola', in Cilliers, J. and C. Dietrich (eds.), *Angola's War Economy: the Role of Oil and Diamonds*, Pretoria: Institute for Security Studies.

Selected Readings on the Political Economy of Conflicts

Alesina, R. and A. Perotti (1996), 'Income Distribution, Political Instability, and Investment', *European Economic Review*, vol. 40, no. 6, pp. 1203–1228.

Booth, J. (1991), 'Socio-economic Roots of National Revolts in Central America', *Latin American Research Review*, vol. 26, no. 1, pp. 33–74.

Buijtenhuijs, R. (2000), 'Peasant Wars in Africa: Gone with the Wind?', in Bryceson, D., C. Kay and J. Mooij (eds.), *Disappearing Peasantries? Rural Labour in Africa, Asia and Latin America*, London, Intermediate Technology Publications.

Collier, P. (2000a), 'Doing Well out of War', in Berdal, M. and D. Malone (eds.), *Greed and Grievance: Economic Agendas in Civil Wars*, Boulder, Co., Lynne Rienner.

——. (2000b), 'Economic Causes of Civil War and their Implications for Policy', Washington, DC: World Bank <http://www.worldbank.org/research/conflict/papers.civilconflict.htm>.

Cramer, C. (2002), 'Homo Economicus Goes to War: Methodological Individualism, Rational Choice and the Political Economy of War', *World Development*, vol. 30, no. 11, pp. 1845–1864.

———. (2003, forthcoming), 'Does Inequality Cause Violent Conflict?', *Journal of International Development*, vol. 15, no. 3, pp. 397-412.

De Soysa, I. and N.P. Gleditsch (1999), *To Cultivate Peace: Agriculture in a World of Conflict*, PRIO Report 1/99, International Peace Research Institute (PRIO), Oslo.

Di John, J. (2002), 'The Effects of Mineral Resource Abundance on Violent Conflicts, Governance, and Growth in Late Developers: A Critical Assessment of the Rentier State Model', Crisis States Programme Working Paper, DESTIN, London, London School of Economics.

Duffield, M. (2001), *Global Governance and the New Wars*, London, Zed Books.

Eckstein, H. (1980), 'Theoretical Approaches to Explaining Collective Political Violence', in Gurr, T.R. (ed.), *Handbook of Political Violence*, New York, Free Press (Macmillan).

Fairhead, J. (1997), 'Conflicts over Natural Resources: complex emergencies, environment and a critique of "Greenwar" in Africa', paper presented to UNU/WIDER conference on 'The political economy of humanitarian emergencies', 3–5 July 1997, Oxford, Queen Elizabeth House.

Fearon, J. and D. Laitin (2002), 'Ethnicity, Insurgency, and Civil War', *American Political Science Review*, vol. 97, no. 1, pp. 75–90.

Fine, B. (2001), 'Economics Imperialism and Intellectual Progress: the Present as History of Economic Thought?', *History of Economics Review*, vol. 32, no. 1, pp. 10–36.

Gleditsch, N.P. (1998), 'Armed Conflict and the Environment: A Critique of the Literature', *Journal of Peace Research*, vol. 35, no. 3, pp. 381–400.

Goody, J. (2001), 'Bitter Icons: How Ethnic is Ethnic Cleansing?', *New Left Review*, 7, January-February.

Gurr, T.R. (1970), *Why Men Rebel*, Princeton, Princeton University Press.

Hirshleifer, J. (1994), 'The Dark Side of the Force', *Economic Inquiry*, vol. 32, pp. 1–10.

Homer-Dixon, T. (1999), *Environment, Scarcity and Violence*, Princeton, NJ, Princeton University Press.

Kaplan, R. (1994), 'The Coming Anarchy: how scarcity, crime, overpopulation and disease are threatening the social fabric of our planet', *Atlantic Monthly*, February, pp. 44–74.

Kaldor, M. (1999), *New and Old Wars*, London, Polity Press.

Kalyvas, S. (2000), *"New" and "Old" Civil Wars: Is the Distinction Valid?*, *La Guerre entre le Local et le Global: Sociétés, Etats, Système*, Colloque, Paris, CERI.

Keen, D. (2001), 'Disqualifying grievance? A response to the Collier/Hoeffler model as an explanation for civil wars', presented to CODEP Conference, June 18–20, School of Oriental and African Studies, London.

Le Billon, P. (2001), 'The Political Ecology of War: Natural Resources and Armed Conflicts', *Political Geography*, no. 20, pp. 561–584.

Marchal, R. and Messiant, C. (2001), 'Une Lecture Symptomale de quelques théorisations récentes des guerres civiles', Working Paper, Paris, CERI/CNRS.

Sambanis, N. (2002), 'Defining and Measuring Civil War: Conceptual and Empirical Complexities', mimeo, Dept. of Political Science, Yale University.

Sanin, F.G. (2003), 'Criminal Rebels? A discussion of war and criminality from the Colombian experience', Crisis States Programme Working Paper No. 27, DESTIN, LSE, London.

Schetter, C. (2001), 'The Chimera of Ethnicity in Afghanistan', mimeo.

Stewart, F. (2000), 'Crisis Prevention: Tackling Horizontal Inequalities, *Oxford Development Studies*, vol. 23, no. 3, pp. 245–262.

Tilly, C. (1978), *From Mobilization to Revolution*, Reading, Addison-Wesley.

———. (1999), *Durable Inequality*, Berkeley, University of California Press.

———. (2000), 'Introduction: Violence Viewed and Reviewed', *Social Research*, vol. 67, no. 3.

CHAPTER TWO

ETHNICITY AND CITIZENSHIP IN SUB SAHARAN AFRICA

Anna-Maria Gentili

Ethnicity is Never What it Seems

When a conflict is proclaimed 'ethnic', it is left to the public to interpret the role of ethnicity according to ideological preference or prejudice (Lemarchand 1999). Some will understand ethnicity as the expression of a mythical entity, the ethnic group, emerging out of a primordial past; others will see it as an entirely modern phenomenon, either the consequence of a colonial plot, instrumental to policies of divide-and-rule, or a false consciousness (Chretien 1997; De Heusch 1997; Dubow 1994).

Those who favour the 'ethnic group' interpretation are divided between believers in ethnicity as the atavistic representation of African 'primordial barbarism',[1] and those who see in it the 'paradise lost', the essence of human nature. Among the people who believe ethnicity to be a modern phenomenon are those who portray ethnicity, be it essential or constructed, as 'imagined' (Amselle and M'Bokolo 1985; Chretien and Prunier 1989; Vail 1989; Vidal 1991; Anderson 1983), or 'invented' as an instrument of (colonial or national) political power (Ranger 1994, 1985; Chretien 2000). Ethnicity is seen as driven by 'greed' in struggles either to control resources or to protect privilege, or as rooted in the 'grievances' of marginalized groups wanting to access scarce resources (Collier 2000). Lastly, it is a form of collective agency, by means of which societies seek to break through or counteract an intolerant, predatory state (Berdal and Malone 2000). In order to claim rights or defend privileges, ethnicity may be used as a strategy of compromise and reconciliation as well as of violent conflict (Reyntjens 1994; Guichaoua 1995; Willame 1997).

---

[1] It is the notion of the collapse of civilization and a return to anarchy or barbarism that has been given much publicity by R. Kaplan (1994).

The meaning of what is ethnic and the relevance of ethnicity in African societies has fostered scores of debates on terminology, which have provided ample opportunity for demonstrating how observations are not pure, but are shaped by our concepts.[2] Research has revealed the complex historicity of social constructions both at the level of identity choices and ideological formulations, showing how ethnicity has been used as an instrument for and against the state (Newbury 1998; Vansina 1998).

Anthropologists have made a distinction between the constituent dimension of ethnicity, that is its structure and organization, and its historical expression. Structure and practice are mutually constitutive through conflict, by the changing material conditions that in turn can either reproduce structural order or change it. Research has shown how ethnicity is constructed by means of language, denominations, symbols and values, how it is the product of history and of specific contextual social situations, including the interests of the elite and policies able to manipulate differences in times of stress or competition for power (Vidal 1998). Nevertheless, we should be aware that: "neither when it is adopted as an ideology nor when it is used as an explanatory concept can ethnicity be passed off as given or necessary, and certainly not as a typical response to modernity" (Fabian 1998).

Research on African societies has been in the vanguard of studies into the role of ethnicity in the construction of social and political identities in colonial and postcolonial states. This was true long before the ethnic question held centre stage at the end of the cold war and the opening up of the Pandora-box of competing national and particularistic identities that has overwhelmed the Balkans, Central Europe and Central Asia. Rediscovered as one of the main causes of the de-structuring and re-ordering of nation-states in the age of globalization, not least in Western countries, ethnicity has ceased to be considered an almost exclusively African 'disease'.

Debates on the meaning of 'ethnic' and 'tribal' in Africa have mostly revolved around investigating the colonial nature of domination: how systems of colonial rule have incorporated and shaped African societies and how ethnicity was constructed as an instrument of subor-

---

[2] Lemarchand (op. cit.) recalls the fortunes of the 'Hamitic hypothesis' in perpetuating and shaping racial stereotypes in the Great Lakes. Sanders (1969). See also Newbury (1995 and 1998), Vansina (1988), Vidal (1998 and 1995), Chretien (1988), Willame (1997).

dination, or became a means of adaptation as well as of rallying resistance to foreign rule. Nevertheless, public discourse, the media and too often the literature on development, continue to reduce to stereotype what are the otherwise complex historical and political dynamics of ethnicity. The study of ethnicity as one of the root causes of conflict should in fact be a distillation of historical trajectory and the carefully researched circumstances of each situation (M'Bokolo 1983; Willame 1995).

It is a matter of record and observation that ethnicity is very relevant to an understanding of African problems, but it is not enough to ask why. It is important to investigate the processes: how ethnicity functions, which are the specific circumstances that unleash 'ethnic' conflict, who are the participants, what is the timing, sequence of events, their interrelation and representation, and in each instance what form it takes.

A current hypothesis regarding the poor economic growth performance of Sub-Saharan Africa (after almost two decades of structural adjustment) is based on the greater ethnic variation or fragmentation of the region as compared to that of other areas in the southern hemisphere (Easterly and Levine 1997).[3] The cross-national samples used to support such theses fail to account for the great diversity within each country, and between states, not to mention how ethnicity has been shaped and institutionalized by historical processes, political choices and changes in social relations. These models do not take into consideration the conceptual ambiguity of the definition of what is an ethnic group, which is intended here to signify a 'primordial' given of the African social and political landscape. Thus the hypothesis relating poor economic growth to ethnic fragmentation is too superficial and should not be taken seriously.

However, the dangerous message it conveys has to be addressed. The conceptual framework, which looms behind this type of research, draws data from an a-historical, out of date ethnic-linguistic enumeration and classification. It thus adopts a racist image of African society in which economic 'marginalization' (economic growth means

---

[3] Ethno-linguistic heterogeneity has been used by other economists to explain growth performance. See a special number of Journal of African Economies 2000 on conflicts in Africa. For a documented critique see Ingrao (2002). Ingrao says that the source of the ETHNIC index was elaborated in the mid-1970s on the basis of linguistic studies and an atlas produced by Soviet scholars in 1964.

lack of success) is deemed to derive mainly from the resilience of 'pri-mordial' forms of ethnic difference, which are then seen as the main obstacle to modernization, first within the state, and then in the context of the global market. Poverty is seen here as a product of backwardness without the dramatic history that goes with it (Ferguson 1990; Stoler and Cooper 1997).

Journalists, aid workers and various 'barefoot' casual observers are, with few exceptions, rarely conversant with the complexities of the historical and political problems of the continent, and have often been instrumental in legitimizing the idea that the main problem is that the continent is prey to 'ethnic struggles'. More and more we are confronted with misinformed cultural explanations for Africa's predicaments, leading to simplistic, reactionary and therefore mostly racist generalizations as has happened in the case of the Rwandan genocide. Too often, even those involved in charity circles and aid organizations, and with a legitimate concern for humanitarian interests, tend to be blind to the political realities or, even worse, consider political motivations secondary, if not irrelevant.

When investigating root causes one needs to be aware that each case is unique and characterized by a different combination of causes (Steward and Vayrynen 2000; Steward 2000). History does not only consist of looking at the past, be it an ancestral or colonial socio-ethnic legacy, or to clarifying the present through the past, but deals with reconstructing how individuals and groups have elaborated their experience and organized their particular field of political action.

Cultural differences alone are not sufficient to bring about violent group mobilization, neither is economic inequality, or poverty *per se* (Goody 2001). Changes in the underlying conditions of power, more specifically with respect to political and economic control,[4] and the role played by political leaders in constructing and activating group identity, have to be investigated to understand how differences and tensions might be transformed into violent conflict.[5] 'Complex emergencies' often arise from failure of governance and are symptoms of a profound crisis of authority in contemporary nation-states (Cliffe

---

[4] Cramer (1998: 19): 'What matters in studying the role of economic inequality in civil conflict of one kind or another is how inequality is institutionalized and shaped by history and changes in social relations'. See also Austin (1996); Storey (1999).

[5] See Lonsdale (1995) for the notion of 'political tribalism' as a creation of 'tribalism' by competition between political elites.

and Luckham 1999). Thus, in order to expose root causes one should start with an adequate understanding of the historical and structural antecedents that have shaped and polarized political identities in the process of state formation. If we look at most cases of contemporary violent conflict we can trace their origins to the growth and dynamic of authoritarian regimes and their explosive turning point in the breaking up of internal legitimacy through corruption, repression and predatory practices (Reno 1995; Lemarchand 1996; Prunier 1996; Ellis 1999; Bazeguissa-Ganga 1999; Braekman 1996). Ethnic identity together with power seeking has played a key role in many conflicts, old and new, and has ideologically informed the perpetuation of wars to the point of near anarchy in many African countries.

The loss of the residual legitimacy of populist projects such as national liberation and socialism, gives us the opportunity to trace the genesis of 'new conflicts' in the interaction between internal and regional participants in their struggle for control of state power as shaped and intertwined with the forces and effects of accelerated globalization (Kaldor and Luckham 2001 and 1999; Duffield 1998 and 2001; Reno 2000; Nafziger and Auvinen 2002). At the same time structural adjustment policies and programmes originating in the 1980s, which were meant to introduce Africa to a mainstream market economy, have contributed to the imbalance and dependency of African polities, along with excessive economic extraversion and unequal access to resources in already very asymmetrical societies, characterized by weak local private entrepreneurship.[6]

Global deregulation and lack of security for investment has mainly attracted speculative capital, and aided by economies plagued with informants and criminals that provide opportunities for rent seeking, rather than incentives for free competition (Sindzingre 2001 and 1998; Bayart, Ellis and Hibou 1999). Intended as a cure against economic 'marginalization' and for the dismantling of patrimonial regimes, liberalization has, up to now, helped to increase rather than reduce structural tensions. The growing gap between the few who are getting

---

[6] Arrighi (2002: 29): "In sharp contrast to East Asia, Sub-Saharan Africa inherited from the pre-colonial and colonial eras a political-economic configuration that left little room for the construction of viable national economies or robust nation states"; Stein (2000) poses the question of structural adjustment and the unwillingness to even consider how colonialism has left African countries with inadequate developmental assets relative to those needed even in the earliest stages of capitalist development.

richer and the majority who are in the process of getting poorer, has deepened the distrust in institutions and laws that only provide guarantees for those who have some direct or mediated access to power and authority.

Democratization and Ethnic Citizenship

Has democratization unleashed "a general obsession with autochthony and ethnic citizenship invariably defined against 'strangers'—that is against all those who 'do not really belong'"? (Geshiere and Nyamnjoh 2000).

Is the entrenchment of identity and belonging, the renaissance under new forms of ethnic linkages, the only real moral fabric of African societies that the state has been incapable or unwilling to 'capture'? (Hyden 1980). Do disorder, anarchy and conflict prove that the state in Africa is not taking root, and what prevails is a neo-patrimonial mode of rule in which ethnicity is the instrument of manipulation by unscrupulous political entrepreneurs who issue from the reciprocal assimilation of both the modern and traditional elite? Or, on the contrary, are the African states, far from being the passive victims of dependency and globalization, even more flexible and inventive in their strategies of assimilating and appropriating extraversion through original ideologies, symbols and rituals than they were in their adapting customs, native authorities and institutions in colonial times? (Bayart 1989, 1996, 2000). Are political 'disorder' and economic informalization constituents of the historical and political originality of African states? (Chabal and Daloz 1999).

Are we saying that almost 40 years into state independence in Africa, the public sphere, the seat of national state politics, is an irrelevant fiction and that African countries are ruled by factional fighting for private gain? Is democratization no more than an exercise in multiparty competition designed to appease or dupe foreign donors?

If we put into context the predicament of African countries we can see how the new, fragile polities, burdened by strong colonial legacies, far from being 'marginal' are facing the storm that shakes the same foundations of the nation-state model all over the world. Conflicts in Africa are the crossroads where the difficult and certainly immature processes of nation building and state formation clash with and are shaped by the struggle for the appropriation of transnational resources in this phase of deregulated globalization. This is even more apparent in multidimensional conflicts where important resources have been used by regimes as the basis not for development but for wielding power, by means of corruption and private appropriation.

The tensions that are driven by strategies of survival as well as by accumulation and are expressed in the, not necessarily violent, manipulation of overlapping and ever moving differences and cleavages, are not necessarily opposed to the contemporary form of state organization. The expansion of so-called 'informal' exchange networks is a case in point. 'Informality' is a survival strategy for the poorer strata of the population as well as being a way to mediate for some sort of access to the 'formal' market. The entrenchment into fragmented autochthonous identities can either be a sign of alienation or of assertiveness. Autochthony may be a strategy against exclusion or a means of claiming rights to full citizenship in situations where formal rules, legislation and rights are accessible only to those who have wealth and connections.

The independence of Sub-Saharan African states has signposted the end of monopoly colonialism. Thus we can say that the nation-state in Africa was born out of the first phase of what today is conventionally call globalization. It was through decolonization that the architecture of equal independent nation-states was completed. The new states had few assets and many liabilities. Their territories were defined by artificially created colonial borders; populations were unequal in terms of productivity potential, access to resources, and national legitimacy. The specific historical trajectory of each nationalist movement produced variable ideologies of national cohesiveness. Nation building and development priorities were intended to reinforce the structures of power and authority on the basis of the composition, organization and ideology of each nationalist movement, which represented the bridge between the modern and the traditional, the rural and the urban, the centre and the peripheries.

African states had few assets to support their basic power structure (Strange 1996). They were states in name only; they had internationally recognized formal sovereignty over a given territory and they were 'nations' mainly because of the trust they had gained in the national struggle for liberation. Their national legitimacy was based on the promise of liberation, democracy and development, by which was meant the equitable extension of rights and justice. This was the original meaning of Kwame Nkrumah's conquest of the 'political kingdom'.

National sovereignty was accepted as the indispensable stepping-stone to attaining the universal entitlement embodied in the notion of progressive and equitable economic and social development.

The African nation-states were legitimized internationally not only by the acceptance of the territorial structure inherited from colonialism but, more relevantly, by the model and ideology of modernization that went with it. This model was based on a number of prescribed stages: national unity, a 'strong' executive with developmental aims, democracy defined by the primacy of 'order and stability', and unity, as opposed to the divisive 'tribal' pluralism. Thus the emphasis was on the necessity of building strong states measured in terms of centralization, vertical power with vast, if not absolute, powers devolved to the executive.

Without entering into a discussion on the meaning and use of the term 'ethnic group' as a more politically correct substitute for 'tribe' and 'race', it should be remembered how the term ethnicity became, both in the social sciences and in political discourse, an acceptable 'neutral' substitute for tribalism with all its implied negative connotations. Ethnicity was acceptable because it was meant to define a social, not a political, group identity that fitted coherently into nation-building ideology. Tribalism had a negative political connotation, insofar as it had pointed to the inferior status of the tribe to which African political societies had been relegated by colonial policies of divide and rule. The national ideologies of independence stressed the solidarity of traditional rural communities, which were presented as egalitarian, and as such morally superior to the class hierarchies prevalent in Western capitalist countries. All nationalist ideologies, those based on culture, such as 'Negritude' and those based on the notion of the natural 'communal' formation of African societies, such as 'Ujamaa', stressed the supposedly egalitarian nature of African communities. This idealization of African tradition was also consistent with the universalism of modernity, whose essence lies in the negation of the principle of hierarchy. 'Communitarism' and modernity were two sides of the same discourse. They supported each other in negating the reality of class hierarchies and struggles, as they had been emerging in their complex identities of African societies and individuals. They were also mutually supportive in conceiving liberation and democracy as nominal extensions of formal political rights to all subjects allegedly transformed by independence into citizens.

While class struggle was negated in that ideological context, ethnicity was considered a residual phenomenon, a remnant of the past
that would dissolve into the national ethos and eventually into the
pan African dream. Political and economic development, whether capitalist or socialist, were projected as the ethos of liberation, reinstat-
ing an equality that had been undermined by divisive, tribal colonial
policies. Colonial 'divide and rule' had to be eliminated through strong,
centralized institutional and political structures. Africanization and
nationalization provided the justification for a drift towards governments dominated by an executive and by the single party.

A challenging analysis of the organization of colonial polities and
the exercise of power underlines how independence did not intend
a rupture with the hierarchical colonial 'mode of rule', characterized
as 'decentralized despotism' (Mamdani 1999: 296). The independent
African regimes although widely different in ideology and organization, ranging from those based on a conservative accommodation to
instrumental alliances with existing authorities to those characterized by radical leaderships pursuing revolutionary agendas, all ended
up either incorporating or negating the legacy of decentralized despotism. Whether adopting state-led initiatives, modernization development models, or the top-down promotion of civil institutions without
any explicit recognition of political affiliations, African regimes proved
unable to overcome the widening gulf and the hierarchy between
national and ethnic citizenship. While the political equality of all citizens through universal suffrage was evidence of liberation, in reality the civil and social rights on which the 'political kingdom' was
postulated mainly affected a minority of the population. As for the
majority of erstwhile African subjects, civil and social citizenship
remained very unevenly distributed, depending on the individual's
position in terms of power, regional or ethnic origin, religion, education or class.

Single-party states did broadly divide between those where ethnic
and tribal constituencies, interests and privileges were the terrain
for consensus, and those in which the intention was either to abol-
ish or prohibit traditional public roles, limiting them to cultural or
ceremonial roles. In both cases, democracy remained an unfulfilled
promise. The mode of power remained basically authoritarian and
functioned either on the basis of a hierarchy of networks and alliances
with local tribal, ethnic constituencies, or through the top-down

absolute domination of institutions, which helped to stifle the very grassroots mobilization that had been the backbone of the process of national liberation.

Mobilization was the object of intense political and intellectual debate during the first years of independent Mozambique, in so far as the foundation of the new state's revolutionary project had been rooted in democratization from below in the liberated areas. However, after independence self-empowerment through mobilization was substituted for the organization and practices of a party that became (through its bureaucratized and dogmatic cadres), the only legitimate dispenser of the people's liberation. Although the debate and the differences of opinion between supporters of the notion of a grassroots party and the party of the vanguard was very intense and quite public, the government's economic and political decisions in fact hindered the possibility of expanding and consolidating the political community at national level. A drift towards dogmatism ensued, aided by the particularly harsh situation of structural backwardness, lack of resource and foreign aggression.

Nation building and development processes embodied a basic contradiction: on one hand, state and nation building ideologies, and the establishment of institutions and organizations failed to recognise the diversity and hierarchical nature of African polities as they emerged from colonial rule; on the other, the same process involved the manipulation and/or repression of those very same identities.

The structural deficiencies of the nation-states and the weight of negative inheritances, made worse by a hostile international environment, since the cold war made Africa one of its main fields of confrontation, have been underlined as causes of the 'failure' of the state. Nevertheless from the second decade of independence it was clear that dissent and the decreasing legitimacy of the government could no longer merely be understood in terms of grievances rooted in the colonial past or in the manoeuvres of neo-colonialism. Ethnicity provided an easy scapegoat for what were inadequate responses to the challenge posed by independence—the drift from politics to manipulative populism.

The emergence of ethnic politics, which seems now to predominate in the discourse on civil and political conflicts, is thus inscribed in the present nature of power in Africa (Wamba-dia-Wamba 1994). The change of emphasis from 'liberation' to 'development' has marked the adoption of top-down approaches both in market-led and in statist polities. The structural quality of African leadership, in so far as no state had an independent economic production base or was in a position to exercise systemic power, was thus fully exposed as undemocratic, and the unfulfilled 'political kingdom' left most African governments without a real popular political base. This loss of legitimacy detracted from whatever residual powers the African states did have as it sought to face the formidable radical onslaught of globalization.

The 1970s signalled the beginning of a global financial order and the emergence of a new international division of labour, with important implications for the nation-state as a form of social, political and economic organization throughout the world. By the end of that decade most African countries, strangled by various political, economic and environmental crises, had no option other than the one provided by mainstream doctrine, that is to negotiate from a position of weakness, stabilization and structural adjustment programmes inspired by the mainstream doctrine of the primacy of market over state led growth.

Whose Modernization?

At the time of independence the modernization theorists had supported 'political order' (Apter 1965; Huntington 1968) as a precondition to economic and political 'takeoff', meaning the ideology and organization of a supposedly 'strong state', be it based on a charismatic leader, single party or a military junta. With the failure of the 'developmental state' discussion turned not so much to the resilience of atavism, but to the excessive intervention of the state in the economy and the authoritarian nature of single-party states. While the first wave of modernization theorists had conceived the state as being in charge of guided development, the second was strongly in favour of a drastic reduction of its role. Under strict international supervision the state, trimmed down and reformed, had to provide the playing field and basic rules so that private entrepreneurs and civil society were left free to act. The political framework for economic liberalization was seen to be the promotion of democracy through pluralism, through multiparty elections, institution building, the adoption of the rule of law and the promotion of civil society (Huntington 1991; Diamond 1997, 1999; Harbeson, Rothchild, Chazan 1994; Doorenspleet 2000).

Democratization was resisted by most single-party leaders and hailed by the majority of the population at large in a wave of what seemed to have been a repeat of the 'revolution of rising expectations'. The electoral laws, the redrawing of constitutions, and elections became a terrain of confrontation. People took to heart the message and promise of pluralist democracy even though the initial popular enthusiasm for suffrage seems largely to have waned, as can be seen from the falling number of voters in recent elections. In recent years evidence from most international organizations has pointed to a persistent and increasing 'democratic deficit' at both national and global level.[7]

The problem in Africa, as elsewhere, is not democracy (Bratton and Mattes 2001) but which democracy (Fabian 1998). When and where the process of democratization has not gone beyond the formal exercise of multiparty elections and reforms, for the most part instigated and financed by international aid, the unfulfilled promise of universal inclusiveness embodied in the notion of democracy is exposed. Even in the few cases considered 'success stories' of democratisation, the possibilities of effective political participation and social inclusiveness are recognized as limited (Ostheimer 2001).

As for development, having declared since the 1980s the failure of the 'developmental state', the possibility of African economies continues to be extremely low. Even in countries considered to be relative success stories, poverty is increasing and becoming more visible. The most recent poverty reduction programmes imply that vulnerable sectors of society will now receive aid administered jointly by international and local, urban and rural civil sources. Initiatives to enhance participation and empowerment included in all packages of institution building and governance lead in the same direction: they are exercises to learn skills meant to be neutral substitutes for politics, if not to contain and constrain political action (Campbell 2000). Top-down technocratic approaches cannot open the way for that freedom of choice, which is the hallmark of citizenship in a democratic state.

---

[7] UNDP (2002) recognizes that 'the wave of democratic-building has stalled with many countries lapsing back into authoritarianism or facing rising economic and social tensions. [. . .] Development policies since the early 1980's have focused largely on economics and markets [. . .] The big lesson of this period is never ignore the critical role of politics in allowing people to shape their own lives. Political development is the forgotten dimension of human development': Mark Malloch, UNDP administrator.

African countries have inherited structural imbalances that are not only due to 'market distortion'. Fluxes in aid or investment have been penalizing the most needy areas of the world, mainly because they are more remote from western political and economic interests. Deregulation in trade and financial markets has had an adverse effect in countries where there are few possibilities of effective normative and juridical control on the predatory practices of transnational alliances of external and internal 'informal' and formal entrepreneurs. Certainly, in many parts of Africa, 'disorder' and 'informality' have become the norm. For many people this situation means death, and for the majority results in a very precarious and limited form of survival, while for a few it is becoming the route to the unscrupulous and often criminal accumulation of great fortune.

African governments, most of which are heavily dependent on external aid and all upon foreign investment, continue to have the monopoly on negotiations with international agencies through which all decisions on access and redistribution of development resources must pass (Brown 2001). Most states have developed very sophisticated skills in the 'presentation game', in order to preserve or gain external 'legitimacy' with bilateral and multilateral aid and investment agencies (Van de Walle 2000). The democratic deficit is evident in the fact that citizens, as electors, do not have a say, through legislative power, in the decision-making process regarding fundamental policy decisions such as the adoption of stabilization and structural adjustment programmes. Current 'participatory' methods are merely techniques designed to convince the 'citizens' to approve the policies and 'development' programmes on which they have had no control in the first place and which will most likely penalize them.

Many observers and many more Africans have become cynical about democracy in Africa. What has happened shows that minimal democracy, including the right to institutionalized multiparty elections, and political citizenship, intended to be universal, and assigned in the same terms to all adults who meet the criteria of nationality, are basically hollow. Nevertheless there is another way of looking at the current process. Elections and what came with them, above all access to some form of independent information with mobilizing effects, have at least opened the way to the reconstruction of a political community. Witness the emergence, even if often repressed, of an independent press, and of intellectuals, workers and peasants organizing and using the language of rights to assert their position on reform, from nationality laws to land ownership, and fighting against exclusion and injustice.

If the experience of democratization has shown that multiparty elections are not enough to build a really democratic state, it has at least revived the notion that as long as African states continue to be funded on the basis of civil rights, which hardly exist and are unevenly distributed at the best of times among individuals, social groups, regions, and above all where social rights have not been promulgated, there is no possibility of equal access to competition for different political identities.[8]

It is not a paradox then that economic liberalization and democratization, intended as deregulation where only the fittest could compete, seems on the one hand to have made the struggle for control of the state more fierce, and on the other has accelerated the display of different forms of factionalism "increasingly dominated by issues of autochthony and of who 'really' belongs".[9] Issues of identity are informed by and at the same time mould the power struggles to redefine in real terms the rights and hierarchies of citizenship at the national, local and transnational level. Examples are to be found in all elaborations of new legislation reforms on nationality rights and land reform access or ownership (West and Kloeck-Jenson 1999) as well as by analyzing how institutions function: the decision-making processes, elections, migration legislation.

In Côte d'Ivoire, Kenya, Zambia, Zimbabwe and Congo/Zaire (one of the hottest questions on the negotiation table regarding the political solution for Congo/Zaire is the contested legislation on nationality rights that helped to unleash the rebellion in Kivu in 1996), the rewriting of nationality laws has brought conflicts out in the open and has shown how the state still matters. The universalism of the first period seems almost everywhere to be losing ground in favour

---

[8] Drawing the connection between civil, social and political rights O'Donnel underlines how most theories of democracy ignore issues such as extreme poverty, illiteracy, disease, malnutrition and constant fear of violence as inhibitors of that individual 'agency' that is minimally reasonable capabilities and options. The perspective adopted in his work leads to a crucial question: to what extent and under what conditions poor and disadvantaged groups may use available political rights as a platform for protection and empowerment for struggles to extend their civil and social rights (O'Donnel 2000).

[9] 'Africa' 68 (3) 1998 is dedicated to 'the politics of primary patriotism', guest editors Geschiere and Gugler; see also Fanthorpe (2001).

of a notion of national citizenship rooted in 'ethnic' citizenship, that is rights deriving almost exclusively from the paternal line to an ethnic community defined as originally indigenous. The best example is that of Côte d'Ivoire, where political debate was followed by violent electoral strife, a coup d'état, the reinstatement of an elected government, and subsequent civil war. Côte d'Ivoire had been a success story from independence to 1978, an example of growth and good, if paternalistic, government. It has since entered a spiralling crisis, almost exclusively centred on the meaning and definition of 'ivoirité'—that is, on the definition of rights belonging only to 'originaires' (Dozon 2000a, 2000b; Sindzingre 2000; Campbell 2000). The conflict on *ivoirité* exploded when the legitimacy crisis combined with tensions produced by the economic crisis, and within the framework of multiparty elections.

The adoption of a new citizenship law inspired by the primacy of ethnic belonging reveals a fundamental change and a reversal of the universal concept of nationalism. This trend towards the reification of the ethnic in the process of nation building is a power strategy by means of which, behind the mask of political citizenship as a legal status assigned only to 'ethnic subjects', 'truncated citizenship' (Mamdani 1996; Halisi 1998) or 'multistrata citizenship' (Ekeh 1995) is redefined and the law, but above all the 'modalities of power' decide the right of access to the political and economic arena.

The loss of legitimacy of African nation-states has been measured by the failure to recognize the diversity and hierarchy of the many political identities and by the political and economic forms of subordination they have suffered. This has led to the inability or lack of will on the part of independent regimes to provide opportunities for the formation of a common political consciousness and for integration from below. The actual processes of democratization, institution building and governance are heralded as the only hope in achieving social transformation; that is, development and sustainable peace in Africa. However, democratization is a playing field on which the players have vastly different assets, where competition functions as the institutionalization of privilege and it is open to the constant manipulation of the most vulnerable sectors of society.

Let us take, for example, the land reform legislation in Mozambique adopted in 1997: it is the product of the alliance between a revised structural adjustment model, which is basically in favour of land privatization, state priorities which are openly bent on maintaining centralized control of this prized resource, and Non-Governmental Organizations pushing the primacy of 'community' as a way of guaranteeing ownership and access to land for vulnerable sectors of the peasantry. This alliance has produced a reformed governance model which is supposed to function to the advantage of all those involved—large local (rural) and foreign entrepreneurs, middle-sized commercial farmers, small subsistence peasantry, nationals, foreigners, men and women—under the supervision of a benign state that networks with a multiplicity of self-governing 'communities'. In this governance model 'communities' are conceived as homogeneous and thus not a problem. The supposed 'neutrality' of this reform, which is supposed to be non discriminatory, is the other side of the coin of the socialism in which Frelimo considers the peasantry as one coherent body. This blindness to the different means of livelihood and class interests of the various strata of farming people is a fatal mistake (O'Laughlin 2000).

What has been missing from the debate on this and other reforms is an understanding of the way institutions which appear to be acting for the common good actually create relations of unequal power and authority, helping to further marginalize those who have no 'voice'. The long history of the survival of the rural population of Mozambique through wars and all kinds of other problems is characterized by mobility and strategies of multiple livelihood. If constrained to a modernized form of 'reserve system', of boundary-making and exclusion, the people will turn to forms of autochthony, ethnic identity, policies of one-man-against-the-other, and finally turn against the state itself.

The struggle over land, with the poor and landless invading and turning to violent appropriation, occasionally with the connivance of national and/or local politicians interested in their vote, has become less and less 'silent'. It is apparent that rural people who subsist on marginal lands are now increasingly exerting their 'agency' in different ways, from not voting, to openly opposing 'development' projects, or practising forms of witchcraft (Moyo 1998). Rural and urban community struggles are developing (Desai 2002). These phenomena are little understood because of the inability of politicians to accept, or deal with, the covert aspects of mobilizing for reform. The root causes of conflict are to be found in the opposition to the notion of democracy as emanating from the people and in the rejection of the model of democratic construction in Africa: that is one that would turn mobilization for reform into a politically recognizable form of agency for its citizens.

Bibliography

Amselle, J.L. and E. M'Bokolo (eds.) (1985), *Au Coeur de l'Ethnie*, Paris, La Decouverte.

Anderson, B. (1983), *Imagined Communities. Reflections on the Origin and Spread of nationalism*, London, Verso.

Apter, D.E. (1965), *The Politics of Modernization*, Chicago, The University of Chicago Press.

Arrighi, G. (2002), 'The African Crisis', *New Left Review*, vol. 15, pp. 5–36.

Austin, G. (1996), *The Effects of Government Policy on the Ethnic Distribution of Income and Wealth in Rwanda, a Review of the Published Sources*, London, LSE/Department of Economic History.

Bayart, J.F. (1989), *L'Etat en Afrique. La politique du Ventre*, Paris, Fayard.

——. (1996), *L'Historicité de l'Etat importé*, Paris, Le Cahiers du Ceri 15.

——. (2000), 'Africa in the World: A History of Extraversion', *African Affairs*, vol. 99, no. 395, pp. 217–267.

Bayart, J.F., S. Ellis and B. Hibou (eds.) (1999), 'The Criminalisation of the State in Africa', *African Issues*, Oxford, James Currey.

Bazeguissa-Ganga, R. (1999), 'The Spread of Political Violence in Congo Brazzaville', *African Affairs*, vol. 98, no. 45, pp. 37–54.

Berdal, M. and D. Malone (eds.) (2000), *Greed and Greviances: Economic Agendas in Civil Wars*, Boulder, Lynne Rienner.

Braekman, D. (1996), *Terreur Africaine: Burundi, Rwanda, Zaire: les racines de la violence*, Bruxelles, Fayard.

Bratton, M. and R. Mattes (2004), 'Democratic and Market Reforms in Africa: What 'the People' Say', in E. Gyimah-Boadi and L. Diamond (eds.), *Democracy and Development in Africa: The Quality of Progress*, Boulder and London, Lynne Rienner Publications, pp. 57–82.

Brown, S. (2001), 'Authoritarian leaders and multiparty elections in Africa: how foreign donors help to keep Kenya's Daniel arap Moi in power', *Third World Quarterly*, vol. 22, no. 5, pp. 725–73.

Campbell, B. (2000), 'Gouvernance: un concept apolitique?', in B. Campbell, F. Crépeau and L. Lamarche (eds.), *Gouvernance, réformes institutionnelles et l'émergence de nouveaux cadres normatifs dans le domaines social, politique et environnemental*, Cahier du CEDIM, Montreal, Université du Québec, pp. 18–28.

——. (2000), 'Réinvention du Politique en Cote d'Ivoire', *Politique Africaine*, no. 78, pp. 142–156.

Chabal, P. and J.-P. Daloz (1999). *Africa works: Disorder as Political Instrument*, London, James Currey.

Chretien, J.P. and G. Prunier (eds.) (1989), *Les Ethnies ont une Histoire*, Paris, Karthala.

Chretien, J.P. (1997), *Le défi de l'ethnisme*, Paris, Karthala.

——. (2000). 'Citoyenneté et ethnie en Afrique', in C. Fievet (ed.), *Invention et réinvention de la citoyenneté*, Pau, J.Sampy, pp. 321–333.

——. (1998), *Burundi entre histoire, memoire et ideologie*, Cahiers d'Etudes Africaines XXXVII.

Cliffe, L. and R. Luckham (1999), 'Complex political emergencies and the state: failure and the fate of the state', *Third World Quarterly*, vol. 20, no. 1, pp. 27–50.

Collier, P. (2000), 'Doing Well out of War', in M. Berdal and D. Malone (eds.), *Greed and Grievance: Economic Agenda in Civil Wars*, Boulder Co., Lynne Rienner, pp. 91–113.

Cramer, C. (1998), *Civil War is not a Stupid Thing: exploring the interlinkages between growth, inequality and conflict*, Working Paper 73. London: SOAS/Department of Economics.

De Heusch, L. (1997), *L'ethnie: les vicissitudes d'un concept*, Archive Européennes de Sociologie XXXVIII.

Desai, A. (2002), *We are the Poor. Community Struggles in Post-apartheid South Africa*, New York, Monthly Review Press.

Diamond, L. (1997), *Consolidating the Third Wave Democracies: Themes and Perspectives*, Baltimore, Johns Hopkins University Press.

———. (1999), *Developing Democracy: Towards Consolidation*, Baltimore, Johns Hopkins Press.

Doorenspleet, R. (2000), 'Reassessing the Three Waves of Democratization', *World Politics*, vol. 52, pp. 384–406.

Dozon, J.P. (2000), 'La Cote d'Ivoire au peril de l'Ivoirité', *Afrique Contemporaine*, no. 193, pp. 13–24.

———. (2000), 'La Cote d'Ivoire entre démocratie, nationalisme et ethnonationalisme', *Politique Africaine*, vol. 78, pp. 45–62.

Dubow, S. (1994), 'Ethnic Euphemisms and Racial Echoes', *Journal of Southern African Studies*, vol. 20, no. 3, pp. 355–370.

Duffield, M. (1998), 'Post-Modern Conflict: Warlords, Post-Adjustement States and Private Protection', *Civil Wars*, vol. 1, no. 1, pp. 66–102.

———. (2001). *Global Governance and the New Wars. The Merging of Development and Security*, London, Zed Books.

Easterly, W. and R. Levine (1997), 'Africa Growth Tragedy: Policy and Ethnic divisions', *Quarterly Journal of Economics*, vol. 11, no. 4, pp. 1203–250.

Ekeh, P. (1995), 'Colonialism and the two Publics in Africa. A Theoretical Statement', *Comparative Studies in Society and History*, vol. 17, no. 1, pp. 91–112.

Ellis, S. (1999), *The Mask of Anarchy: the Roots of Liberia's war*, New York, New York University Press.

Eyok, D. (1998), 'Through the prism of a local tragedy: political liberalisation, regionalism and elite struggles for power in Cameroon', *Africa*, vol. 68, no. 3, pp. 338–359.

Fabian, J. (1998), *Moments of Freedom. Anthropology and Popular Culture*. Charlottesville, London, University Press of Virginia.

Fanthorpe, R. (2001), 'Neither Citizen nor Subject? 'Lumpen' Agency and the Legacy of Native Administration in Sierra Leone', *African Affairs*, vol. 100, no. 400, pp. 363–386.

Ferguson, J. (1990), *The Anti-Politics Machine: 'Development', 'Depoliticization' and Bureaucratic Power in Lesotho*, Cambridge, Cambridge University Press.

Geschiere, P. and J. Gugler (1998), 'The Urban-Rural Connection: Changing Issues of Belonging and Identification', *Africa*, vol. 68, no. 3, pp. 313–320.

Geschiere, P. and F. Nyamnjoh (2000), 'Capitalism and Authoctony, the Seesaw of Mobility and Belonging', *Public Culture*, vol. 12, no. 2, pp. 423–452.

Goody, J. (2001), 'Bitter Icons: How Ethnic is Ethnic Cleansing?', *New Left Review* 7, pp. 5–15.

Guichaoua, A. (1995), *Les crises politiques au Rwanda et au Burundi*, Lille, Université des Sciences et Technologies.

Halisi, C.D.R. (1998), 'Citizenship and Populism in the New South Africa', *Africa Today*, vol. 45, nos. 3-4, pp. 337–351.

Harbeson, J., D. Rothchild and N. Chazan (eds.) (1994), *Civil Society and the State in Africa*, Boulder Co., Lynner Reinner.

Huntington, S.P. (1968), *Political Order in Changing Societies*, New Haven, London, Yale University Press.

———. (1991), *The Third Wave: Democratization in the Late Twentieth Century*, Norman, University of Oklahoma Press.

Hyden, G. (1980), *Beyond Ujamaa in Tanzania: Underdevelopment and the Uncaptured Peasantry*, Berkeley, University of California Press.

Ingrao, B. (2002), 'Ethnicity and Development in Economic Discourse'. *Paper presented at the 6th Eshet Confrence Conference on Social Change and Economic Development in the History of Economic Thought*, Reythimo, Crethe, 14–17 March.

Kaldor, M. and R. Luckham (2001), 'Global Trasformation and New Conflicts', *IDS Bulletin*, vol. 32, no. 2, pp. 48–70.

Kaldor, M. (1999), *New and Old Wars. Organised Violence in a Global Era*, London, Polity Press, Blackwell.

Kaplan, R. (1994), 'The Coming Anarchy: How Scarcity, Crime, Overpopulation and Disease are Rapidly Destroying the Social Fabric od our Planet', *Atlantic Monthly*, no. 2, pp. 44–76.

Leach, M., R. Mearns and I. Scoones (1997), 'Challenges to Community-Based Sustainable Development, Dynamic, Entitlement Institutions', *IDS Bulletin*, vol. 28, no. 4, pp. 4–14.

Lemarchand, R. (1996), *Burundi: Ethnic Conflict and Genocide*, Cambridge, Cambridge University Press, Woodrow Wilson Center Studies.

Lemarchand, R. May (1999), *Ethnicity as Myth. The View from Central Africa*, Centre of African Studies, University of Copenhagen, Occasional Paper.

Lonsdale, J. (1995), "Listen while I read': orality, literacy and Christianity in the Young Kenyatta's making of the Kikuyu', *Paper presented for the Conference on Ethnicity in Africa-Roots, Meanings and Implications*, May, Edinburgh.

Mamdani, M. (1999), *Citizen and Subject. Contemporary Africa and the Legacy of Late Colonialism*, London, James Currey.

———. (2001), *When Victims become Killers, Colonialism, Nativism and the Genocide in Rwanda*, Kampala, Dar Es Salaam, Fountain Publishers.

M'Bokolo, E. (1983), 'Historicité et Pouvoir d'Etat en Afrique Noire', *Relations Internationales*, vol. 34, pp. 197–213.

Moyo, S. (1998), 'Land Entitlements and Growing Poverty in Southern Africa', *Sapem*, vol. 11, no. 5, pp. 15–22.

Nafziger, E.W. and J. Auvinen (2002), 'Economic Development, Inequality, War, State and Violence', *World Development*, vol. 30, no. 2, pp. 153–163.

Newbury, C. (1995), *The Invention of Rwanda: the Alchemy of Ethnicity*. Orlando: Asa.

———. (1998a), 'Ethnicity and the Politics of History in Rwanda', *Africa Today*, vol. 45, no. 1, pp. 7–24.

Nyamnjoh, F. and M. Rowlands (1998), 'Elite associations and the politics of belonging in Cameroon', *Africa*, vol. 68, no. 3, pp. 320–337.

O'Donnel, G. (2000), *Democracy, Law, and Comparative Politics*, IDS Working Paper n. 118, Brighton, IDS.

O'Laughlin, B. (2000), 'Class and the customary: the ambigous legacy of the indigenato in Mozambique', *African Affairs*, vol. 99, no. 394, pp. 5–42.

Ostheimer, A.E. (2001), 'The Permanent Entrenchment of Democratic Minimalism?', *African Security Review*, vol. 10, no. 1, pp. 25–43.

Prunier, G. (1995), *The Rwanda Crisis, 1959–1994: History of a Genocide*, London, HurstandCo.

Ranger, T. (1985), *The Invention of Tribalism in Zimbabwe*, Gweru, Mambo Press.

———. (1994), 'The Invention of Tradition Revisited: the Case of Colonial Africa.', in P. Kaarsholò and J. Hultin (eds.) *Invention and Boundaries: Historical and Anthropological Approaches to the Study of Ethnicity and Nationalism. International Development Studies*, Roskilde, Roskilde University.

Reno, W. (1995), *Corruption and State Politics in Sierra Leone*, Cambridge, Cambridge University Press.

———. (2000), 'Liberia and Sierra Leone: The Competition of Patronage in Resource-Rich

Economies', in E.W. Nafziger, F. Steward and R. Vayrynen (eds.) *Weak States and Vulnerable Economies: Humanitarian Emergencies in Developing Countries. vol. 2*, Oxford, Oxford University Press, pp. 231–261.
Reyntjens, F. (1994), *L'Afrique des Grands Lacs en crise: Rwanda and Burundi (1988-1994)*, Paris, Karthala.
Richards, P. (1996), *Fighting for the Rainforests: War, Youth and Resources in Sierra Leone*, Oxford, James Currey.
Sanders, E. (1969), 'The Hamitic Hypothesis: its Origins and Functions', *Journal of African History*, vol. 10, no. 4, pp. 521–32.
Sindzingre, A. (1998), *Dimension Economique des Reformes de l'Etat en Afrique Sub-Saharienne*, Bordeaux, Ecole d'été Aegis.
——. (2000), 'Le contexte économique et social du changement politique en Cote d'Ivoire', *Afrique Contemporaine*, no. 193, pp. 27–38.
——. (2001), *States, Networks and Rents: Constrasting Corruption in Africa and Asia*, Paris, Cnrs.
Stein, H. (2000), *The Development of the Developmental State in Africa: a Theoretical Inquiry*, University of Copenhagen, Center of African Studies. December.
Steward, F. and R. Vayrynen (eds.) (2000), *War hunger and Displacement: the Origins of Humanitarian Emergencies*, Oxford, Oxford University Press.
Steward, F. (2000), *Weak States and Vulnerable Economies: Humanitarian Emergencies in Developing Countries, vol. II*, Oxford: Oxford University Press.
Stoler, A.L. and F. Cooper (1997), 'Between Metropole and Colony: Rethinking a Research Agenda', in F. Cooper and A.L. Stoler (eds.) *Tensions of Empire. Colonial Cultures in a Bourgeois World*, Berkeley, Los Angeles, London, University of California Press.
Storey, A. (1999), 'Economics and Ethnic Conflict: Structural Adjustment in Rwanda', *Development Policy Review*, vol. 17, pp. 43–63.
Strange, S. (1996), *The Retreat of the State: the Diffusion of Power in the World Economy*, Cambridge, Cambridge University Press.
UNDP, *Human Development Report 2002*.
Vail, L. (ed.) (1989), *The Creation of Tribalism in Southern Africa*, London, James Currey.
Van de Walle, N. (2000), 'The Impact of Multi-Party Politics in Sub-Saharan Africa', *Annual Conference of the Norwegian Association of Development Research, 'The State under Pressure'*, 5–6 October, Norway.
Vansina, J. (1998), 'The Politics of History and the Crisis in the Great Lakes', *Africa Today*, vol. 45, no. 1, pp. 34–77.
Vidal, C. (1991), *Sociologie des passions*, Paris, Karthala.
——. (1995), 'Le genocide des Rwandais tutsi: trois questions d'histoire', *Afrique Contemporaine*, no. 174, pp. 8–33.
——. (1998), 'Le génocide des rwandais tutsi et l'usage public de l'histoire', *Cahiers d'études africaines*, nos. 150–152, pp. 331–347.
——. (1998), 'Questions sur le role des paysans durant le genocide des Rwandais tutsi', *Cahiers d'études africaines*, vol. 38, nos. 2–3, pp. 331–345.
Wamba-dia-Wamba, E. (1994), 'Africa in Search of a New Mode of Politics', in H. Himmelstrand (ed.) *African Perspectives in Development*, London, James Currey.
West, H.G., S. Kloeck-Jenson (1999), 'Betwixt and between: traditional authority and democratic decentralisation in post-war Mocambique', *African Affairs*, vol. 98, no. 393, pp. 455–485.
Willame, J.C. (1995), *Aux sources de l'hecatombe rwandaise*, Les Cahiers Africains, no. 14, Paris, L'Harmattan.
——. (1997), *Banyarwanda and Banyamulenge: Violences ethniques et gestion de l'identitaire au Kivu*, Paris, L'Harmattan.

CHAPTER THREE

NATURAL RESOURCES, SCARCITY AND CONFLICT:
A PERSPECTIVE FROM BELOW

Mirjam de Bruijn and Han van Dijk[1]

> At least 23,000 Fulbe herders have fled Nigeria's eastern Taraba
> State to Cameroon in order to escape clashes, which broke out
> in the Mambila plateau with farming communities at the begin-
> ning of the year, a pastoral association said. [. . .] Clashes between
> pastoral and farming communities revolving around disputes
> over grazing land became frequent in various parts of Nigeria's
> central and northern regions in recent years. Some analysts have
> blamed the trend on increasing desertification further north,
> which is pushing herders southwards in their search for pasture,
> often putting them in conflict with farming communities (AFROL
> News, 23 February 2002).

Clashes between farmers and herders are being reported everywhere
in the drought-prone regions of Sub-Saharan Africa. In some cases
they are extremely violent, in others conflict is limited to social, political and ethnic tensions. The origin of these conflicts often lies in the
decreasing, or finite, availability of natural resources in combination
with increasing population pressure resulting from, for example, the
immigration of groups of different ethnic origins. This is leading to
a scarcity of resources and increasing competition for any that are
available: violent (ethnic) conflict is the inevitable result. This fits
with the image of a neo-Malthusian disaster in Africa caused by high
birth-rates, the irresponsible use of ecological environments and inter-
ethnic hostility based on age-old tribal conflicts. It seems to address
the concerns of policymakers and development agencies dealing with
sustainable development and ecosystem management.

---

[1] This article is the result of various discussions. A first draft of the text was presented by Mirjam de Bruijn at the AEGIS summer school in Leipzig in August 2001.
Discussions during this meeting were helpful in sharpening our ideas and further
discussions with Karen Witsenburg, who did her field research in northern Kenya
and who is struggling with the same basic questions, were also inspiring (see Witsenburg
and Adano 2001).

However, many questions remain unanswered. Why do conflicts between herders and farmers occur in one instance and not in another? Is conflict inevitable? Are there no other intervening factors involved such as climate variability, technology, and conflict mediating institutions? Furthermore, do these conflicts really arise at the local level and are they based on ethnic affiliation as the primordial basis for political allegiance in Africa, or are there multiple levels of conflict, and ramifications for regional and national politics?

This chapter compares different cases of conflict and non-conflict between herders and farmers in ecologically fragile areas. Competition for scarce resources should not be neglected in the debate, but the analysis should allow ample space for a study of the problems from the perspective of the people involved in the conflicts themselves. Scarcity is relative and must be understood in a local context and from a local perspective. The main question to be considered here is, therefore, how important is resource competition to an explanation of farmer-herder conflict in the Sahel-Sudan region in West Africa, and what other factors are involved in these conflicts.

Scarcity and Conflict—A Debate

A predicted decrease in rainfall in the dry regions of Africa has put the question of the relationship between resource scarcity and political and ethnic conflict high on the agenda of policymakers and scientists (see Dietz et al. 2004, Van Den Born et al. 2000). The idea that increasing resource scarcity leads to more (violent) conflict has gained currency and analytical credibility in past decades. Rapid population growth, ecological decline and an increasing number of violent conflicts seem to confirm the causal relationship between these phenomena.

The implicit assumptions underlying this hypothesis are derived from a neo-Malthusian frame of reference. Poverty, lack of adequate technology and knowledge, as well as the slow growth of employment in other sectors of the economy have caused a poverty spiral. People are moving to the cities and trying to expand agricultural and industrial activities at the expense of already vulnerable ecosystems (UNEP 1999). Consequently, these people have no choice but to engage in a Darwinian struggle for survival and challenge others who compete with them for the use of the resources they need for their own survival.

Homer-Dixon (1994) who coined the phrase 'environmental scarcity'—defined as a scarcity of renewable resources—is a prominent analyst in this field. Scarcity is the result of environmental degradation and most observers regard degradation as the result of land-use systems becoming maladapted because of population growth, technical inadequacies when dealing with soil erosion, and high levels of exploitation of soil nutrients. Scarcity is, therefore, induced by human action. Environmental change can be defined as a "human-induced decline in the quantity or quality of a renewable resource that occurs faster than it is renewed by natural processes" (Homer-Dixon 1999: 64). Similar definitions emphasizing the human factor in environmental decline circulate in policy circles around desertification, deforestation and other phenomena related to ecological degradation (see UNDP 1991). Large areas of semi-arid Africa are defined as severely degraded, implying that the current condition of the land is the result of the impact of human activity (Dietz et al. 2004).

However, the relationship between human agency, resource scarcity and conflict is hotly debated (see Gleditsch 1998; Schwartz et al. 2000), with discussion centred on the notion of causality. To establish the precise relationship between environmental scarcity and violent conflict, one needs, firstly, to ascertain whether there is indeed a growing scarcity of natural resources and that cases of violent conflict are in fact on the increase. Secondly, this scarcity needs to be perceived as such by the parties involved in violent conflict. Thirdly, is scarcity one of the reasons why the various stakeholders are engaging in conflict and resorting to violence?

The relationship between population growth, ecological degradation and increasing resource scarcity has recently been seriously challenged by evidence from research on ecological changes in more densely populated zones and semi-arid areas in East and West Africa. African ecological environments display much more variety than commonly assumed and processes of environmental change are more varied and complex. What appears to be degradation may well be part of the normal natural variability resulting from fluctuations in rainfall and other drivers of the ecosystem. For example, rainfall fluctuations have been shown to be the main driving force for oscillations in pasture production in dry-land Africa to the extent that it is hard to detect the influence of intensive grazing on the vegetation in the long run, and to establish ecological degradation (Ellis and Swift 1988).

Local people, especially resource-poor farmers, actively manage and anticipate future changes and demands. Historical reconstruction has shown that what was taken to be a degraded ecosystem with an increasing population, actually shows a remarkable improvement compared with the past, the reason being investment by local people who are always supposed to be the unwilling victims of ecological decline and population growth (Tiffen et al. 1994; Fairhead and Leach 1996; Basset and Koli Bi 1999; Mortimore and Adams 1999). Quite remarkably, in the Sahel, where one would expect environmental degradation and scarcity of resources to be critical factors in the lives of an increasing number of people, the level of conflict is relatively low compared to other regions in Africa.

Scarcity, far from being an absolute phenomenon, has to be set within its socio-political and legal context. Various groups have different forms of access to resources and are affected differently by drought, rainfall variability, population growth and ecological degradation. As Adams (1992: 87, cited in Salih 2001) argues: "the environment [i.e. scarcity of resources] is not neutral in its effects on the poor; environmental quality is mediated by society, and society is not undifferentiated. Access to and the distribution of environmental 'goods' is uneven". People occupy uneven 'risk positions' *vis-à-vis* ecological calamities (cf. Beck 1992), and are differently affected by resource scarcity, oscillations in resource availability and ecological decline. Due to their status, certain groups may be denied access to economic assets and specific ways of resource use, or may be excluded when it comes to the distribution of resources and/or income over society (De Bruijn and Van Dijk, 2003a). Their responses to ecological constraints will differ, as will their predisposition to conflict. Therefore, a study of the relationship between environmental change and violent conflict should also take into consideration the differential distribution of the costs and benefits of conflict and violence, and the social and political divisions leading to conflict, concentrating on those who benefit from these events.

Models derived from political science that take large-scale phenomena as the basis for analysis and presuppose a linear relationship between scarcity and conflict are essentially flawed. Conclusions drawn at the national and international level cannot be downsized to the regional and local level. Actors at these lower levels do not react in the same way to assumptions postulated at international and national levels. For one thing, ecological change is not a predictable and linear phenomenon. Consequently, local actors cannot be expected to respond accordingly. Detailed research is needed to investigate the dynamics of small- and medium-sized changes in the ecological environment and their relationship to violent conflicts and the behaviour of local actors under these conditions. Focusing on violent conflict leads to the neglect of other types of responses to environmental scarcity and decline, such as migration to urban areas and more fertile regions (Westing 1992; Suhrke 1994; Lonergan 1998).

Herders and Farmers in the Sahel: Increasing Conflict and Violence?

An investigation into farmer-herder conflicts in West Africa may reveal a good deal about the relationship between resource scarcity and violent conflict. Over the past decades there have been a number of studies on this topic, mainly dealing with the Fulbe and their sedentary neighbours.

On the surface, there seems to be good reason to suppose that conflicts are on the increase. The population in West Africa is growing at an enormous rate and cultivators are expanding their fields and putting large tracts of pasture into production. Ecological problems in the form of drought, bad harvests, famine and massive losses of livestock have plagued the region over the past decades. Rainfall figures for the past 40 years show a very irregular pattern, with periods of drought and a reduction in average rainfall figures since the 1960s (Put et al. 2004).

Consequently, millions of farmers and herders from the areas affected by ecological calamities have left their homeland to settle in more fertile regions. Ecological stress is an important determinant of life. Scarcity of natural resources is thus an important factor in shaping the lives of the inhabitants of the Sahel, and seems to have become more important over the course of the 20th century. Studies of farmer-herder relations suggest that violent conflict is on the increase, and that increasing resource scarcity (both man-made and natural) forms the basis for clashes between different user groups.[2] However, Hussein et al. (1999) argue convincingly that evidence for this statement is lacking. They asked the authors of studies on herder-farmer conflicts

---

[2] See Delgado 1979; Benoit 1984; Marchal 1983; Bernardet 1984, 1999; Bassett 1988; Diallo 1995; Van Driel 1999; Hagberg 2001.

whether they had any figures on the frequency of past and present conflicts. No one could provide a satisfactory answer. The three cases presented below demonstrate that an answer to such a question is difficult to give, but that any explanation of conflict should include an historical analysis and an examination of present-day social relations.

Periods of resource scarcity in the Sahel have always been linked to variations in climate (see, for example, Gado 1993; Tymowski 1978; Cissoko 1968). In the course of time individual and collective strategies have been developed, and positions *vis-à-vis* the ecological risks have been taken. The Sahel has not enjoyed a peaceful and harmonious past: tensions, raids, conflict and political unrest have always been present. The source of conflict can often be explained in relation to the vagaries of the ecological environment. Social and political hierarchies have functioned to some extent to secure access to resources at the expense of those at the bottom of the social scale, who suffer the uncertainties of rainfall and resource scarcity in ways that can be said to be a form of institutional violence against the powerless. Even today, the old relationship between these subjugated people and their masters plays a role in the division of labour and in status hierarchies (De Bruijn and Van Dijk 1995, 2001, 2003a).

The development of complementary strategies is another institutionalized way of dealing with limited accessibility to natural resources. Farmers and herders have co-managed the available resources and maintained good relations in order to profit from each other's expertise.

However, during the 20th century profound changes took place in the relationship between herders and farmers in West Africa that may have weakened the mechanisms for containing conflict and violence. The abolition of slavery, the incorporation of political hierarchies into the colonial state and the relative peace that was brought to the area by the colonial regime resulted in an expansion of cultivation to pastures that had previously been the ambit of pastoral groups. The livelihood of farmers and herders grew increasingly similar. Consequently, the degree of complementarity of farming and herding decreased and they became direct competitors for land.

This transformation of land use and farmer-herder relations was further exacerbated by the droughts of the 1970s and 80s. Large numbers of herders lost most of their livestock and turned to the cultivation of cereals, to herding for the new post-drought livestock owners or migrated to the Sudan, with or without livestock. Investments in labour-saving technology, the large-scale introduction of cash crops and a population growth over the past decades of more than two per cent per annum resulted in the expansion of cultivation in the West African savannah region.

Three Cases of Interaction between Herders and Farmers

Northern Côte d'Ivoire

At first sight, the conflict between Fulbe herders and Senoufo farmers seems a classic example of competition for resources and space by two rural population groups. The Fulbe, victims of the droughts, have been compelled to create a new existence among a hostile farming population. The Senoufo farmers, for their part, feel threatened by the pastoralists who occupy the bush land around their villages and whose herds destroy their fields. However, the situation is much more complicated than it first appears, and current conflicts result from a complex interaction between government policies, internal contradictions in Fulbe and Senoufo society and ecological change.

The wave of migration began well before the droughts of the 1960s with pastoralists from Boboola in Burkina Faso (Diallo 1995; Bernardet 1999). Later, pastoralists from Mali followed. Initially, they (and their animals) were welcomed as there was a shortage of meat in the Côte d'Ivoire and imports from Argentina and the European Community were required for the country's fast-growing cities. Local production in the north of the country, where population numbers were relatively low, seemed to be a good strategy for replacing meat imports and improving the balance of trade. The local Senoufo farmers also welcomed the herders with their cattle, seeing their presence as a means of increasing their capacity to produce cereals and cotton with the help of organic manure produced by the livestock of the Fulbe. Fulbe oxen could draw their ploughs, and they sometimes hired Fulbe herdsmen to manage their personal herds.

However, an extremely significant factor for the hostility against Fulbe pastoralists was the role of the government in creating the conditions for conflict. The Ivorian government promoted the settlement of pastoralists and livestock production: large investments were made to open up forest reserves and to encourage Fulbe pastoralists to settle there via SODEPRA (SOciété de DÉveloppement des PRoductions Animales), a parastatal charged with the development of livestock production in the north of the Côte d'Ivoire. Vaccination programmes were set up for the cattle, pasture was upgraded, feed concentrates were provided, and the water situation was improved with the construction of hundreds of dams to retain water during the dry season. Despite a few planning disasters (Bernardet 1999), improvements in the water situation and the provision of services to combat infectious diseases and ticks certainly contributed to a spectacular growth in livestock numbers (Diallo 1999).

The policy to promote the keeping of livestock was very successful and by 1994 the density of the livestock population in the north of the Côte d'Ivoire (19 head of cattle per km^2) was comparable to that of Mali and Burkina Faso. Growth figures over the 1970s and 80s varied between 9.3 per cent between 1975 and 1982, to 5.2 per cent from 1982 to 1986. However, the growth rate for Fulbe herds was even higher, between 15 per cent and 7.5 per cent (Diallo 1999). Private Ivorian investors, such as urban traders and civil servants who invested in livestock and the construction of dams for their own purposes promoted further growth.

The local Senoufo farmers have felt threatened by this state of affairs and have tried to limit access, preventing the Fulbe from tending their herds, and by having hunting associations patrol the bush to track down Fulbe whose herds destroy their fields. The populations from the north also feel neglected within the national context of the Côte d'Ivoire.

On several occasions, the area has been the scene of violent conflicts between Fulbe and Senoufo. In 1974, this had required the intervention of the Ivorian head of state. In 1986 Fulbe had been expelled from the Côte d'Ivoire and in 1993 similar incidents had occurred just after the death of President Houphouet Boigny, who had always promoted immigration into the Côte d'Ivoire. The political situation has recently deteriorated further, following the presidential elections in 2000, the xenophobia that erupted and was manipulated by southern politicians to promote their own interests. Many Fulbe have returned to Mali and Burkina Faso because they no longer feel safe in the Côte d'Ivoire.

A further factor in the deterioration of farmer-herder relations is the internal structure of Fulbe society: the Fulbe have changed their system of servitude for one of salaried labour. The rich Fulbe in northern Côte d'Ivoire often employ salaried herdsmen—young and impoverished Fulbe who have no other means of employment in their home areas in Mali or Burkina Faso—to look after their herds. Relationships between these patrons and their herders are extremely exploitative (Bassett 1988). Minor incidents, such as cattle trampling a Senoufo-owned field, entitle the patron to withhold the already very low salary of the herder or reduce his material income (grain). The herdsmen, who are already often living on the edge of starvation, can no longer make a living and are forced to steal cattle or commit other crimes. They do not dare steal livestock from their own patrons but steal, for example, from a Senoufo cattle owner, which leads to further conflict between the Senoufo and the Fulbe (Bernardet 1999: 427–34).

Within Senoufo society there are conflicts between those who own cattle and those who do not, in regard to natural resource management and livestock keeping (Bernardet 1999: 432–43).

The ecological situation also plays a role in these conflicts. Over time, the area cultivated by Senoufo farmers has expanded significantly. Bassett and Koli Bi (1999: 154) report that in their research area in northern Côte d'Ivoire the cultivated area increased from 23 per cent in 1956 to 36 per cent of the total surface area in 1989. They also report a considerable increase in types of vegetation where trees dominate instead of grasses. They explain this change as resulting from different burning practices, the influence of grazing and cattle manure promoting the growth of trees, and the alternation of cultivation and fallow periods (ibid.: 158). Their study shows that this type of savannah ecosystem was highly unstable as only one quarter of the land remained in the same land-use classification unit between 1956 and 1989 (ibid.: 157). The results of their study are confirmed by local perceptions of ecological change and Fulbe herders have responded by changing their location for transhumance to ensure sufficient grazing for their cattle.

Another important factor contributing to the increase in conflict in northern Côte d'Ivoire is the exploitation of ethnic contradictions by politicians, who manipulate the hostile relations between the groups to their own advantage in their election campaigning. A heated debate has also emerged around the question of immigration, focusing on the issue of *Ivorité* (i.e. Côte d'Ivoire citizenship and entitlement to participate in politics and run for political office). The Fulbe, as immigrants, are finding that their position has seriously been undermined by this debate on autochthony.

Burkina Faso: The Example of the Mossi Plateau

Most cases of violent conflict are reported from areas in the Sudan region where immigration from the north is a relatively recent phenomenon, but even in areas where farmers and herders have been living next to each other, conflict is also a part of daily life. It is said that conflicts are on the increase (Delgado 1979; Benoit 1984; Marchal 1983). The case of the Mossi Plateau in Burkina Faso seems to prove the thesis of increasing farmer-herder conflicts. For a long while this plateau has been inhabited by Mossi farmers and by Fulbe herders, 82.5 per cent and seven per cent of the population respectively. The area is known for its resource problems. Population density is very high, and since the 1970s observers have drawn attention to the continuing degradation of natural resources due to ill-adapted agricultural technologies and the overexploitation of pasture and forest resources.

The question is whether this is indeed a new situation or just a continuation of old relationships, old ways of managing problems and conflicting interests in a new context. Underlying the thesis of increased conflict is the assumption that in the past farmers and herders had complementary land-use strategies and lived in a kind of symbiosis. Because of the increasing pressure on resources and the gradual convergence of land-use strategies, it is reasoned that the symbiosis has been jeopardized and conflict increased.

Breusers et al. (1998) argue that this present interpretation is based on an incorrect understanding of the past. A study of the records concludes that in the 20th century conflict between herders and farmers had been much more common than assumed. It is thus difficult to prove that today's conflicts are different in principle from those in the past, or that there are more conflicts today. The question that needs to be asked is whether conflict is not in fact an integral part of the relationships between farmers and, if so, whether the increase in hostility should not also be questioned. In the past the strategies of farmers and herders were complementary in the sense that the farmers made use of the arable land and the herders made use of the bush, with sufficient space for both. After the cereal harvest, the Fulbe herders' livestock grazed on the harvest residues, were penned on Mossi agricultural land, and supplied them with manure to maintain soil fertility. This relationship altered when the Fulbe also took up cereal cultivation.

This decrease in complementarity was compensated for by another trend: the growing numbers of cattle owned by the Mossi were guarded by the Fulbe. Publicly, the Mossi uphold a negative image of the Fulbe and their ability as cattle guardians, accusing them of theft and the illegal selling of their animals, and regard them as uncivilized bush people (Breusers et al. 1998). In cases of crop damage inflicted by a Fulbe-managed herd on a Mossi farmer's field, there is a very open display of hostility by the Mossi. It appears, however, that there is a difference between the way herders and farmers present their case to outsiders (front-stage) and the way things are done in private (back-stage). To the public, the discourse is on contested interests and conflict, as though both groups hated each other. Relationships between individuals, however, have sometimes existed for generations. Fulbe often participate in Mossi naming and marriage ceremonies and may maintain fictive kinship relations with Mossi families. This does not exclude conflict but it does explain the exaggerated situation maintained in the presence of outsiders.

According to Breusers et al. (1998), this difference between front-stage and backstage displays of hostility and mutual friendship can be explained by internal contradictions in Mossi society. Cattle ownership among the Mossi is surrounded by secrecy: those owning cattle want to keep it secret to avoid the curse of other Mossi. To prevent others from knowing they have entrusted their cattle to Fulbe they will even go so far as to publicly denounce their own Fulbe herder or chase him from the village wells. To a casual observer it may seem that interethnic relations are strained and characterized by enmity and conflict, whereas in reality Mossi and Fulbe, individually, maintain longstanding relations of trust and collaboration with respect to cattle management.

The Hayre in Central Mali

The Hayre, a region in Central Mali in the middle of the Sahel, is regularly affected by drought and climate variability. It consists of a rocky plateau with a mountainous area extending towards the northeast to Hombori. Adjacent to the mountains and at the foot of the Bandiagara escarpment the plateau gives way to sandy plains. The plateau is a harsh environment mainly consisting of bare rock, and cultivation is only possible on around 10 per cent of the land. Most of the population is concentrated on the escarpment where water gathers, and more land is available on the plains. Resource scarcity is the main complicating factor of daily life and has ramifications in all aspects of life (De Bruijn and Van Dijk 1995). Analysis of rainfall figures shows a deterioration in rainfall over past decades (Put et al. 2004). Droughts in the 1970s and 80s have had a profound impact on the productivity of ecological resources. From one year to the next six-fold increases and decreases in biomass production can be observed. Economically it is one of the poorest areas in the Republic of Mali, which in turn is one of the poorest countries in the world. Child mortality is around 35 per cent for under fives (Hildebrand 1985; De Bruijn and Van Dijk 1995) and life expectancy was below 40 during the 1980s (Harts-Broekhuis and De Jong 1993). Resource scarcity and the extreme poverty of the population are the reasons for intervention by a number of NGOs. The area is mainly inhabited by semi-nomadic pastoralists who cultivate millet and herd cattle and small ruminants, which they regard as their main activity. In reality, a large number of these so-called pastoralists have become more dependent on cereal cultivation because they have lost most of their livestock through drought. The other main population group consists of cultivators who grow millet and sometimes sorghum. Increasingly they keep livestock to fertilize and plough the fields.

Given this situation, the Hayre seems the perfect stage for conflict over resources. During drought years, production is only able to feed a small portion of the human as well as animal population. This problem has been aggravated over the years by a number of changes. During the 20th century enormous tracts of land were taken into cultivation by agriculturalists to deal with the growing population and declining productivity of their land. The introduction of ox-drawn ploughs has expanded cereal cultivation and this labour-saving technology has enabled farmers to compensate for the declining productivity of their fields due to the decrease in rainfall and soil fertility. Some have even been able to expand cereal production for commercial purposes (Maas 2001; Rutgers Van Der Loeff 2001). Since the droughts, however, an increasing number of outside commercial herds have come into the area during the rainy season, again increasing the pressure on grazing resources.

Contrary to expectations, conflicts between herders and farmers and within Fulbe and Dogon societies are not very frequent. As everywhere else, there are conflicts relating to crop damage by livestock, and there have been a number of larger territorial disputes, but the amount and level of violence does not compare to situations reported elsewhere. The explanation for this lies with the historical actors and the internal organization of the societies in the area.

The Fulbe have been politically dominant for centuries. They vested small chiefdoms in the area in the 17th and 19th centuries, who controlled the area under the influence of the Fulbe Empire of Maasina, and which had its base in the Inland Delta of the Niger. The Fulbe subjugated other people there, making them slaves or dependants. The main reason for their 'success' was the protection they provided against invading and pillaging groups from other regions: against the Tuareg from the north, for example, and the Mossi from the southeast. Because of the military superiority of the Fulbe they controlled the plains and could prevent agricultural colonization by cultivating groups. The cultivation of cereals by their subordinates was organized in accordance with the needs of nomadic livestock herding (De Bruijn and Van Dijk 2001).

When the French colonized the area at the beginning of the 20th century the Fulbe were seen as the people in power and the political hierarchy they imposed on the population was accepted. However, the Fulbe lost control of the organization of land use. Although the hierarchy has changed, the division and regulation of access to resources still exists today. Former slaves are still dependent on their former masters for access to land for cultivation. At times of drought, therefore, it is clear who will have to leave the area, and during times of scarcity it is equally clear who has and does not have access to resources. As long as this balance of power exists and is accepted by everyone, violent conflict over resources is less likely to occur.

However, the Fulbe could not prevent the Dogon farmers, who had been contained in their refuge areas during the pre-colonial era, from expanding cultivation into the Fulbe pastures on the plains. With the colonial government in firm control, this process of colonization took place relatively peacefully. Even within the core areas of the chiefdoms, farmers who descended from the mountains occupied land. Many Fulbe, especially those on the southern plains, had no choice but to move away. They settled on the Bandiagara Plateau but also went as far as Burkina Faso or the Inland Delta of the Niger. In many places villages emerged where Fulbe and Dogon lived together, though in separate quarters.

With independence and drought, these trends continued. The first government of the Republic of Mali was keen to put an end to the feudal structures of pre-colonial society, and was not in favour of the traditional control over land. After the first drought in the 1970s, outside intervention in the form of a livestock development programme further undermined the traditional power base of the Fulbe elite. The political position of the herding groups within Fulbe society, which was already weak, further deteriorated and many lost their livestock and moved away. The position of former slaves, who were able to respond to ecological fluctuations with more flexibility, improved somewhat.

The strategies of individual herders during and after a drought or because of the gradual change in their environment indicates an intention to avoid conflict. Herders who have a mobile way of life prefer to migrate and search for new pasture areas rather than stay where there is not enough space for their animals. Although the movement of pastoral nomads was largely restricted in the 20th century, it appears that in the Hayre migration was still one of the important options in times of poverty and resource scarcity.

In many cases they settled near farming villages where they might be invited to herd their own or the farmer's livestock in their fields during the dry season to provide manure to restore soil fertility. In the past few decades, however, farmers have expanded their fields and it has become more difficult to feed animals. So, pastoral nomads have sought to obtain agricultural land to ensure a place within these villages, or they have moved on to become marginalized nomads, often deriving most of their income from non-agricultural activities such as petty trade, religious services and casual labour. Many families have had to separate, with individual males moving away to look for work as salaried herders, even though it is badly paid (De Bruijn and Van Dijk 2003b).

These patterns of mobility are embedded in the specific fabric of social institutions that shape relations between members of different guest and host communities. These social institutions allow guests to find a host, someone to act as patron in a new area. Migrants are often welcomed when they provide knowledge or services that are in demand in the host community. Especially in the Sahelian areas, where people are more mobile than elsewhere, these relations are critical. They are also important for the prevention and mediation of conflicts over resources.

Technological innovations are also central to this discussion on resource scarcity. People inhabiting these regions are not passively sitting and waiting to starve. They import new technologies and creatively invent new relations. For instance, in the Hayre herders have taken increasing numbers of camels into their herds. They are both more resistant to drought and are a good means of transport. The reason for adopting these animals is indeed ecological, but it is the immigrating Tuareg who acquainted them with their possibilities. From 1990 to 2000 the number of camels increased considerably and they have now become an important traction animal for farmers in the area.

Discussion

Conflicts between herders and farmers can be seen as the result of incompatibility between different land-use strategies and cultural and social factors, as well as the growing similarity in their respective system of land use. However, as the situation in the Hayre shows, differences as well as similarities do not necessarily have to lead to conflict as long as both groups are able to develop complementary strategies and have ways to mediate conflicts of interest. Even in cases of extreme resource scarcity, such as in the Sahel during and after periods of drought, the level of conflict can remain low. This situation points to the importance of an historical view of resource conflict. Shared experiences between population groups and long-term relationships can create a foundation for the mediation and resolution of conflicts before they get out of hand.

In the Burkinabé case, farmer-herder conflicts seem to have emanated from the internal contradictions in Mossi society, and are not so much a result of resource scarcity. In the Burkina case, conflicts seem to have been controllable, at least over the period studied in this paper, because of the long history of relationships between Mossi and Fulbe on the Central Plateau in Burkina Faso. Groups of Fulbe herders were often an integral part of the Mossi hierarchy, performing a specific role within this political constellation, while at the same time remaining strangers. Today, the Fulbe are tied to Mossi society in an entirely different way: they are no longer the cattle herdsmen of the sovereign, but anybody's herdsmen. At a distance, they appear to be an integral and historical part of Mossi society. It would be interesting to see whether the attitude of the Mossi is different towards newly immigrant Fulbe who entered the area during and after the droughts of the 1970s and 80s.

Past experiences do not have to be peaceful. Relations between the Dogon and the Fulbe have been very hostile at times but both groups have developed mechanisms to deal with conflicts. Differences are expressed through ritual and if necessary the Fulbe and Dogon perform complementary roles in these rituals (De Bruijn et al. 1997). Relations between herders and farmers are multi-stranded and are even formalized in organizations such as the *njaatigi* (Mali) and *zoogo* (Burkina Faso). The social fabric woven in this way prevents conflicts from getting out of hand. It would be interesting to examine the differences between newcomers and long-time Fulbe residents in these areas to assess their relative contributions to farmer-herder conflicts.

The situation in northern Côte d'Ivoire reveals a different kind of dynamics. The recent arrival of the Fulbe in this area and the conflict created by government involvement have created grudges and resentments among the autochthonous population who have not been able to accept these 'strangers' on their own terms. The organization of livestock production on the one hand, and the internal organization of the Fulbe on the other, were important contributing factors, because they resulted in unruly behaviour on the part of the young, badly paid, herdsmen.

Immigration into northern Côte d'Ivoire is fairly recent, and multi-stranded ties between host and 'strangers' have not had time to develop. Over the past few decades, especially since the death of Houphouet Boigny, the first president, the political situation in the Côte d'Ivoire has become extremely tense. Immigrants in particular have become the scapegoats in the country's internal political struggles. In this context, violence against the Fulbe has been tolerated. In some areas in south-western Burkina the manipulations of regional politicians have also contributed to a more tense political climate, where the possibility of violence is never far away.

What is the role of resource scarcity in farmer-herder conflicts? The paradox is that violent conflicts are most frequent in precisely those areas with the best resource availability. In all three case studies described above resources are diminishing. On the Mossi Plateau, high population density and underlying technological changes seem to be enhancing absolute and relative resource scarcity. In northern Côte d'Ivoire, bush encroachment, a growing population and increasing numbers of cattle are creating greater scarcity. In the Mali case, scarcity is a recurrent phenomenon because of rainfall failure.

However, in none of these is there a direct link between scarcity—such as drought or excessive localized pressure—and conflict. It seems that, for example, herders adapt their herding strategy to scarcity. They try to avoid situations of scarcity by moving their herds to better grazing areas. This is the major mechanism for diminishing the potential for resource conflict.

When conflicts arise frequently, it can be shown that they are sparked off by a set of conditions that enhance the potential for violence. In the Ivorian case, relations within Fulbe society contributed significantly to conflict as did the asymmetrical technical support for the herders by the government. In this case, many herders were not able to move, since they were not the owners of the herds they tended. Moreover, the Senoufo were deliberately provoking conflict by developing fields so near to Fulbe camps that it was almost inevitable that cattle would damage their fields. In the Malian case the situation is slightly different. There it is still possible to move cattle around when scarcities occur but limitations are imposed on livestock mobility.

However, this does not mean that ecological factors are not important for an understanding of the presence or absence of conflict. In the first place, fluctuations in the availability of resources are an important explanation for many of the changes that Sahelian and Sudanic societies have undergone over the past decades. Temporary resource scarcity is one of the basic parameters of life. The massive immigration of Fulbe herdsmen into the savannah area can only be explained as a response to recurrent drought in the Sahel. However, people engage as social beings in these conflicts and not in isolation. The relationships people have with those whom they regard as their own kind and with other groups always affect access to and the use of resources. Explanations for conflict have to be sought in the nature of these relations combined with the relevant ecological features of the resources in question.

The scarcity model is a logical sequel to discussions on the colonial period in which deterioration is seen as part of the discourse of civil servants (see, for instance, Fairhead and Leach 1996). In the 1930s there were already warnings about the advancing desert and French colonial officers were denouncing the wasteful use of natural resources. This has always served as a justification for the imposition of greater control over farmers and herdsmen (De Bruijn and Van Dijk 1999). In a similar vein, the categorization of various population groups into, sometimes invented, ethnic identities was a way for the colonial administration to gain more control over the people (see Amselle 1990). This is precisely what happened to Fulbe cattle-keeping people and Mande cultivating people from the area where these case studies were drawn (see De Bruijn and Van Dijk 1997).

The anthropologist's incursions into these cultures have for a long while contributed to the essentialist perception of these opposing identities (Breusers et al. 1998: 377). In view of this intellectual tradition, the idea of isolated ethnic groups coming into conflict over deteriorating and scarce resources is a logical contemporary variant. As we have shown, internal contradictions in these societies are just as important for explaining conflict. Moreover, a direct causal relationship between scarcity and conflict cannot be proven in the three above-mentioned cases of farmer-herder conflict.

Bibliography

AFROL News (2002), 'Masses of Fulani flee from Nigeria to Cameroon', see <http://www.afrol.com/news2002/nig008_bororo_cam.htm>.

Amselle, J.-L. (1990), *Logiques métisses, anthropologie de l'identité en Afrique et ailleurs*, Paris, Payot.

Bassett, T.J. (1988), 'The political ecology of peasant-herder conflicts in northern Ivory Coast', *Annals of the Association of American Geographers*, vol. 78, no. 3, pp. 453–472.

Bassett, T.J. and Z. Koli Bi (1999), 'Fulbe livestock raising and environmental change in Northern Côte d'Ivoire', in V. Azarya, A. Breedveld, M. de Bruijn and H. van Dijk (eds.), *Pastoralism under Pressure? Fulbe Societies Confronting Change in West Africa*, Leiden, Brill, pp. 139–159.

Beck, U. (1992), *Risk Society. Towards a New Modernity*, London, Sage.

Benoit, M. (1984), *Le Seno-Mango ne doit pas mourir: pastoralisme, vie sauvage et protection au Sahel*, Paris, ORSTOM.

Bernardet, P. (1984), *Association agriculture élevage en Afrique: Les Peuls semi-transhumants de Côte d'Ivoire*, Paris, l'Harmattan.

———. (1999), 'Peuls en mouvement, Peuls en conflits en moyenne et haute Côte d'Ivoire, de 1950 à 1990', in R. Botte, J. Boutrais and J. Schmitz (eds.) *Figures peules*, Paris, Karthala, pp. 407–444.

Breusers, M., S. Nederlof and T. van Rheenen (1998), 'Conflict or Symbiosis? Disentangling Farmer-Herdsman Relations: The Mossi and the Fulbe of the Central Plateau, Burkina Faso', *Journal of Modern African Studies*, vol. 36, no. 3, pp. 357–380.

Cissoko, S-M. (1968), 'Famines et épidémies à Tombouctou et dans la Boucle du Niger du XVIe au XVIIIe siècle', *Bulletin de l'IFA*, vol. 30, no. 3, série B, pp. 806–821.

Delgado, C.L. (1979), 'The Southern Fulani Farming System in Upper Volta: A Model for the Integration of Crop and Livestock Production in the West African Savannah', *African Rural Economy Paper 20*, Department of Agricultural Economics Michigan State University.

Diallo, Y. (1995), 'Les Peuls, les Sénoufo et l'État au nord de la Côte d'Ivoire. Problèmes fonciers et gestion du pastoralisme', *Bulletin APAD* 10, pp. 35–45.

——. (1999), 'Dimensions sociales et politiques de l'expansion pastorale en zone semi-humide ivoirienne', in V. Azarya, A. Breedveld, M. de Bruijn and H. van Dijk (eds.) *Pastoralism under Pressure? Fulbe Societies Confronting Change in West Africa*, Leiden, Brill, pp. 211–236.

De Bruijn, M. and H. van Dijk (1995), *Arid Ways, Cultural Understandings of Insecurity in Fulbe Society, Central Mali*, Amsterdam, Thela Publishers.

——. (eds.) (1997), *Peuls et Mandingues, Dialectiques des constructions identitaires*, Paris, Karthala.

——. (1999), 'Fulbe Mobility: Migration and Travel into Mande', *Mande Studies* (1), pp. 41–62.

——. (2001), 'Ecology and Power in the Periphery of Maasina: The Case of the Hayre in the Nineteenth Century', *Journal of African History*, vol. 42, no. 2, pp. 217–238.

——. (2003a), 'Risk Positions and Local Politics in a Sahelian Society. The Fulbe of the Hayre in Central Mali', in B. Moseley and B. Ikubolajeh Logan (eds.), *African Environment and Development: Rhetoric, Programs, Realities*, London, Ashgate Publishing, pp. 140–158.

——. (2003b), 'Changing Population Mobility in West Africa: Fulbe Pastoralists in Central and South Mali', *African Affairs*, vol. 102, no. 407, pp. 285–307.

——. (1997) 'Antagonisme et solidarité: les relations entre Peuls et Dogons du Mali central', in M. de Bruijn and H. van Dijk (eds.), *Peuls et Mandingues, Dialectiques des constructions identitaires*, Paris, Karthala, pp. 243–267.

Dietz, A.J., R. Ruben and A. Verhagen (eds.) (2004), *The impact of climate change on drylands, with a focus on West Africa*, Dodrecht, Kluwer Academic Publishers.

Ellis, J.E. and J. Swift (1988), 'Stability of African Pastoral Systems, Alternate Paradigms and Implications for Development', *Journal of Range Management*, no. 41, pp. 450–459.

Fairhead, J. and M. Leach (1996), *Misreading the African Landscape: Society and Ecology in a Forest Savanna Land*, Cambridge, Cambridge University Press.

Gado, B.A. (1993), *Une histoire des famines au Sahel: Étude sur des grandes crises alimentaires (XIXe-XXe siècles)*, Paris, l'Harmattan.

Gleditsch, N.P. (1998), 'Armed Conflict and the Environment: A Critique of the Literature', *Journal of Peace Research*, vol. 35, no. 3, pp. 381–400.

Hagberg, S. (2001), 'À l'ombre du conflit violent. Réglement et gestion des conflits entre agriculteurs karaboro et agro-pasteurs peul au Burkina Faso', *Cahiers d'Études africaines*, vol. 161, no. XLI-1, pp. 45–72.

Harts-Broekhuis, A. and A. De Jong (1993), 'Subsistence and Survival in the Sahel: Responses of Households and Enterprises to Deteriorating Conditions, and Development Policy in the Mopti Region of Mali', *Netherlands Geographical Studies*, no. 46, Amsterdam, KNAG.

Hildebrand, K. (1985), 'Assessing the Seasonal Stress amongst Fulani of the Seno-Mango, Central Mali', in: A.G. Hill (ed.) *Population, Health and Nutrition in the Sahel: Issues in the Welfare of Selected West African Communities*, London, Routledge Kegan Paul Inc., pp. 254–283.

Homer-Dixon, T.F. (1994), 'Environmental Scarcities and Violent Conflict: Evidence from Cases', *International Security*, vol. 19, no. 1, pp. 5–40.

——. (1999), *Environment, Scarcity and Violence*, Princeton, NJ, Princeton University Press.

Hussein, K., J. Sumberg and D. Seddon (1999), 'Increasing Violent Conflict between Herders and Farmers in Africa: Claims and Evidence', *Development Policy Review*, no. 17, pp. 397–418.

Lonergan, S. (1998), 'The Role of Environmental Degradation in Population Displacement', *Environmental Change and Security Project Report*, Issue 4, pp. 5–15.

Maas, P. (2001), *L'influence des changements climatiques sur l'exploitation du mil à Wayre, village dogon du Mali central*, Leiden, Afrika Studies Centre, ICCD/ASC Working Paper.

Marchal, J-Y. (1983), *Yatenga, Nord Haute Volta: La dynamique d'un espace rural Soudano-Sahelien*, Mémoires de l'ORSTOM, section de géographie.

Mortimore, M. and W.M. Adams (1999), *Working the Sahel. Environment and Society in Northern Nigeria*, London and New York, Routledge, Routledge Research Global Environmental Change.

Put, M., J. Verhagen, E. Veldhuizen and P. Jellema (2004), 'Climate change in dryland West Africa?, in A.J. Dietz, R. Ruben and A. Verhagen (eds.), *The impact of climate change on drylands, with a focus on West Africa*, Dodrecht, Kluwer Academic Publishers.

Rutgers van der Loeff, M. (2001), *Between Hardship and Abundance: Caravaneers and Caravan Trade in Central Mali*, Amsterdam, Dept. of Geography and Planning, Leiden, Afican Studies Centre, M.A. Thesis in Human Geography.

Salih, M.A.M. (2001), 'Introduction: Elements of Local Environmental Change and Society', in M.A.M. Salih (ed.), *Local Environmental Change in Africa*, Dordrecht, Kluwer Academic Publishers, 2nd ed., pp. 1–16.

Schwartz, D.M., T. Deligiannis and T.F. Homer-Dixon (2000), 'The Environment and Violent Conflict: A response to Gleditsch's Critique and Some Suggestions for Future Research', *Environmental Change and Security Project Report*, Issue 6, pp. 77–94.

Surhrke, A. (1994), 'Environmental Degradation, and Population Flows', Journal of International Affairs, vol. 47, no. 2, pp. 473–496.

Tiffen, M., M. Mortimore and F. Gichuki (1994), *More People, Less Erosion: Environmental Recovery in Kenya*, Chicester, John Wiley.

Tymowski, M. (1978), 'Famines et épidémies à Oualata et à Tichit XIXᵉ siècle', *Africana Bulletin*, no. 27, pp. 35–53.

UNDP (1991), *Assessment of Desertification and Drought in the Sudano-Sahelian Region 1985-1991*, United Nations Sudano-Sahelian Office.

UNEP (1999), *Global environmental outlook 2000*, Nairobi, UNEP with Earthscan.

Van den Born, G.J., M. Schaeffer and R. Leemans (2000), 'Climate Scenarios for Semi-Arid and Sub-Humid Regions: A Comparison of Climate Scenarios for the Dryland Regions in West Africa from 1990-2050', *NRP report 410 200 050*.

Van Driel, A. (1999), 'The End of the Herding Contract, Decreasing Complementary Linkages Between Fulbe Pastoralists and Dendi Agriculturalists in Northern Benin' in V. Azarya, A. Breedveld, M. de Bruijn and H. van Dijk (eds.), *Pastoralism under Pressure? Fulbe Societies Confronting Change in West Africa*, Leiden, Brill, pp. 191–211.

Westing, A. (1992), 'Environmental Refugees: a Growing Category of Displaced Persons', *Environmental Conservation*, vol. 21, no. 2, pp. 201–207.

Witsenburg, K. and W.R. Adano (2001), *Population Growth, Resource Scarcity and Armed Violence in Northern Kenya: Flawed Causal Relationship*, Draft Paper, Amsterdam.

CHAPTER FOUR

EMPIRICAL PERSPECTIVES ON AFRICAN CONFLICT RESOLUTION

Klaas van Walraven

Introduction

There are, perhaps, few concepts that can count on such faithful lip service from politicians, NGOs and interested social scientists as the notion of 'conflict prevention'. Since the end of the Cold War, this notion has been perceived as relevant to the maintenance of the new world order, which materialized when the super powers not only stepped back from the nuclear abyss, but also saw diminishing advantage in sustaining wars by proxy in their Third World theatres of confrontation. With its twin notion of 'early warning', conflict prevention entered the vocabulary of international diplomacy, ostensibly giving rise to a new way of handling human conflict. This was facilitated not only by a collusion of interests between policy-makers forced to provide answers to humanitarian crises and social scientists eager to sustain public investment in social science research, but also by what this chapter argues is the rather ill-defined nature of the notion of conflict prevention.

The rise of what could be called the conflict prevention *discourse* also affected the style, if not the practical functioning, of Africa's diplomatic community. African policy-makers, diplomats and international civil servants began to refer to early warning, conflict prevention and peace-building in their public pronouncements, their thinking and their search for strategies that could improve the continent's declining effectiveness in handling its own—especially intra-state—conflicts. Such thinking on new strategies, tactics and policies had begun in the late 1980s to early 1990s and resulted from a growing awareness of the ineffectiveness of Africa's own international organizations in ending wars.

Thus, the reforms undertaken in the Organization of African Unity (OAU) in 1992–93 rested squarely on the specifics of the experiences of the organization in the mediation of conflicts in the preceding decades. The measures taken, however, were to some extent affected by and couched in the language of the policy concepts that, by then, were *en vogue* in international diplomacy: that is, early warning, conflict prevention, peace-keeping and peace-making. The same was true, possibly even to a greater extent, for the institutional reforms that were introduced in regional organizations such as the Economic Community of West African States (ECOWAS), in 1998–99, and the Southern African Development Community (SADC), from 1996.

It is far from certain, however, that these interests, reforms and institutional mandates were actually informed by the rationale of the conflict prevention discourse as it originated in Western policy circles. As is well known from studies of African societies, their political systems differ considerably from those in the West, something that has not fundamentally changed since the onset of multi-party rule.[1] Consequently the rationale for, and actual performance of, (non-)governmental African institutions—including those operating on an international level—could very well be driven by other objectives, considerations and interests. In that respect, one could even argue that the discourse of conflict prevention has tended to blur our understanding of the working of Africa's international politics. This chapter therefore analyses the problem of conflict prevention in Africa from an empirical, rather than a normative, perspective. In so doing, it focuses on some of the continent's inter-governmental institutions, since these structures, being controlled by African state elites, represent some of the (potentially) more powerful international institutions on the continent.[2]

Theoretical Observations on Conflict Prevention, Mediation and Intervention

Before these international organizations and their role are analysed, some comments are necessary on the concept of conflict prevention and mediation. The emergence of a conceptual framework incorporating conflict prevention and early warning owed much to the with-

---

[1] See, for example, Bratton and van de Walle 1997.
[2] A comprehensive study of the role of conflict prevention in Africa would, of course, require inclusion of the various non-governmental institutions and groups working in this field, but this would go beyond the remit of a chapter in a book.

drawal of the superpowers from Third World theatres of conflict. Of course, during the era of superpower confrontation external interference in many of these conflicts had been prompted not so much by a desire for settlement, irrespective of which belligerent party would come on top or benefit most, as by the desire to advance the interests of the superpowers themselves, and intervention was dependent to a considerable degree on the extent to which these interests corresponded with those of one of the belligerents. This led, more often than not, to an intensification of local conflicts and, sometimes, to escalation into full-blown regional conflagrations. Indo-China, Angola, the Horn of Africa and Afghanistan are typical cases in point.

Yet, the end to what might be called conflicting forms of intervention was not an unambiguous blessing. The decline of Western and Eastern bloc interest in Third World problems meant that many—though not all—conflicts could linger on interminably (Zartman 1991: 299–319). Liberia, Sierra Leone, and the Democratic Republic of Congo (DRC) could be cited as examples. In other conflict situations the end of superpower meddling resulted not in peace, but in a substantial deterioration in security, developing into comprehensive humanitarian crises, in part due to the Cold War. Somalia is a good example of this.

The strategic marginalization of these countries by the North meant that, if these conflicts were to be settled by parties other than the belligerents themselves, action had to be taken by international organizations and/or regional powers. International organizations such as the UN were, thus, confronted with a daunting challenge, not only because they did not really have 'power' themselves and had to rely on member states and their willingness to put their forces at their disposal, but also because many of the conflicts were very complex, intra-state wars. In many cases the United Nations proved unable to make a difference—especially if the individual member states were pursuing their own, conflicting interests. The history of UN intervention in the Balkans is a telling example.

Consequently, social scientists, policy-makers and NGO representatives began to argue that it would be easier and cheaper if outside actors—so-called 'third parties'—were to intervene *before* a stage of armed conflict had been reached. This required timely warnings of impending trouble, which in turn demanded the systematic collection and analysis of data on the basis of which warnings could be given to decision-makers, recommending the requisite steps to pre-empt the eruption of violence. While this represents, in short, the core of the conflict prevention argument, it should be realized that the essence of the concept involves pre-emptive action being taken *before* a conflict develops into armed violence. One should otherwise refer to conflict 'mediation', 'intervention' or 'management' (i.e. 'reduction' of the level or intensity of violent conflict), conceptually older terms that refer to activities *vis-à-vis* conflicts that have already led to violent exchanges. It is important to realize the difference, as many politicians and diplomats refer to conflict prevention in the context of *existing* violence—where conflict *mediation* would be more appropriate.

The conflict prevention discourse ignored one hard fact of international politics, namely that action by third parties (whether mediation or real prevention) seldom occurs if self-interest is not involved. This has two implications. Firstly, action will not be taken on the sole basis of a financial cost-benefit calculation being implicit in the conflict prevention argument. Secondly, one could argue that theoretically humanitarian concerns should indeed be sufficient ground for action if, and to the extent that, the third party perceives that putting an end to human suffering in another country is in *its* interest. With the instant transmission of televised pictures of human misery across the globe, the pressure of public opinion could become a factor in the calculations of decision-makers.

However, *as a matter of fact*, human suffering has seldom proved to be sufficient reason for third party actors to intervene forcefully (that is, militarily) with a view to putting an end to hostilities in another country. In Africa, for example, the ECOMOG's intervention in Liberia was driven not only by humanitarian considerations (Van Walraven 1999c: 40–45); contrary to accepted wisdom, televised pictures of human suffering did not prove crucial in the intervention in Somalia.[3] Rwanda, despite ample warning, had to content itself with president Clinton's apology for US inaction years after the genocide that was not prevented; and, finally, UN intervention in Sierra Leone, Eritrea-Ethiopia, and the DRC came well after the outbreak of hostilities and the death of innumerable victims. In other words, neither financial nor humanitarian considerations are (solely) decisive in decisions to mediate in or prevent conflicts.

---

[3] See Ph.D. by P.G. Robinson (Liverpool). Personal communication to the author, 4 September 2001.

Hence, in order to understand current realities one needs to return to more sobering reflections on the theory of social science, and notably the political power approach to conflict mediation.[4] This perspective assumes that both parties to the conflict and the mediating third party have their own specific agendas. The third party will intervene principally in pursuit of his own interests, in whatever way these are formulated—which means that it is rarely appointed by the belligerent parties, who in principle have an interest in winning. Initially, therefore, the third party often acts on its own initiative.

From this it follows that a third party may not observe strict neutrality but may profit from a certain bias towards one or other party as this may provide some influence over the belligerents—although this should not lead to partisanship either, since this would result in the loss of influence over parties not benefiting from support. Leverage is crucial to the third party, usually resulting from a mutually disadvantageous stalemate between the belligerents and their perception of this continuing stalemate as being unacceptable and that it should be substituted for a mutually agreeable—mediated—formula, rather than outright victory for one of the parties concerned. The outcome of such mediation usually depends on the balance of power between the belligerent parties and the third party.[5]

Since the third party has his own interests to consider, mediation or, better still, intervention,[6] might also be achieved for reasons other than the peaceful settlement of the conflict or any settlement, irrespective of which belligerent would profit most (also Herbst 2000: 318–320). As argued below, conflict intervention may even represent a manifestation of conflict itself. The substance of the *factual* rationale—or motivation—of the intervening parties must therefore be studied, since these impinge heavily on the character, execution and outcome of intervention. Here it should suffice that the publicly aired

---

[4] Another approach, not examined here, is the intermediary perspective, which focuses on the role of persuasion, the personal qualities and rank of the mediator and subtle forms of influence over the belligerents. However, this perspective is difficult to prove empirically, while the outcome of the intermediary's work still depends, ultimately, on the balance of power. See Princen 1992.

[5] Touval and Zartman, 1985; and more recently, Zartman and Rasmussen 1997.

[6] 'Intervention' is used here in a broad sense, that is signifying any kind of activity (military, economic, political, cultural) by a third party intended to affect the course, intensity, scope or outcome of a conflict and/or activity geared to attenuating the effects of conflict. See Van Walraven 1999b: 12–13.

motives for intervention are not *ipso facto* evidence of the rationale
of the third party actor, more especially because these are often
couched in the righteous language of humanitarianism. Such normative discourse is even more likely if intervention involves more
than mere diplomatic mediation: for example, military intervention.
Lastly, if multilateral intervention does occur there is a good possibility that there is more than one reason for a third party to inter-
fere in a conflict.

While strictly speaking the political power perspective on mediation refers to violent conflicts that have already broken out, it is also
relevant to situations that have not yet erupted into violence. At that
stage, third party intervention would probably be even more difficult, as it would be less clear what interests might be involved that
would warrant third party interference in someone else's (still non-
violent) dispute. If such interference involved some form of military
action—that is action against the sovereignty of another state—then
the measures involved would require even greater political will on
the part of the third party and would-be belligerents. Since the would-
be belligerents would not yet be at the stage of a seriously disadvantageous stalemate, successful mediation by a third party would
be even less likely.

While politicians and diplomats have, nevertheless, made the conflict
prevention discourse part of their expanding diplomatic vocabulary,
in terms of concrete actions and institutional innovation international concern with conflicts has remained ambivalent (Van Walraven
1998b and ibid., with van der Vlugt, 1996). Thus in Africa, inter-governmental organizations are only called on when conflicts become
violent.[7]

African Conflict Policies at the Continental Level

Although frequently overlooked, the structure of international relations in Africa has always affected the functioning of the continent's

---

[7] Perhaps only NGOs can boast a record of preventive action with regard to the
continent's potential conflicts, although this is inevitably accompanied by many glaring failures, as well as difficulty in establishing evidence of an unequivocal link
between their efforts and the absence of violence.

international organizations to a considerable degree.[8] Without undue simplification one could argue that Africa's international relations have been marked by three major features: external dependence, marginalization, and the absence of undisputed African hegemonic leadership in the relations between the African states themselves (or, rather, the state elites).[9] The third feature, together with contradictory patterns of external dependence, has often impaired the functioning of Africa's international institutions. Without strong leadership, provided either by a particular member state or group of powerful states, it has been difficult to generate inter-state cooperation on many issues. In view of the large number of actors involved and various levels of cooperation, this lack of hegemonic leadership is most evident in the OAU (Van Walraven 1999a). Thus, it has always been difficult for the Pan-African body to execute forceful strategies in conflict mediation. It has also lacked the clout—which could only be provided by a powerful member state—to impose the degree of financial discipline necessary to develop strong institutions and stage decisive operations, such as military intervention.

In this context the OAU has always pursued a pragmatic strategy. In conflict mediation it has followed a minimalist strategy focused on persuasion, the use of delaying tactics, and the containment of hostilities. Employed on a decentralized, *ad hoc* basis, this strategy was, contrary to popular perception, moderately successful in the management of inter-state conflicts. It had one glaring defect, however, which was evident in times of crisis: limited reactive capacity. Consequently, when the organization was confronted with increasingly serious (especially intra-state) conflicts, it looked for institutional alternatives to improve its performance. From the late 1970s, proposals were made to enhance the OAU's effectiveness in conflict management. These ranged from reviving the defunct Commission of Mediation, Conciliation and Arbitration to the establishment of a semi-permanent Ad Hoc Committee for the settlement of inter-state disputes and the formation of a Political and Security Council similar to the UN (Van Walraven 1999a: ch. 7).

---

[8] This becomes particularly evident if one looks at the literature published on the OAU. See Van Walraven 1999a.

[9] On international relations, for example, see Harbeson and Rothchild 2000; Clapham 1986.

Without hegemonic leadership these proposals never stood a chance. Yet, by the late 1980s—early 1990s the changed international climate forced Africa's state elites to take action. This involved, first of all, a formal arrogation of intra-state conflicts to the OAU's mandate (1990),[10] then the introduction of a Conflict Management Division within the secretariat to improve the organization's monitoring and fact-finding capabilities (1992), and, in 1993, the approval of a new "Mechanism for Conflict Prevention, Management and Resolution".[11] The question here is whether the rationale underlying these reforms really stemmed from a conflict prevention logic and whether the institutional changes can be interpreted as the operation of an early warning system, or of conflict preventive policies.

There are reasons to think that the OAU genuinely embarked on conflict prevention strategies. Firstly, when the Conflict Management Division was introduced into the Secretariat, the stated objective was to improve the monitoring of conflicts and collection of data as a first step to establishing an 'early warning' system.[12] By the mid 1990s, the division was renamed the 'Conflict Management Centre',[13] and given the task of developing strategies for conflict prevention, management and resolution; service the 'central organ' (on which, more below); monitor political developments and manage an "Early Warning System through research and the establishment of a network of information sources and a data bank"; and promote negotiations aimed at preventing and resolving conflicts.[14] The centre would include a small conference room, a library and documentation department and a 24-hour 'situation room', to be equipped with modern telecommunications technology. It would be manned by personnel from the Secretariat, with further staff following at a later date (Matthies 1996: 56). Secondly, the mechanism introduced in 1993 was originally part of a more comprehensive proposal from the Secretary-General, which entailed a

---

[10] It had been concerned *de facto* with such conflicts in certain circumstances in the past. Van Walraven 1999a: ch. 8.

[11] Much has already been written on this mechanism. See, for example, Wembou 1994; Matthies 1996; and Edimo 1997.

[12] CM/1710 (LVI) Rev. 1: Report of the Secretary-General on Conflicts in Africa: Prospects for an OAU Mechanism for Conflict Prevention and Resolution (June 1992) and letter by Dr. C.J. Bakwesegha, Head of Conflict Management Division to the author, 7 December 1992.

[13] Note 'management', not *prevention*.

[14] See the description of tasks on the organization's website <http://www.oau-oua.org>.

process of prevention, management and resolution with the aid of political, judicial and military support (Van Walraven 1999a: 299).

However, the changes in the Secretariat were not unconnected with—and in fact very similar to—the responsibilities of staff well before the 1990s: these pertained to the monitoring of events, in a broad sense, so as to enable the Secretary-General to engage in policy-making and mediate in armed conflicts, but they had been hindered by the constraints of limited staffing and financial-material resources. Since the 1960s, therefore, appeals had been made regularly for improvements in the Secretariat's resource base, but these were usually in vain (Van Walraven 1999a: 173–174 and 299; Amate 1986). The 1992 reforms could therefore be seen as a logical response to past institutional underdevelopment, the realization of which continued to be dubious in view of the organization's persistent resource weakness (Matthies 1996: 61).

Thus, by March 2000—almost eight years after these institutional alterations—the Secretary-General confronted member states with what many African observers thought began to sound like a broken record: lamenting the OAU's chronic budget deficit against a background of expanding objectives. The OAU managed to get approval for a one-year budget—in contrast to the biennial ones first introduced in 1994—with funds limited to 29 million dollars, i.e. just four million dollars above the level at which the organization had operated more than fifteen years before. Rather than allowing an expansion of its staff base, this forced a restructuring programme that made some 140 professional and general service staff redundant. It would therefore be dubious to conclude that the secretariat's 1992 reforms amounted to operation of early warning and conflict prevention capabilities. It is more likely that they were part of the normal process of politicking between secretariat and member states over minimal resources. In the end, these are usually realized, but at levels precluding a radical departure from past institutional practices.[15]

The 1993 mechanism, moreover, carefully built on existing institutions and past practices. It consisted of improved cooperation between the Secretary-General, now with a formally upgraded political role, and the Bureau of the Assembly of Heads of State and Government,

---

[15] See *Africa Research Bulletin* (Political Series), 2000, 13894. For the OAU's budget practices, see Van Walraven 1999a: ch. 5.

which was turned into a semi-permanent institution meeting at ambassadorial level at least once a month—the 'central organ' referred to above. Key to acceptance of the mechanism was the fact that it would operate from existing institutions and let bureau membership rotate between member states, which precluded claims for additional funding and forestalled old objections that member countries were treated differently (Van Walraven 1999a: 299–301).

With the Secretary-General supposed to provide a speedy response to events and the bureau giving political backing to his mediation activities, the bureau's fundamental *raison d'être* was not so much the prevention of conflict as the improvement of the OAU's reactive capacity while continuing to employ the old minimalist tactics geared to reducing existing armed conflicts. A cursory look at its operating practices during the last decade would suggest that reactive capacity did, indeed, improve. More generally, the OAU's mediatory, monitoring and diplomatic activities increased considerably. However, capacity *vis-à-vis* high intensity conflicts continued to be deficient, and inevitably in Africa's conflict-ridden environment so long as the OAU operated within the constraints of existing resources it was inevitable that the organization would continue to react to any eruption of violence rather than pre-empt conflict. That its 'new' strategy was couched in the language of conflict prevention only brought it into line with prevailing international fashion and might elicit additional Western funding (Van Walraven 1999a: 299–301 and 343–346; Matthies 1996: 56–58).

African Conflict Policies at the Regional Level

Before any observations are made about the OAU's transformation into the 'African Union' (AU), it is necessary to refer to the conflict strategy of Africa's regional organizations. In terms of official strategy and practice the OAU has, for some time, allowed the regional institutions—principally the ECOWAS, SADC and the Inter-Governmental Authority on Development (IGAD)—to bear the brunt of interventions, or countries operating on a bilateral or trilateral basis. Theoretically, this can be explained as a form of actor reduction tactics to facilitate decision-making. According to game theory, the fewer actors there are in a decision-making context, the easier it is to arrive at a

decision.[16] By delegating responsibility to the regional institutions—
or, rather, acquiescing to them—the Pan-African body could in principle improve Africa's decision-making record in conflict interventions,
since these institutions have fewer participating states and usually a
relatively powerful regional actor in their midst (Van Walraven 1999a:
371–372).

Whereas this argument is sustainable in terms of game theory, it
has limited practical application with regard to actual conflict intervention in Africa. Experience shows that, while hegemony continues
to be a much-contested concept in the political culture underlying
continental politics, the same appears to be true for regional organizations, which have frequently been hampered by challenges to
regional leaders from the membership at large. Consequently, the
financial state of organizations such as the ECOWAS and SADC, as well
as their ability to function in areas as disparate as common trade policy and security cooperation, have not proved any more successful
than the OAU's continental record.[17]

The performance of the 'ECOWAS Cease-fire Monitoring Group' (ECO-
MOG) in Liberia is illuminating.[18] Three fundamental features stand
out. Firstly, Nigeria's leadership in the ECOMOG was hotly disputed
by certain West African countries—Burkina Faso and the Côte d'Ivoire—
and also, to a lesser extent, France and Libya. The contrary actions
of these countries go some way to explain the difficulties that the
Nigerians had in successfully pursuing their objectives. Even such a
comparatively powerful African actor as Nigeria encountered problems with funding—with the ECOMOG requiring donor assistance[19]—
while upon arrival in Monrovia it was found to be so poorly prepared
for any military operation that it almost immediately ran into trouble.
ECOMOG operations later conducted in Sierra Leone failed to defeat
the rebels of the Revolutionary United Front, and in several instances
required back-up from mercenary forces, narrowly averting the ran-
sacking of the capital. The ECOMOG intervention in Guinea-Bissau

---

[16] See, for example, Oye 1986.
[17] For the ECOWAS, for example, see Gershoni 1993; Hanink and Owusu 1998. For
SADC see Evans et al. 1999; Khadiagala 1998: 140–144.
[18] There has been a flurry of publications on this. See, among others, Gershoni
1993; Adeleke 1995; Aning 1994 and 1996; Howe 1996/97; also the bibliography in
Van Walraven 1999c.
[19] See also Van Walraven 1999b.

hardly fared any better. This may come as a surprise when Nigeria's *potential* leverage is taken into account, given its influence in a continental body such as the OAU.

Secondly, it appears that the objectives pursued by the Nigerians through the ECOMOG differed considerably from the conventional mandates of peace keeping forces. Careful reconstruction of the rationale underlying the ECOMOG's deployment in Liberia yields the following observations.[20] While, as with every intervention undertaken in a multilateral structure, the ECOMOG's deployment took place for a variety of reasons, the driving force behind the Liberian operation as determined by the Nigerians was *not* the desire to pursue a peaceful settlement of the civil war irrespective of which side came out victorious, but to come to the aid of Liberia's embattled president, Samuel Doe, and, upon his execution, to thwart Charles Taylor's rise to power. The reasons for this, however, are not relevant here.[21] What is important is that with this built-in bias against one of the belligerent parties, the ECOMOG had almost totally compromised its neutrality. With a vague and all-encompassing mandate which covered any military contingency, it could pursue its own objectives by whatever means it chose—including such unorthodox methods as assisting in the formation, arming and splintering of rival warring factions.[22]

Thirdly, the implementation of Nigeria's strategy was made possible because relevant decision-making violated and by-passed ECOWAS regulations and institutions. Thus, the initial decision to establish and despatch the ECOMOG to Liberia was *ultra vires* under existing ECOWAS regulations,[23] and in legitimating itself by reference to the ECOWAS military institutions that *did not yet actually exist*, kept its execution outside the organization's purview. By the time this situation was legally remedied, the Nigerians had confronted the ECOMOG's opponents with a military *fait accompli*. In this way, they continued to determine the goals of military operations not only through the ECOMOG's Nigerian Field Commander and the 'Committee on ECO-

---

[20] This is based on ibid.: 1999c.

[21] [See extensively] Ibid.: 38–49; Herbst 2000; and further below.

[22] Nigeria's participation in looting and exploiting the surplus of Liberia's expanding war economy could probably not be interpreted as part of its original objective. Rather, this aspect became more significant when the intervention was deadlocked. Van Walraven 1999c: 64–68.

[23] Curiously, this is often overlooked—even in legal analyses, which usually focus on international (humanitarian) law.

MOG' inside the Nigerian Ministry of Defence, but also by furnishing the larger part of the force's financial-material requirements and providing seventy per cent of its rank and file and half its officer corps.

Thus, instead of a genuinely multilateral intervention force fielded under the auspices of the ECOWAS, the ECOMOG represented an almost entirely Nigerian entity, controlled by Nigerians, with the objective to engage in Liberia's civil war as a (de facto) belligerent rather than a third party—its final exit strategy being similarly affected by partisan considerations, but this time to Charles Taylor's advantage. Most observers agree that, rather than contributing to a rapid settlement, it is likely that the ECOMOG's deployment in Liberia helped to prolong the conflict (Van Walraven 1999c: 59–64 and 93–104; ibid. 1999b: 43–47).[24]

Such unconventional actions can also be seen at times in the functioning of Africa's other regional organizations. IGAD's mediation in the Sudanese civil war ostensibly led to attempts, in 1994, to reach a peaceful settlement on the basis of a so-called 'Declaration of Principles' (DOP), which among other things allowed the south of Sudan to opt for independence. Genuine acceptance of the DOP would have entailed the Sudanese government's political suicide, not just because the regime upheld the interests of a narrowly constituted group of northerners who defined themselves by their aggressive concept of Islam, but because acceptance of the terms of the DOP—potential secession— would have been intolerable for *any* government under *any* circumstances save military defeat (Douma and Van Walraven 2000: 17 and Van Baarsen 2000).

Of course, the DOP could be interpreted as an attempt to redress the military balance inside the Sudan to the advantage of the southern rebel forces and, in the process, create a mutually disadvantageous stalemate that would force the government back to the negotiating table (El-Affendi 2001: 590–591). Yet, failing this, the attempt by the mediators to get the government side to accept the DOP's conditions destroyed any attempt at neutrality *vis-à-vis* the belligerents. Their bias destroyed any leverage they might have had over the government in Khartoum (Douma and Van Walraven 2000: 17).

In fact, the motives for the IGAD mediation initiative had been partisan all along—beginning with the desire to contain the Sudanese

---

[24] Relevant ECOWAS institutional reforms are discussed in the next section.

government in the interests of regional stability, and quickly degen-
erating into open hostility and partisan intervention. IGAD member
states actually favoured, or were prepared to accept, the idea of southern independence and were motivated by the desire to eliminate
Sudanese government support to their own dissidents. While they
sought to make a distinction between their own actions and the sub-
version that has long characterized the conduct of foreign affairs in
the Horn, their intervention did not in fact differ fundamentally from
the old subversive activities—although now they took place in the
guise of a peace process. Consequently, the mediators got sucked into
and exacerbated the conflict (El-Affendi 2001).

Finally, SADC's experience with conflict mediation has hardly fared
any better. In 1996, member states aimed to establish an autonomous
'Organ on Politics, Defence and Security', which was officially charged
with cooperation in regional security and defence through conflict
prevention, management and resolution; preventive diplomacy to pre-
empt conflict in the region and the mediation of existing conflicts,
both inter-state and intra-state. To this purpose, an 'early warning
centre' was established in the Zimbabwean capital Harare (Breytenbach
2000: 86).

From the beginning, the Organ was hampered and postponed as a
result of powerful disagreements between South Africa, which saw
the Organ as being subordinate to SADC as a whole, and Zimbabwe,
which became the first country to assume the Organ's rotating presidency. Zimbabwe, however, resented South African hegemony in the
region and preferred to let the Organ operate as a separate entity to
allow for the continuation of regional alliance building through idio-
syncratic means (Khadiagala 1998: 141–143).

Thus, when troops from Rwanda and Uganda aided a rebellion
against the DRC government in 1998, its president, Laurent Kabila,
sent a request for assistance to other SADC members to repel the
invading forces. With this request ostensibly activating the SADC
Organ, its presiding member state, Zimbabwe, convened a meeting of
regional heads of state.[25] In conformity with the Organ's protocol, a
commission was set up to mediate a settlement, which was made up
of the foreign ministers of Zimbabwe, Angola, Namibia and Zambia.
The commission met with Ugandan and Rwandan officials, Congolese

---

[25] Through Art. 5 (1) of its Protocol.

rebels and DRC government leaders. It concluded that the DRC had been invaded and unanimously recommended that military material and manpower be sent "to restore peace and stability".[26] Within a fortnight of the meeting of the heads of state troops from Zimbabwe, Angola and Namibia began pouring into the Congo to rescue the Kabila regime from collapse.

While this scenario allowed for defence and security cooperation in rather broad terms, the problem was that the draft protocol of the SADC Organ had not yet been officially adopted by the SADC Summit and, consequently, had not been ratified by sufficient numbers of member states and, therefore, was not actually enforceable.[27] If the protocol emphasized political and diplomatic mechanisms for the resolution and prevention of conflict, in practice countries relied heavily on military means during their intervention in the DRC, and in the political crisis in Lesotho.[28] Of course, one might defend the deployment of Zimbabwean and other forces on the basis of the request of Congo's legitimate head of state and hence, through application of Article 51 of the UN Charter, which stipulates the right of individual and collective self-defence (Chigara 2000: 62 ff.). The point is, however, that the intervention was not a SADC operation (Meyns 2002: 17), but came about through bilateral lines of communication (Breytenbach 2000: 88); it did not constitute a mediation effort on the part of genuine third parties. Rather, in the process of saving one particular belligerent it helped to widen the conflict to a point where observers began to speak of 'Africa's First World War'—marked by deadlocked negotiations, a semi-permanent division of the Congo between external powers and their involvement in the exploitation of its mineral riches.[29]

Some Interpretative Comments

While intervention practices have therefore deviated very substantially from official policies and agreed institutions, later institutional

---

[26] Chigara 2000: 59, quoting the foreign minister of Zimbabwe.
[27] It was only adopted by the SADC Summit in Blantyre, August 2001. Meyns 2002: 9. With thanks to Peter Meyns for this source.
[28] Breytenbach 2000: 85–89. See also Kadima 1999: 65–82.
[29] *Africa Confidential*, 26 May 2000 and *The Namibian*, 23 February 2001 (accessed via <http://www.namibian. com.na>). With thanks to Jan-Bart Gewald for the latter source.

reforms moved into an even higher gear. In 1998 the ECOWAS Authority approved the establishment of a Mediation and Security Council with a mandate for peace and security issues. The organization's Executive Secretariat acquired new departments for political affairs, security and peace-keeping operations and was assisted by a network of information bureaux within member states with the task of collecting data on (impending) conflict and developing conflict preventive strategies. The ECOMOG, made up of national contingents, would become the standing military institution of the Community.[30] A protocol detailing these arrangements was adopted in December 1999 and made enforceable, provisionally, upon signature. A new Defence and Security Commission held its first meeting in July 2000, making recommendations on the stand-by units of the ECOMOG. The Mediation and Security Council also went into formal operation, approving the arrangements of stand-by units and engaging in a flurry of diplomatic activity to contain and reduce several violent crises, such as those in Sierra Leone, Liberia-Guinea and the Côte d'Ivoire.

Amidst its financial problems the OAU also engaged in new institutional reforms. In May 2001 the 'Constitutive Act of the African Union' came into force. This document combined the old OAU Charter with the treaty that established the 'African Economic Community' (AEC) a decade earlier. While containing truly novel objectives—such as an explicit commitment to democratic government; rejection of *coup d'états*; and the right to intervene in countries in the event of war crimes, crimes against humanity and genocide[31]—the Union treaty also stipulated the formation of a Pan-African Parliament and a Court of Justice. The Council of Ministers was transformed into an 'Executive Council' and the General Secretariat was renamed the 'Commission'. The Union treaty also stipulated the far-reaching objective of full continental economic integration, accompanied by institutions in common such as an 'African Central Bank'.[32] In 2001–02, African leaders

---

[30] Decision A/Dec. 11/10/98 and Economic Community of West African States: ECOWAS Mechanism for Conflict Prevention, Management and Resolution and for Peace-Keeping and Security; Meeting of Ministers of Defence, Internal Affairs and Security, Banjul, 23–24 July 1998, Draft Mechanism (Executive Secretariat: Banjul, July 1998).

[31] That prerogative, however, is not automatic, but dependent on a (political) decision of the Assembly, decided by consensus or a two-thirds majority.

[32] Constitutive Act of the African Union, Lomé, Togo, 11 July 2000, *passim*. It also contains some tightening of sanctions against defaulting states, financially or otherwise. See Art. 23. For details on the AEC project, see Van Walraven 1999a: 360.

launched the well-publicized economic recovery programme 'NEPAD', which aimed, among other things, to reduce by half the number of African poor (those living on less than a dollar a day) by 2015, an annual growth rate of seven per cent for the next fifteen years, and a foreign aid input of 60 billion dollars a year in exchange for Africa's self-monitored commitment to peace, security, respect for human rights and the rule of law.[33]

It would be dangerous to take all these projects simply at face value, because some (notably the economic ones) appear outlandish and, more especially, because of the substantial discrepancies between official policy and actual practice, as noted in the preceding sections. Thus, while formally adopted by the (O)AU, the NEPAD plan received only moderate support from the G-8 and met with considerable scepticism, particularly because of African reticence to condemn the fraud and violence that marred the presidential elections in Zimbabwe. In ECOWAS, emphasis has so far been placed on the containment of existing violent conflict by diplomatic or military means, even though its early warning network, while requiring a huge investment (financial as well as political) to make it effective, attracted some Western funding.[34] The organization's highest priority continued to be in the area of actual armed conflict, namely the worsening civil strife in the Côte d'Ivoire—a situation in which by the spring of 2003 it had failed to intervene effectively.

Moreover, in the seemingly grander transformation of the OAU into the African Union, the structures of the 1993 mechanism were left essentially intact,[35] notwithstanding proclamations on an early warning arrangement and more military oriented provisions such as a Pan-African Standby Force made up of national contingents, which in view of current arrears in contributions would—like the OAU's existing Peace Fund—depend on substantial input of foreign aid.[36] While previously announced organs such as the Parliament and Court of Justice

---

[33] See, among others, Patat 2002: 81–88 and *Afrika Jahrbuch* 2001.

[34] ECOWAS Press Release, no. 72/2001, 28 August 2001.

[35] The OAU's central organ (i.e. the semi-permanent Assembly Bureau) is now known as the 'Peace and Security Council'. Cilliers and Sturman 2002: 31 and 37; Meyns 2001: 63.

[36] A protocol, approved at the AU summit in Durban (July 2002), replaced AHG/Decl.3 (XXIX)/Rev.1, which introduced the 1993 mechanism. Cilliers and Sturman 2002: 32; Meyns 2001: 63.

had already been outlined in the AEC treaty,[37] the Union treaty also confirmed the aim of the AEC document, which had called for full continental economic and financial integration, with monetary institutions in common, to be realized in six stages over a 30-year period.[38]

Although the Union treaty wisely omitted reference to any deadline or the introduction of a common currency, the reiteration of these objectives pointed, firstly, to the lack of progress on these issues since the early 1990s. Secondly, the reference to what in the actual context of continental underdevelopment amounted to a fantastic scheme, also characterized the OAU's functioning in preceding decades and could be interpreted as a psychological rationalization of—or escape from—the despair felt over Africa's predicaments. If in the past the OAU's leaders lamented the continent's marginalization and hoped to bring Africa into the mainstream of world affairs,[39] now the Union treaty referred to 'the challenges posed by globalization' and found solace in a terminology bearing astonishing resemblance to the language of the integration process of the European Union.[40]

Herein, too, may lie part of the key to understanding the yawning discrepancies between the theory and practice of Africa's international institutions. The functioning of these institutions may to some extent be affected by the influence of 'cognitive scripts'. In the modern world, societies may be tempted to copy the behaviour of other countries, theirs being the accepted way of doing things, of formulating aspirations or of responding to problems. Consequently, most modern countries have, for example, a national parliament, a trade union confederation, an airline or a national academy of science, in part because others also have them. The introduction of these institutions, however, takes place in different political and cultural contexts. The concepts underlying such institutions may therefore differ from those underlying similar institutions elsewhere and lead to a split between the original paradigms and actual behavioural patterns. In such a case, output becomes separated from formal institution (Van Walraven 1998a: 172–173).

---

[37] Admittedly, a protocol stipulating details of the functioning of the Pan-African Parliament entered into force in December 2003. African Union: Press Release no. 093/2003, Addis Ababa, 14 November 2003.

[38] Treaty on the African Economic Community, Abuja, Nigeria, 3 June 1991, Art. 6.

[39] On this psychological role see Van Walraven 1999a: 351–355.

[40] Such as 'Union', 'the Commission', 'Permanent Representatives Committee', 'the Court of Justice'.

International organizations may be particularly sensitive to such 'cognitive scripts', because as a result of their historical origins they are usually analysed from an unduly instrumentalized perspective. These institutions were founded in the nineteenth century with the object of solving the problems that states share in common but could not tackle on their own. Since international organizations were meant to provide solutions, their function is usually understood in terms of problem-solving potential and seldom in the light of their ability to *create* problems—or even problems inherent in their being at the *heart* of the matter. Hence, there may be a tendency, in Africa as elsewhere, to perceive international institutions and their projects as the means of achieving not just goals that have not yet been realized but also objectives that were never part of the formal paradigm. The latter is made possible by the psychological function of international organizations that is usually overlooked. Since these institutions are controlled by their member states, they do not really have objectives in themselves, but only those attributed to them by those in control (Claude 1964). Because of this and their instrumentalist origins international organizations serve as a focus for people outside the corridors of power for articulating ideas on international politics. Consequently, institutions such as the OAU are often criticized on the basis of objectives they do not actually have.

If part of the function of Africa's international institutions is informed by 'cognitive scripts', this means that there is something else, something fundamental, behind their formal structure. In the case of Africa's sub-state politics, this is readily acknowledged by those who recognise that the post-colonial state is radically different in practice from its Western counterpart, with political power devolved through patronage and clientelism rather than through formal public institutions *per se*, leading to the personalization of political power, the exercise of which serves mainly private interests. In certain cases this turns the state into a façade concealing the real sources of political power, i.e. the exploitation of economic resources for the benefit of private clientele (Reno 1995).

In view of the above, there are good reasons to believe that Africa's *international* institutions are also driven, to an indeterminate degree, by objectives other than the publicly acknowledged aims widely attributed to international organizations in the West. They may share the same structure as these institutions, including charters, secretariats and even multilateral intervention forces, but they are actually driven by other objectives, which are not necessarily deviant or unusual, but just *different*. Thus, a cursory look at international relations in Africa, in the realm of both politics and economics, suggests that the conduct of foreign affairs is usually informal and based on personal relations—paralleling more closely political practice at the sub-state level.[41] The point is not that personal relations are important to formal institutions—the same is true in the West—but that these personal relations are centred around the pursuit of private interests to a significantly greater degree than is usually possible in the West, and often take precedence over public interests.

This has two consequences. Firstly, foreign affairs are usually conducted privately. There is evidence, for example, that African heads of state establish foreign relations by creating bonds of friendship, business relationships and marriage arrangements with other heads of state and their families, on which, unfortunately, there is still little systematic research.[42] Secondly, the personal interests of heads of state and their followers affect their position in foreign affairs and their relations with international organizations.

Thus, the attitude of certain countries on the ECOMOG was informed by their different interests in Liberia, many of which were of a private nature involving friendship and business deals (again, between the embattled Doe and the Nigerian head of state); private security arrangements (between Burkina's president and Charles Taylor); and private liaisons (again, between Burkina's leader and a niece of the Côte d'Ivoire head of state who had married into Liberia's presidential family and been widowed by Doe). Much of this accounts for the apparent aberration in ECOMOG's deployment of troops, which actually concealed the pursuit of private and other interests behind a façade of multilateral intervention to an extent that conflict began

---

[41] While, as elsewhere, one should not assume a dichotomy between sub-state and international politics, this is especially true for Africa in view of the personalized nature of politics and the concomitant underdevelopment of formal institutions such as the state and its organs.

[42] So far, this has been the province of journalism, as exemplified by the news sheet *Africa Confidential* and the work of French journalists such as Smith and Glaser 1992 and Pean 1983. For the importance of the role of marriage ties and sexual liaisons in Africa's international politics, see Bourmaud 1995: 148–149; also Clapham 1986: 249–266 for a more general insight, and 88 ff. on personal ties in the Francophone world.

to masquerade as conflict resolution (Van Walraven 1999; Herbst 2000: 318–319).

In the case of IGAD, state elites sought to defend security interests *vis-à-vis* dissident opposition forces and their regional backers by pursuing mediation initiatives that did not differ significantly from the subversive methods used in the past. This was even more evident in the DRC, where regional mediation amounted to partisan military intervention through ordinary bilateral channels. The objective was to save one particular regional ally—the *quid pro quo* of which was, in the case of the Angolans, greater military security against their own dissidents and, for Zimbabwe and Namibia, greater influence and a share of Congolese mineral resources for government officials.[43] The supposed diplomatic involvement of Southern Africa's regional organization thus concealed, but only thinly, the naked pursuit of narrow elite and personal interests.

Finally, in the past the OAU had not really functioned as a formal, public, international organization working towards objectives common to the entire African continent, but as an exclusivist forum catering to the psychological needs of Africa's top brass.[44] Even if more recently the (O)AU has been widening its representative role, communicating more, for example, within non-governmental circles, it cannot be more than a marginal actor in conflict intervention. Seen from the perspective of regional organizations, however, its present impotence and lack of continental leadership has the advantage of precluding its use for socially exclusive interests in the brutal ways that have marked the functioning of the regional institutions.

In conclusion, the formal structures prevalent in Africa's international relations are probably not the crucial variables determining the trajectories of conflict settlement. These lie elsewhere, among the network of personal relationship and private interests tat influence African politics, the international repercussions of which require thorough analysis. Furthermore, if Africa's formal inter-governmental institutions are not conducted in the main on behalf of the disinterested aspirations for conflict settlement, it would be treacherous for

---

[43] DRC diamond mines/concessions are owned respectively by 'Osleg', a company controlled by the Zimbabwean Ministry of Defence, and the 'August 26 Company', a parastatal [resorting] under the Namibian Ministry of Defence, in both cases involving numerous government officials. Sources in note 29 above.
[44] For extensive details see Van Walraven 1999a.

the international community to graft its policies onto the institutions as they now stand.[45]

Bibliography

Amate, C.O.C. (1986), *Inside the OAU: Pan-Africanism in Action*, New York, St Martin's Press.

Adeleke, A. (1995), 'The Politics and Diplomacy of Peacekeeping in West Africa: The ECOWAS Operation in Liberia', *Journal of Modern African Studies*, vol. 33, no. 4, pp. 569–593.

Aning, E.K. (1994), 'Managing Regional Security in West Africa: Ecowas, Ecomog and Liberia', *Centre for Development Research Working Paper 94.2.*, Copenhagen.

————. (1996), 'Ghana, ECOWAS and the Liberian Crisis—An Analysis of Ghana's Role in Liberia', *Liberian Studies Journal*, vol. 21, no. 2, pp. 259–299.

Bourmaud, D. (1995), 'Le pouvoir au risque du sexe', *Politique Africaine*, no. 59, pp. 145–152.

Bratton M. and N. van de Walle (1997), *Democratic Experiments in Africa: Regime Transitions in Comparative Perspective*, Cambridge, Cambridge University Press.

Breytenbach, W. (2000), 'Failure of Security Co-operation in SADC: The Suspension of the Organ for Politics, Defence and Security', *South African Journal of International Affairs*, vol. 7, no. 1, pp. 85–95.

Chigara, B. (2000), 'Operation of the SADC Protocol on Politics, Defence and Security in the Democratic Republic of Congo', *African Journal of International and Comparative Law*, vol. 12, no. 1, pp. 58–69.

Cilliers J. and K. Sturman (2002), 'The Right Intervention: Enforcement Challenges for the African Union', *African Security Review*, vol. 11, no. 3, pp. 29–39.

Clapham, C. (1986), *Africa and the International System: The Politics of State Survival*, Cambridge, Cambridge University Press.

Claude, I.L. (1964), *Swords into Plowshares: The Problems and Progress of International Organization*, New York, Random House.

Douma, P. and K. van Walraven (2000), *Between Indifference and Naïveté: Dutch Policy Interventions in African Conflicts. A Synthesis Report*, Clingendael Occasional Paper, The Hague.

Edimo, J.E. (1997), 'Le rôle des Etats membres de l'OUA et le défi du nouveau mécanisme sur la prévention, la gestion et le règlement des conflits', *Afrique 2000*, no. 27/28, pp. 89–102.

El-Affendi, A. (2001), 'The Impasse in the IGAD Peace Process for Sudan: The Limits of Regional Peacemaking?', *African Affairs*, vol. 100, no. 401, pp. 581–599.

Evans, D. et al. (1999), *SADC: The Cost of Non-Integration*, Harare, SAPES Books.

Gershoni, Y. (1993), 'From ECOWAS to ECOMOG: The Liberian Crisis and the Struggle for Political Hegemony in West Africa', *Liberian Studies Journal*, vol. 18, no. 1, pp. 21–43.

Hanink, D.M. and J.H. Owusu (1998), 'Has ECOWAS promoted trade among its members?', *Journal of African Economies*, vol. 7, no. 3, pp. 363–383.

---

[45] Also Herbst 2000: 319–322. Whether one can make an exception for NGOs remains to be seen. Their practices are possibly not as much affected by calculations of power politics. Yet, their limited leverage probably hinders the realization of settlements. It is also doubtful that NGOs are themselves immune to the rationalities of African politics. See f.e. Clapham 1986: 257–265; Ndegwa 1996; and Patterson 1998.

Harbeson, J.W. and D. Rothchild (eds) (2000), *Africa in World Politics: The African State System in Flux*, Boulder, CO, and Oxford, Westview Press.

Herbst, J. (2000), 'Western and African Peacekeepers: Motives and Opportunities', in J.W. Harbeson and D. Rothchild (eds), *Africa in World Politics: The African State System in Flux*, Boulder, CO, and Oxford, Westview Press, pp. 308–323.

Howe, H. (1996/97), 'Lessons of Liberia: ECOMOG and Regional Peacekeeping', *International Security*, vol. 21, no. 3, pp. 145–176.

Kadima, D. (1999), 'The DRC and Lesotho Crises: Some Lessons for the SADC', *Lesotho Social Science Review*, vol. 5, no. 1, pp. 65–82.

Khadiagala, G.M. (1998), 'Prospects for a Division of Labour: African Regional Organizations in Conflict Prevention', in K. van Walraven (ed.), *Early Warning and Conflict Prevention: Limitations and Possibilities*, The Hague, London and Boston, Kluwer Law International, pp. 131–148.

Matthies, V. (1996), 'Die friedenspolitische Rolle der Organisation der Afrikanischen Einheit: Der OAU-"Mechanismus für die Prävention, das Management und die Lösung von Konflikten"'. *Afrika Jahrbuch*, pp. 49–62.

Meyns, P. (2001), ‚Die "Afrikanische Union"—Afrikas neuer Anlauf zu kontinentaler Einheit und globaler Anerkennung', *Afrika-Jahrbuch*, pp. 51–67.

———. (2002), *The Ongoing Search for a Security Structure in the SADC Region: The Re-Establishment of the SADC Organ on Politics, Defence and Security*, MS.

Ndegwa, S.N. (1996), *The Two Faces of Civil Society: NGOs and Politics in Africa*. West Hartford, CT, Kumarian Press.

Oye, K.A. (ed.) (1986), *Cooperation under Anarchy*, Princeton, Princeton University Press.

Patat, J.P. (2002), 'Le NEPAD n'est pas un nouveau plan Marshall', *Géopolitique Africaine*, no. 6 (May), pp. 81–88.

Patterson, A.S. (1998), 'A Reappraisal of Democracy in Civil Society: Evidence from Rural Senegal', *Journal of Modern African Studies*, vol. 36, no. 3, pp. 423–441.

Pean, P. (1983), *Affaires Africaines*, Paris, Fayard.

Princen, T. (1992), *Intermediaries in International Conflict*, Princeton, Princeton University Press.

Reno, W. (1995), *Corruption and State Politics in Sierra Leone*, Cambridge, Cambridge University Press.

Smith, S. and A. Glaser (1992) *Ces Messieurs Afrique: Le Paris-Village du continent noir*, Paris, Calmann-Levy.

Touval, S. and I.W. Zartman (1985), *International Mediation in Theory and Practice*, Boulder and London, Westview Press.

Van Baarsen, M.V. (2000), *The Netherlands and Sudan: Dutch Policies and Interventions with respect to the Sudanese Civil War*, Clingendael Occasional Paper, The Hague.

Van Walraven, K. (1998a), 'Conclusions', in K. van Walraven (ed.), *Early Warning and Conflict Prevention: Limitations and Possibilities*, The Hague, London and Boston, Kluwer Law International, pp. 163–174.

———. (1998b), 'Inter-governmental Organizations and Preventing Conflicts: Political Practice Since the End of the Cold War', in K. van Walraven (ed.), *Early Warning and Conflict Prevention: Limitations and Possibilities*, The Hague, London and Boston, Kluwer Law International, pp. 19–44.

———. (1999a), *Dreams of Power: The Role of the Organization of African Unity in the Politics of Africa, 1963-1993*, Aldershot, Ashgate.

———. (1999b), *The Netherlands and Liberia: Dutch Policies and Interventions with respect to the Liberian Civil War*, Clingendael Occasional Paper, The Hague.

———. (1999c), *The Pretence of Peace-keeping: ECOMOG, West Africa and Liberia (1990-1998)*. Clingendael Studies, 10, The Hague.

Van Walraven, K. and J. van der Vlugt (1996), *Conflict Prevention and Early Warning in the Political Practice of International Organizations*, Clingendael Occasional Paper, The Hague.

Wembou, M.C.D. (1994), 'A propos du nouveau mécanisme de l'OUA sur les conflits', *Afrique 2000*, no. 16, pp. 5–20.

Zartman, I.W. (1991), 'Conflict Reduction: Prevention, Management, and Resolution', in F.M. Deng and I.W. Zartman (eds), *Conflict Resolution in Africa*, Washington, Brookings Institution, pp. 299–319.

Zartman, I.W. and J.L. Rasmussen (eds) (1997), *Peacemaking in International Conflict: Methods and Techniques*, Washington, United States Institute of Peace Press.

CHAPTER FIVE

AREA STUDIES, THE ANALYSIS OF CONFLICTS AND THE
EVALUATION OF PREVENTIVE PRACTICE IN AFRICA[1]

Andreas Mehler

Introduction

For several decades mainstream research on peace and conflict dealt primarily with Europe. Most explanatory models today still focus on European experience.[2] Although some universal thinking is stimulating and helpful in identifying aims for peaceful conflict resolution in Africa, it has by and large failed adequately to capture the African reality—the particularities of the root-causes of violence, and the factors aggravating or prolonging conflict on the continent.

It took a long time for peace studies and policy makers to recognise the challenge of dealing with apparently 'small scale' wars in the Third World. This has dramatically changed over time.[3] However, so far, little systematic use has been made of area studies as an entry point for understanding, prediction and possible prevention of violent conflicts in Africa (Mehler 2002a) while the assumption that an insight into the regional nature or dynamics of violent conflict could help in better targeting the problem is obvious. The lack of communication between policy-makers and regionalist researchers is deplorable; and the responsibility is a shared one. Even objectively it

[1] This contribution draws on a paper originally prepared for the 44th African Studies Association (ASA) meeting, Houston, TX, 18 November 2001 (Area Studies and the Analysis of Conflicts in Africa: An underrated potential for practical conflict prevention) and a lecture given at the AEGIS summer school in Leipzig, 29 August 2001 (Preventing Violent Conflicts: Can best practices be identified?). I am grateful to the Stiftung Wissenschaft und Politik, Berlin, in enabling me to come up with a final text.
[2] See e.g. for the German debate the widely discussed 'Civilizational Hexagon', Senghaas 2001.
[3] There is a growing body of scientific literature on wars 'of the third kind' (Holsti 1996) and 'low intensity conflict' inter alia in Africa—see e.g. Clapham 1998; perhaps more significant is that the UN Secretary General and different EU bodies are now issuing regular reports on the subject that cannot be exhaustively quoted here.

could be difficult to bring together two worlds that are too often apart, but—as will be argued—efforts can be made.

The main concern of this chapter is to give some hints on how to escape this mutual disregard. A first step is the identification of relevant research topics for both practitioners in the field of conflict prevention and area studies experts. Some proposals are made here, based on the author's experience and his work with both sides. Area studies can also leave their mark and influence the course of peace research and conflict prevention. This article proposes the subject of conflict-prolonging factors as a (broad enough) subject of particular interest where research could take into account already existing civil society engagements. Scholars could become more interested in the major general flaws of donors' Africa policies (and be more vocal in their constructive critique). Area studies representatives should be aware of the intrinsic difficulties of a dialogue with practitioners and of practice-oriented research itself—while practitioners could show an interest in adjusting their own behaviour in order to make maximum profit out of any exchange with researchers. And finally, Africanists might get involved in the identification of 'best practices' and the analytical tools enabling practitioners to build healthy routines.

But why should this be done at all? For several years, conflict prevention and peace building has been constantly moving up in the list of priorities of policy makers in the industrialised world and more particularly concerning their policy towards Africa (south of the Sahara). However doubts remain as to whether this is just rhetorical (Engel 2001). The overall impression is that conflict prevention is still not 'mainstreamed' in either development and foreign policy bureaucracies or international organisations. There are several indicators that prove this. The policy planning process has—at best— changed only slightly in order to take care of conflict and peace. Embassies and representatives on the ground are not sufficiently prepared to implement a conflict prevention policy, in terms of human resources and expertise, training, supervision, analytical tools. There are few efforts to reconcile the most prominent objectives of a) conflict prevention and b) poverty reduction. Only rarely does 'political dialogue' use appropriate procedures to mitigate conflict risks. 'New' or regionally specific challenges to peace and security in Africa are not appropriately addressed.

There is no doubt that a learning process on these issues has begun in some countries and organisations, but it may not have made sufficient progress. The main reasons for this lack of progress are bureaucratic in nature and there are doubts as well about political will—at least for some actors. Practitioners remain sceptic (or over-optimistic) as to their room for manoeuvre when faced with unfamiliar conflict patterns. Informed advice may help, although it might sometimes lead to the same conclusion: that there is no viable conflict-preventive option at a given point in time. The risk is slim, however, that it will lead to the conclusion that windows of opportunity will remain closed forever.

Conflict prevention offers a potential field for close co-operation between foreign policy and development experts on the one hand, and area studies and country experts on the other. A sometimes vague, but often massive, demand for regionalist expertise is growing in development agencies, but are they 'well served'? And are the area specialists 'well treated'? In the end, expectations at both ends are frequently frustrated. This contribution aims to identify opportunities for and obstacles to co-operation at both ends. It is based on personal experiences with the EU Commission and the German actors in conflict and crisis prevention.[4]

The Analysis of Conflicts in Africa: Focusing on Relevant Subjects

The first part of this contribution makes the case for the potential usefulness of the approaches used and the results achieved within area studies for practical conflict prevention. In a recent paper (Engel and Mehler 2000) we have argued that the limited number of dominant paradigms in political research on Africa since 1960 have all provided insights into the nature of authority and therefore on the nature of political conflict in Africa as well (we focused here on 'African presidentialism', 'neo-patrimonialism', 'prebendal politics', 'hegemonic exchange, 'weak state'/'collapsed states'). This reflection led us to a limited number of research categories, reflecting on 'structure' and 'agency'. This discussion needs not be repeated here. It may even no longer be necessary to prove that there is valuable scientific insight that can be distilled into the political process. In fact, the necessity of observing the empirical evidence and regional particularities more

---

[4] In Germany the term crisis prevention is preferred to conflict prevention. For an overview see Mehler and Ribaux 2000; van Walraven 1999.

closely (instead of building highly abstract rational choice models) was acknowledged following the events of September 11: policy makers asked themselves: do we know enough about foreign cultures, hostile communities, regions at war? The answer was obvious: no. However, it is unclear whether this new mood will boost the attention paid to area studies; instead intelligence and journalism might be held in higher esteem. To be properly acknowledged clearly depends on the readiness of the area specialists to respond to the questions of potential 'consumers' who doubt whether they can be served properly.

Obviously, the first step, which is likely to be of interest to policy-makers, is to focus on subjects that are conflict-relevant and will—with some plausibility—be on the agenda of North-South relations in the foreseeable future. The following—non exhaustive—points might be indicative of relevant areas—some of them are already high on the agenda, others not yet.

Political Economy of Violent Conflict

This notion has become prominent in recent years, starting arguably with the edited work by Jean and Rufin 1996. The work of Paul Collier, and more particularly his 'greed and grievance' thesis (Collier 2000; Collier and Hoeffler 2000)[5] has been well promoted and widely received (although not always positively by Africanists), while it remains true that "the micro-linkages that tie the presence of lootable natural resources to conflict have yet to be adequately developed" (Herbst 2000a: 271). Some subjects remain or will increasingly be on the practitioner's agenda. The general issues are, firstly, networks for trading resources (diamonds, hardwood, gold, etc.) connected to violent conflicts and, secondly, the global economy and local conflicts. And more specifically the following topics are of importance: the role of the private sector in unstable areas,[6] the economy of borderlands,[7] resource flows between diasporas in industrialised countries and African country of origin,[8] but also the management and access to

---

[5] Collier claims that he would have predicted the DR Congo war with his model—without taking into account the external factor of the Rwanda imbroglio!

[6] This is a domain where some NGOs are particularly active (International Alert, Prince of Wales Business Leader Forum, Collaborative for Development Action, Global Witness, etc.). For an introductory article see Champain 2002.

[7] Mainly micro-studies are available, although rarely linked to the subject of conflict and peace; some explicit thoughts in Duffield 2000.

[8] Some research findings are extremely disturbing: studies conducted by the

natural resources (water, land, firewood, etc.),[9] drugs (production, trade and consumption),[10] small arms,[11] and, finally, population flows and human trafficking.[12]

Sociology of Violence

This involves areas where an exchange between Africanists and practitioners seems to be confined to small sections of both camps. The issues are the social legitimacy of violence, ideologies or 'cultures of violence',[13] the role of religion in this area[14] and traditional and modern adapted conflict resolution/management/reconciliation mechanisms.[15]

Political Power

The 'hard core' political science issues seem to form a residual category for economists and practitioners: institutions do matter, but how and why is rarely explained. Legitimacy is frequently implicitly and incorrectly presumed ('partner government', 'partners'). The following

---

Refugee Studies Centre of the University of Oxford (drawing on research conducted in Ghana, Sri Lanka, Afghanistan, and Palestine) led to the conclusion that "remittances have sometimes helped sustain the very conditions that lead to forced migration, both directly by funding war, and indirectly by giving at least some of the recipients of transfers an implicit interest in these conditions continuing" (Hear, no date). The role of diasporas in neighbouring African states is particularly important in the Great Lakes region; see Lemarchand 2001.

[9] There is a wealth of studies in this area, mostly arguing for the inter-relatedness of ecological and other (political) factors. Given the general projection that resource conflicts will gain prominence in the future, there is reason to invest continuous attention in that area.

[10] Some work on African cases has been done by the Observatoire Géopolitique des Drogues (see <http://www.ogd.org>).

[11] There are numerous studies on this issue, but mainly by NGOs (e.g. Saferworld) and universal peace research (e.g. Bonn International Center for Conversion), but rarely by Africanists.

[12] The debate is dominated by policy papers of international organisations; specific Africanist research is rare.

[13] The subject was addressed at the Third 'Stuttgarter Schlossgespräch' ('Mit Kultur gegen Krisen'), but has certainly not yet been exhaustively examined. Instructive contributions in English by John Abbink and Paul Richards can be found on the website of the Institut für Auslandsbeziehungen <http://www.ifa.de/z/crisis/ezinhalf.htm>. See as well Abbink 2000. From the perspective of indigenous identity see Bayart, Geschiere and Nyamnjoh 2001.

[14] Rare contributions by Africanist; an exception is Ellis 1999.

[15] A sample of case studies can be found in Zartman 2000; a detailed constructive critique of sometimes naive approaches remains necessary.

points remain or will probably become of prime importance: the nature of the state in Africa,[16] consolidation and reform of 'hybrid regimes',[17] forms of legitimate authority in new settings (such as refugee camps, squatter zones, mega-cities),[18] security concepts (national, sub-regional)[19] and regional integration (i.e. the capacities of organisations, prerequisites, etc.).[20]

Development Policies

Finally there are subjects that were or still are on the development policy agenda and fail to be adequately reflected in African Studies: impact assessment (i.e. aid and conflict),[21] chances and risks associated with the expansion of cyberspace,[22] entitlement approach to poverty reduction (Verstegen 2001; Schmitt 2001), environmental degradation (e.g. Baechler 1999), and the spread of communicable diseases.[23]

The demand for such insights is frequently not explicit on the part of the policy makers and a clear understanding of what would be the core zone of mutual interest is part of a difficult process of searching

---

[16] This is an all-time classic of political science in Africa; see e.g. Bayart 1989; Villalón and Huxtable 1998; Herbst 2000b. In practical politics and development assistance this literature has had remarkably little impact so far.

[17] There is some general literature on hybrid regimes which still merits reception in Africanist circles; in the African context the paradox of concomitant democratisation and persistence of neo-patrimonial rule is an obvious research subject. 'Reforming neo-patrimonialism' is an evident practical problem of democracy assistance.

[18] So far, few political scientists and peace researchers have worked on these issues [so far]. Humanitarian organisations feel concerned; some geographers have worked on the political implications of mega-cities, but efforts of conceptualisation are rare.

[19] This is a subject apparently confined mostly to 'securocrats' and might contain a strong dose of ideology. The assumption that 'ideology does not matter' in post-Cold War Africa might prove premature, while a denial of strategic thinking by African military elites is both condescending and dangerous. A broader approach can be found in Wohlgemuth et al. 1999.

[20] The literature on regional integration is dominated by economic considerations. Much less scientific attention has been devoted to 'security architectures' with some notable exceptions (the military side, particularly in the case of ECOMOG; the OAU mechanism for conflict prevention and resolution).

[21] Most of the literature is not regional-specific, while the empirical record of development aid in different world regions points to marked differences. For an overview of the general debate on conflict impact assessment, see Lund and Rasa-moelina 2000. For an African case study (Tanzania) see Klingebiel et al. 2000.

[22] This is mainly a subject debated in international organisations (e.g. European Parliament) and less explored by Africanist research.

[23] Different dimensions play a role: the spread of diseases as an effect of armed conflict, the infection of security forces with its effect on their abilities (Heinecken 2001) and behaviour, the use of HIV infection as a 'weapon', etc.

for common ground. Establishing the links between these issues or associated research projects/results and conflict prevention could represent a great leap forward. For example, an important step in the direction of conflict prevention would be the acknowledgement that political elites in a large number of African countries are oriented to the neo-patrimonial model: privileging themselves and their supporters, not taking care of national welfare, building clientelist networks, not formal institutions, in times of crisis excluding large sectors of society and political competitors, etc., while the official policy operates—often cynically—with a terminology of committed 'partner governments', 'sovereignty' and 'participation' where there is none of those. It can be argued that the euphemisms in development assistance have been a major obstacle to development itself. It is high time to enter a phase of 'enlightened realism' with regard to the goals set out and the expected effects of an adapted Africa policy.[24]

Changing the Peace Research Focus: Conflict Prolonging Factors

Another, more pro-active approach would be an attempt by researchers to re-focus attention on specific types of conflict factors. By doing this, area studies specialists would not fail to engage in peace research debates themselves. Current thinking on African conflicts is influenced by a tendency to focus predominantly on 'root-causes' of violence, whose resolution is frequently beyond reach. Africa's wars are among the most enduring in the world: some of the most striking examples are the armed conflict in the northeast of Ethiopia, 1962–91, or civil war and rebellion in Southern Sudan, 1955–72 and from 1983 till today; the war that began as a liberation war in 1961 in Angola only ended in 2002. Some of these conflicts change their nature over time, new actors and factors add to those already in existence; to determine the origin of a conflict sometimes becomes an academic exercise.

   Various analyses of the root causes and aggravating factors of violent conflict in Africa exist. But some of the most important features of contemporary warfare in Africa in terms of material and human costs are rather those factors that prolong conflicts. Some of these

---

[24] Such a policy might be better oriented towards 'structural stability' instead of 'development' or 'poverty reduction'; see Mehler 2002b.

are even associated with the aid business (Uvin 1998, 2001), others with military intervention (Korte and Kappel 2000: 98–101). The ideal-type conflict cycle suggests that an 'unstable Peace' transforms over time and is made worse by 'aggravating factors' into a situation of 'high tension' and ultimately 'open conflict'—and the de-escalation pattern would be the same process in reverse. Mainstream thinking on conflict resolution suggests that conflicts attain a moment of 'ripeness for resolution' (Zartman 1985). But these moments arrive late, if at all. De-escalation in a lot of contemporary conflicts is often temporary, while the antagonists prepare for the next battle. In contrast to outside expectations some belligerents might even not prefer their outright victory.[25] The effects should be clear: prolonged war can deny people access to their land for dozens of years with obvious effects on agricultural production. Prolonged war means that whole generations will have experienced nothing but war. This is not yet sufficiently clear to policy makers and researchers alike. More original ways to address some of those war-prolonging factors are important.

A few reflections on some conflict prolonging factors can be made, while it seems premature to give the elements of a potential response strategy.

Oil and Warfare

The links that can be established between oil and conflict are numerous. Oil resources are reasons to circumvent democracy, since governments gain far more from royalties (from major companies) than from taxes from their own ordinary citizens. Thus, they tend to be less responsive to demands for participation (virtually all oil economies in Africa: Libya, Algeria, Gabon, Angola, Congo Brazzaville, Cameroon, Nigeria, Sudan, and newcomer Chad).[26] Royalties or other oil-related

---

[25] Addison et al. explain the rationality of "an avoidance of 'total war' and instead a form of conflict ('low-intensity') that minimises direct losses (thereby reducing the cost of conflict to the belligerent) and increases the direct gains (booty)" (2001: 3).

[26] Ross is unequivocal: "oil inhibits democracy even when exports are relatively small, particularly in poor states" (2001: 356). His findings support the theory that three effects are functional for authoritarianism: a 'rentier effect' (no need for taxes coupled with pressure for democracy), a 'repression effect' (ability to strengthen internal security) and a 'modernization effect' (fewer people going into industrial and service sector jobs which would be positively related to democracy).

transfers can also be used to buy arms or reinforce military capacity to continue violent conflict (Chad, Angola, Sudan). Oil producers in conflict zones get involved in on-going wars or state repression of community protests.[27] Their facilities are used for military interventions as in Sudan (Gagnon and Ryle 2001; Christian Aid 2001; Africa Confidential 2001), and they may side willingly or unwillingly with conflict parties (Congo-Brazzaville).[28]

Trafficking of Precious Resources

Precious resources, such as diamonds, gold, hardwood or other rare natural resources are transiting national frontiers illegally.[29] Warlords are generally military entrepreneurs in search of control of the production sites and trade routes of these commodities, but regular armies might tie in, as in the case of Coltan and other resources from Eastern Congo.[30] Trade profits permit a continuation of such politico-commercial strategies, particularly if both sides of a conflict have access to them (the classic case being Angola—UNITA: diamonds, government: oil—Le Billon 2001). Governments in weak states tend to be corrupted slowly, but pervasively by criminal networks and might become actors of violent conflict.

Small Arms and War as a Profession

Small arms are available at low cost in expanding zones around escalated conflicts. The most common approach to the problem is the regulation of arms exports from Northern countries. However, small arms and ammunition are produced in others as well, including African countries (e.g. South Africa). The destruction of weapons necessitates

---

[27] The Niger Delta in Nigeria is the best-known example; see e.g. Frynas 2001.

[28] Mainstreaming Conflict Prevention in the corporate world is a major issue (as mentioned above). Typically the oil industry is very much the focus of the 'business in conflict' approach. Classic development projects portrayed as acts of 'corporate social responsibility' (as in the Shell case in Nigeria) could easily be a mere PR strategy and fall prey to the prevalent corruption in the country (Frynas 2001: 53).

[29] Addison et al. 2001 claim that countries that are abundant in 'point resources' (oil, gas, diamonds, uranium, rubber etc.) are more likely to experience conflict than countries that possess only 'diffuse resources' (timber, ivory, cattle, etc.). However, there is no doubt that timber played a role in Liberia/Sierra Leone.

[30] The Report of the UN Panel of Experts on the Illegal Exploitation of Natural Resources and other Forms of Wealth of the Democratic Republic of Congo (<http://www.un.org/Docs/sc/letters/2001/357e.pdf>) sheds some light, particularly on the role of Uganda, Rwanda and Burundi in this exploitation (dated 12 April 2001).

their prior collection, an activity which frequently necessitates material input by donor organisations ('arms for cash'), which in turn may be an incentive for becoming a fighter in the first place ('demobilisation rent'): arms collection, demobilisation and reintegration schemes might have perverse (conflict prolonging) effects, if beneficiaries are exclusively those who took up arms in the first place. In enduring conflicts enrolment as a fighter is a rational alternative to less promising opportunities on the labour market for male youth. Fighters may not necessarily be paid, but live from armed blackmail and outright robbery. The traumatising effects of large-scale violence are particularly harmful for children and adolescents. It may be the starting point for a 'career' from victim to perpetrator and thus a 'conflict-prolonging factor' or a 'conflict reproducing factor'.

Declining States

Some African states were simply juridical fictions at independence, others had clearly made progress on the road to informality. 'Horizontal' and 'vertical legitimacy' (Holsti 1996: 84) crucially are missing. This has consequences for conflict and peace. In the absence of responsible governments there are often no credible partners for peace negotiations. The monopoly of violence is gradually replaced by an oligopoly that results in a multiplication of actors and the 'need' to prove their capacity for violence. Security sector reform, high on the agenda of some donor countries, is an important element of structural conflict prevention, but those countries most concerned are the least likely to implement reform.[31] Somalia remains an extreme case where the absence of a state—despite numerous efforts to support local 'peace constituencies'—clearly proved to be a disincentive for peace in large parts of the country (while the reconstitution of an authoritarian state would certainly not help the situation).

Sustaining the War Effort From Abroad: The Role of Diasporas

African diasporas in neighbouring states, in the USA or in Europe may work actively to overthrow regimes in their countries of origin; haphazard internal reform processes may be even less sufficient to appease

---

[31] Aside from Southern African countries Sierra Leone is on the list of recipients.

these communities than the local population. Money transfers from diasporas in Europe (and the US) are fuelling wars in Africa and websites of armed and unarmed opposition movements inciting violence are based in Northern states. On the other hand, there are some (rare) examples where diasporas engage positively in peace processes in their home country/region, an area where outside support could be given. The need to develop a coherent policy (Justice and Home affairs/ foreign policy and development co-operation) towards diasporas is a clear challenge to Northern governments. This should not be a reason for censoring creative thinking on the issue! Some Africanists already work on African diasporas, but are frequently inspired by 'solidarity', taking care of the 'victim perspective' instead of an 'actor perspective'.

Translation Into Practice

However, all the work on paper and the oral expertise researchers can offer may not have the desired effect, and this for two major reasons. Firstly, the opportunities to influence internal conflicts from outside are limited and depend largely on the will of local actors. In many African cases their will to wage war is more pronounced than their readiness to promote peace (e.g. Great Lakes region). Raising expectations might therefore be counter-productive in the end. And, secondly, donor policies are far from having conflict preventive effects in practice.

Where could the insights of area studies help in redefining and implementing policies in order to become conflict preventive? Let us take a quick look at some of the major elements of North-South relations.

Poverty Reduction

Poverty reduction as a core paradigm in donor relations towards Africa clearly needs a more political focus to become a conflict preventive policy. According to the author of a recent study a closer look at the relationship between both objectives is necessary:

> Current policy thinking (. . .) tends to be underpinned by the assumption that 'poverty' and 'social exclusion' cause conflict. Poverty eradication is then justified as a form of conflict prevention. The relationship,

however, is more complex and hence needs refinement. Conflict is as much a consequence of development as it is a constraint on development (Verstegen 2001: 5).

And she offers a different perspective:

> In short, entitlement analysis argues that there are many ways of gaining access to and control over resources, such as the market and kin networks. There are, furthermore, many ways of legitimating such access and control not only through the formal legal system, but also through customary law, social conventions and norms. The nature and 'rules' of each political and economic system produces a set of entitlement relations, governing who can have what in that system. The nature of the entitlement of a person would thus depend on the legal, political, economic and social conditions in society and the person's position in it (ibid.: 12–13).

Indeed, the appropriate way to address conflict prevention via poverty reduction would be an entitlement approach. This is far from being the dominant understanding. A closer analysis of 'entitlement relations' in specific social settings (squatter zones, marginal rural zones) would certainly be useful. Existing anthropological as well as micro-political studies or new research projects involving an area studies approach can help to identify those. What are frequently lacking in these studies are operational recommendations. A translation into practice is therefore needed.

Political Dialogue

Decision-makers should acknowledge the interest and seek to get to know the elites from partner governments in Africa south of the Sahara. This is particularly important when adapting 'political dialogue' to realities.

In the case of the EU the procedure as such has already been elaborated: Art. 96 of the Cotonou agreement between the EU and the ACP countries has established a mechanism in the event that a party considers that the other party has failed to fulfil an obligation in respect of human rights, democratic principles and the rule of law, requiring the Commission to consult member states on its application.[32] This article does not specifically address conflict prevention (this subject is dealt with in Art. 11—there might be a need to make

---

[32] ACP-EU Partnership Agreement, signed in Cotonou on 23 June 2000.

this article operational), but since violent conflict violates human rights a link is easily established.

This provision is currently used extensively and sometimes with success. Beginning in September 2001 17 (mostly African) out of 77 ACP countries have been under consultation, preparing for consultation or under sanctions.[33] This procedure is potentially a rather efficient instrument.[34] It has accounted for some success in Côte d'Ivoire (so far) under the Cotonou Agreement, while a first procedure (under the predecessor Lomé Agreement) was considered to be a failure. It will be interesting to see whether stubborn leaders in, for instance, Zimbabwe could be motivated to change course through political dialogue as well. Now what are the reasons for the different outcomes? A recent study suggests that experience was gained, some lessons learned and the new provisions more conducive to success, but it also made the case for differentiating between governments. In the case of Côte d'Ivoire it is obvious that the Gbagbo government by its nature was more responsive than the military regime of Général Robert Guéi (Hartmann 2001). This question needs more systematic and comparative examination.

Overcoming Sectoral Approaches

A different problem arises when acknowledging the contradictions of sectoral donor policies. The absence of a comprehensive view on conflict and peace, including the acknowledgement of the inter-relatedness of its own activities, has led the international community into a situation where conflict-prevention effects take place only at random. To have a long-term impact, the paradigm of structural stability should finally be taken seriously.[35] This means helping societies

---

[33] According to ACP Assistant Secretary-General Pa'o Luteru during an EPLO/EP conference (Towards a Coherent EU Conflict Prevention Policy in Africa: Challenges for the Belgian Presidency, Brussels 17 September 2001).

[34] The ACP-Secretariat was critical of some processes including those in the case of Haiti; it is certainly right to demand that the consultation procedures under Article 96 of the Cotonou Agreement should be further clarified.

[35] "Structural stability is to be understood as a term denoting a dynamic situation, a situation of stability able to cope with the dynamics inherent in (emerging) democratic societies. Structural stability could thus be defined as a situation involving sustainable economic development, democracy and respect for human rights, viable political structures, and healthy social and environmental conditions, with the capacity to manage change without to resort to violent conflict", cited in:

to build their own capacities in order to manage change without resort to violence.

Difficulties in Making Use of Area Studies Expertise in Practice

Why is there still so little co-operation between decision-makers and researchers? Some insights based on personal experience might give an answer.

Dependency

There is a unilateral dependency of researchers on the funding by donor organisations when deepening their understanding of the research subjects cited above. Alternatives are rare: funding by national research programmes frequently favour 'pure' scientific approaches, disregarding practice-orientation. Consequently, it is simply easier to pursue research in an area where the funding process is an established routine, missing the practice-relevant focus of research. In the case of the CPN,[36] funding was decided at a political level (European Parliament), but in day-to-day practice, and finally in the decision on structure and orientation, the CPN depended too much on one single unit in the DG RELEX (Directorate General for Foreign Relations) of the European Commission. In the context of a lack of content-related competence on the side of its counterparts and a lack of a 'policy advice culture' this institutional construction proved to be too weak to assure sustainability of what remains a good idea: a 'go-between' approach associating a network of (mostly academic) experts with practical needs.

Bureaucratic Obstacles

Practitioners in the field of conflict prevention are mostly members of bureaucratic organisations. They have to deal with a lot of constraints and prerequisites to make a career in a given apparatus. This includes not giving priority to any outside signal when there is clear opposition from somewhere inside the apparatus, whether legitimate

---

Commission of the European Communities 1996. A slightly different definition is given by the OECD DAC. For a discussion of the term see Mehler 2002b.

[36] The Conflict Prevention Network (CPN) was a consultative service for the European Union in conflict prevention matters.

or appropriate or not. Independent research results can be very unpleasant for bureaucratic organisations and therefore tend to be ignored or sidelined.

The Vicious Cycle of Lacking Awareness and Lacking Training

Bureaucratic organisations still lack awareness of conflict risks associated with their own behaviour in African countries. They often do not acknowledge the need to be better trained in issues of conflict prevention or only the need to be better informed by analytical support from area studies specialists—while this accounts in turn for a lack of awareness. In some respect, these organisations remain hermetic and try to deal with new challenges on a mere rhetorical level.

Arrogance of Each Community

Bureaucrats believe they know 'their' country better than independent researchers, particularly those who rarely travel to Africa. After all it is they who get daily reports from their embassies or delegations in the case of the EU (quality control of those reports is rare). They often feel 'badly served' by academic experts who use a hermetic language, too many qualifications, footnotes and far fewer recommendations than would fit their needs. There is some truth in these allegations. On the other hand, researchers fail to find a satisfactory level of refinement in the intellectual discourse of their counterparts, disregard practitioners who usually work only for a limited period of up to three years on a given country and hate to simplify complex issues. They frequently feel badly treated by practitioners who ask for immediate solutions where the range of open questions is expanding on a daily basis. Here as well, these allegations are true to a large extent.

Some researchers raise a number of fundamental ethical questions: they do not want to be associated with a policy based on their (selectively chosen and partly implemented) advice that fails in the end, they do not want to be exploited as an 'intelligence' service, giving up neutrality, serving the 'dirty politics' of a mistrusted government agency. But the ethical question can be turned around: don't researchers with rare or exclusive insights have a moral obligation to try to influence decision-making processes for the better?[37]

---

[37] These issues were discussed at the AEGIS plenary meeting in Bayreuth, 26 May 2001.

Adversity to Conflict Prevention

Doubts remain as to the effectiveness of conflict-prevention approaches on both sides even though these are barely tested. It is true that there are some fundamental methodological problems in proving that individual outcomes and developments can be ascribed to specific causes with any precision, given the large number of actors, projects and other factors involved. It is in fact difficult to know whether a preventive measure prevented an event that would not have occurred in the absence of this measure (Miall 2000). Co-operation on such a subject therefore seems filled with doubt as to the usefulness of the overall approach, while only a deeper involvement on both sides would help to refine a) practical approaches and measures, b) methods of evaluation, and c) quality of scientific research on these topics.

The Best Practice Approach—of Interest to Africanists?[38]

Bureaucratic organisations look for routine procedures, hence the temptation quickly to come to a certain set of activities that can be standardised. And of course, this routine should be the best routine. It might well be that here is the first contradiction in this approach: can a routine ever be the best practice? Probably not. However, an identified best practice might be the reference point for building routines—and routines are unavoidable. This is particularly true in conflict prevention and for a very simple reason: if actions to prevent escalation into violence are to be more timely (as everybody wants), they cannot be created from scratch each time an early warning signal is received. By the time the situation has been properly analysed, choices made, and core actors and needed resources mobilised, the conflict may have reached a situation of open conflict. Without well-established routines this will be a very slow process. Ideally, systems need to be in place that routinely monitor potential conflict situations, review the stakes and decide whether to respond, formulate options how to do this, and draw on an appropriate mix of programmes and projects to implement a targeted strategy. Unfortunately, this is not the case in most national and international bureaucracies. Would such a routine approach hamper a case-by-case judgement? No, it

---

[38] This paragraph is very much influenced by Lund 1998 and by my own experience at the CPN.

would not, if you are faced with an enlightened user. The decision-maker would be able to make an informed decision, but he would still have to make it.

The best practice approach involves different levels or stages of a decision-making process: best practice in *early warning*, in *conflict analysis*, in *agenda-setting*, in *resource mobilisation*, in *programming* and *project implementation*. This chapter will not go into all details. The best practice approach assumes that we know quite a few things about the impact of different modes of action. Some knowledge has been accumulated over time, while gaps remain. It is of particular interest how far regional variations matter, whilst a systematic assessment of the applicability of lessons learned elsewhere in Africa is a task insufficiently undertaken by Africanists. Governments and other bodies can certainly no longer claim that 'nobody' knows what needs to be done, but lessons have yet to be consolidated and presented as policy guidelines that can be digested by policy-makers.

And methodological questions remain unanswered: a study commissioned by the OECD DAC Informal Task Force on Conflict, Peace and Development in 1999 stated that development co-operation always creates both incentives and constraints to both violent and peaceful settlement of conflicts (Uvin 1999). Consequently, the aim must be to isolate and reduce the negative effects, while strengthening the positive impact and—follow best practice. Therefore, lessons have first to be learned before they can be translated into best practice.

The first step is certainly to take stock of past and present experiences. In this field there has been a lot of development in the past decade. Particularly with regard to Bosnia and Rwanda the international community was concerned with its own failure and a number commissioned evaluation studies. These studies looked closely at the chronology of events and identified missed opportunities, doubtful decisions and failing actors. Obviously, this enabled decision-makers to learn a lot about actors and their behaviour in particular situations, but can they draw general conclusions beyond the country—which may be valid for entire African sub-regions?

Looking at several cases with a common analytical framework would avoid a dubious generalisation from what may be specific to a single case. Drawing lessons from Bosnia and Rwanda alone could be misleading. And since decision-makers would learn predominantly 'worst practice' it might be better to look into successful cases such as the Baltic region, and maybe Northern Mali as well. However, the same cautionary comment may apply here: do not generalise too quickly on the basis of individual cases; nor should you transplant an approach that has worked under specific cultural, political and economic conditions (say in several Southeast European states) to a different setting (say the Great Lakes region). Regional variations can be of great significance here.

Michael Lund promotes a method of close systematic comparison of different preventive efforts taken in very similar settings that failed in some cases, but succeeded in others. Notwithstanding the fact that each instance is unique in its situational details, the close comparison of several similar cases of 'success' and 'failure' can help to isolate and continually test variables—and potentially the preventive efforts themselves—that seem to be consistently associated with these divergent outcomes (Lund 1998: 50).

A second method proposed examines comparatively the effects of the same policy instruments applied in distinct conflict settings. There are some studies following those lines; for instance, there is some literature on the effectiveness of sanctions in different settings (South Africa being cited frequently as a successful case, Burundi as a doubtful one). To bring some scientific rigour into the existing literature is effectively an obligation for serious researchers.

After all, these are mainly academic concerns. It would be good if the respective organisations would care about best practice themselves since they have better access to critical information than outsiders, at least concerning the type and assessment of projects or measures. Currently a lot of actors have engaged in taking stock of what can be termed conflict prevention. There is no doubt that part of this exercise is propaganda. Some actors claim always to have done conflict prevention and simply want to prove this now by pointing to a random sample of projects. The good thing is that they feel compelled to do so and this might be an impetus as well to become genuinely concerned about conflict prevention. Whatever the motivation, information is gradually being centralised and evaluated, sometimes internally, sometimes additionally by outside experts. No doubt this approach is painstaking and will only be successful if the respective organisations have enough manpower, a capacity for self-criticism and a structure that permits them to translate the lessons drawn from such a stock taking of projects and instruments into better practice.

Again, however, model projects and instruments are usually not in and of themselves 'conflict preventive'—i.e. wherever, whenever, and however they operate—but only when they are applied in places and times with a potential for more or less imminent violence (frequently this can best be judged by area studies experts) and if they are targeted towards conflict prevention.

This brings us back to the policy level. Best practice is not only to be sought and found at the measure level, but also at the decision-making level. Here a central tool would be to have an operational early warning system. Only a few actors have achieved this so far. There are a lot of competing early warning models on the market, some of them quite academic, others suited to some actor's need. After all, an early warning system must be tailor-made for each client. Governments, NGOs and international organisations have different kinds of mandates, different information sources, process information differently (e.g. involving a varying number of administrative levels), and their decision-making processes function in very different ways. They live in varying organisational cultures. In addition, a regional-specific list of indicators might be appropriate. In order to be relevant and practical (short enough), conflict indicator lists must be close to the empirical evidence of sources of conflict and peace, which means that they probably have to be region-specific.[39]

The ideal situation would be to have an adapted early warning system that makes inroads into the decision-making process by suggesting a number of units and committees that should be concerned with a conflict case and how it should be advanced to a decision-making level. Then a specific unit with substantial standing inside the organisation would drive the process forward until a decision is made as to if, when, what and how preventive action needs to be taken.

Some general rules of good practice stand out.

Good Practice in Conflict Prevention

Here, the following are important:

– Timeliness of concern: put conflict cases on the agenda early, which implies identifying potential crisis early on and monitoring conflict indicators continuously.

---

[39] The Forum on Early Warning and Early Response (FEWER) is using different sets of indicators in its regional programmes, e.g. the Great Lakes region and the Caucasus region.

- Early action: exert firm, unequivocal, and sustained influence on parties to the conflict before a level of escalation is attained that makes any return to stability unlikely.
- Ownership: the responsibility for conflict prevention, management and resolution rests primarily with the people concerned. Outside actors should primarily support their conflict preventive efforts, notably by enhancing the capacities of relevant organisations and institutions at all levels.
- Co-ordination: try to combine and co-ordinate efforts since this would signify a broad international concern and potentially maximise the chances of success.
- Coherence: this is one of the most important principles. Different sectoral programmes and projects should have a coherent peace-building strategy and should be appropriately sequenced. Diplomatic action should be in line with other involvements. If applicable, coordination between civilian and military action is of utmost importance.
- Comparative advantage: actors involved in prior unilateral actions (e.g. former colonial powers) might not be best suited to take a lead role in conflict prevention. Multilateral intergovernmental organisations are usually regarded as being neutral to a conflict.
- Realism I: assess the chances of success. This is certainly a rare lesson to find in textbooks, but it could be regarded as good practice to refrain from being involved in conflict prevention exercises that have no chance of succeeding, while it is best practice effectively to use windows of opportunities in hopeful cases.
- Realism II: to build a coalition of the able and the willing is another necessary prerequisite for collective preventive action, particularly if this involves military means as well.
- Realism III: a mix of 'carrots' and 'sticks', of pressure and reward, is needed most of the time.
- Regional approach: neighbouring states with stakes in a given conflict should be closely watched and persuaded not to fuel a conflict.
- 'Do no harm': be aware of the potential negative impact of the whole range of activities on the conflict.
- Monitoring and evaluation: it is good practice prospectively to assess and then retrospectively evaluate conflict prevention activities in order to get more insight into the question of what works and what does not. Supervision of activities while they are on-going

is another important element that would permit on the spot re-orientation of a project or strategy.

- Training: working in conflict places high demands on personnel on the ground; working with violent conflict places high demands on personnel in decision-making bodies. Good practice involves appropriate training of the different strata within an organisation.

Bureaucratic and Political Obstacles

These rules are not exhaustive, and they may sound simple. Why then do the main actors fail to pursue a best practice approach? The main obstacles are of a bureaucratic nature, others of a political nature.

Bureaucratic and Political Obstacles to Good Practice

Building routines is a long-term process: guidelines must be accepted first—this is not so difficult on paper—but lessons must finally enter the bureaucratic routine. This is a painstaking exercise. The following are obstinate hurdles on the way:

- Contradicting principles and competition: resource competition among different actors is diverting resources away from developing coherent conflict prevention strategies. Conflict prevention is not the only option in relevant organisations, and it is not yet 'mainstreamed' everywhere.
- Organizational overload: some actors simply surrender when faced with so many different challenges from outside. Conflict prevention is then only one of many concerns, such as gender sensitivity, human rights and environmental concerns.
- Incoherence: we observe that countries that go to war frequently get more aid resources than countries that remain at peace (consider the cases of Rwanda, Uganda and Ethiopia). The institutional inertia of agencies leads them to a simple continuation of what they have done in the past. This might be one reason why there has been so much international engagement in post-conflict situations rather than in conflict prevention (Rwanda might be a case in point).
- Deeply entrenched scepticism about effectiveness of conflict prevention: examples are accumulating of how diplomacy, democracy-building, or other responses, even if relatively prompt, are nevertheless

irrelevant or sometimes harmful. Indeed, the need for reliable knowledge about what is likely to work under what conditions is perhaps the most pressing current question.

- Predilection for symbolic policy: it is important to understand that politicians prefer the obvious reward—which may take the form of delivering a couple of tons of food aid long after the escalation of a war or to visit a refugee camp—than, for example, stimulate a discussion on a forward-looking migration policy that might prevent a violent conflict.
- Lack of an evaluation culture: a number of actors simply would not want independent researchers looking into their information and decision-making systems. This remains a black box, sometimes to the actors themselves. Accordingly, it is difficult to introduce best practice on this level. Furthermore, the efforts to evaluate lesser known preventive tools such as election observation, initiation of an Accession Strategy to regional or international organizations, security sector reforms, etc., have only begun and we don't know enough about them.
- Lacking the capacity for self-criticism. A best practice approach may imply that a given organization has not followed such good practice in the past, which seems to be difficult to admit for some of them.
- Lack of appropriate institutional capacity: only a minority of the important actors already have appropriate units to deal with conflict prevention. Where they have, they might quickly overestimate their own capacity and in practice even work against the promotion of best practice.
- Cost of conflict prevention: conflict prevention might be cheaper than post-conflict reconstruction or military adventure, but it will come at some cost. In times of budget constraints this means that the issue has to compete with others. Best practice may cost more than bad practice.

It is easy to find reasons why the other good or best practice rules are not applied or why they fail: diverging agendas of major actors hamper co-ordination efforts. Using sticks is not making you popular with partner governments. Additionally, regional approaches are not easily compatible with a focus on individual countries, which are usually covered by country desk officers and country strategy papers. In light of these difficulties a lot remains to be done to change attitudes. Analytical tools or instruments could be of some help if they are given appropriate weight in the decision-making process. They are developed (some of those by CPN) under the explicit assumption that best practice needs to be turned into routine. Africanists ought to be aware of the adaptation of such instruments and approaches to regional particularities and social change. What is good practice in one environment might be doubtful in other circumstances.

Conclusion

'Thinking conflict' (or 'thinking conflict prevention'!) should become automatic for those who are concerned with the continent. Africa has become an area of conflict and the outlook for altering this picture is not very promising. A drastic change towards research on associated topics and practical activities at least in countries/sub-regions at risk seems unavoidable. It is still desirable to overcome numerous obstacles and to foster synergies between research and practice. Both sides ought to attempt to take the necessary steps, including the institutionalisation of discussion forums. Concrete areas of co-operation include the regional adaptation of Early Warning Indicators and Conflict Impact Assessment tools for specific regions or conflict patterns, in addition to the whole range of other subjects cited above. For area studies the paradigm of conflict prevention offers a rare opportunity to get the outside attention they merit—if they can prove to be relevant.

Bibliography

Abbink, J. (2000), 'La violence, l'Etat et l'ethnicité dans la Corne de l'Afrique: au niveau local et mondial', *Autrepart*, no. 15, pp. 149–166.

Africa Confidential, 23 March 2001, Opening new front in the oil war. Petrodollars are financing Khartoum´s diplomacy and its war against the south, vol. 42, no. 6.

Addison, T., P. Le Billon and S.M. Murshed (2001), 'Conflict in Africa. The Cost of Peaceful Behaviour', United Nations University/WIDER Dicussion Paper No. 2001/51, Helsinki, WIDER.

Baechler, G. (1999), *Violence through Environmental Discrimination*, Dordrecht, Kluwer.

Bayart, J.-F. (1989), *L'Etat en Afrique*, Paris, Fayard.

Bayart, J.-F., P. Geschiere and F. Nyamnjoh (2001), 'Autochtonie, démocratie et citoyenneté en Afrique', *Critique Internationale*, no. 10, pp. 177–194.

Champain, P. (2002), 'Assessing the Corporate Sector in Mainstreaming Conflict Prevention', in L. van de Goor and M. Huber (eds.) *Mainstreaming Conflict Prevention. Concept and Practice*, CPN Yearbook 2000/2001, Baden-Baden, Nomos, pp. 145–163.

Christian Aid (2001), *The scorched earth: oil and war in Sudan*, London, Christian Aid.

Clapham, C. (ed.) (1998), *African Guerillas*, Oxford, James Currey, Bloomington, University of Indiana Press, Kampala, Fountain Publishers.

Collier, P. (2000), 'Doing Well out of War: An Economic Perspective', in M. Berdal and D.M. Malone (eds.) *Greed and Grievance. Economic Agendas in Civil Wars*, Boulder/CO, Lynne Rienner, pp. 91–111.

Collier, P. and A. Hoeffler (2000), *Greed and Grievance in Civil War* (= CSAE Working Paper 2000/18), Oxford and Washington, D.C., World Bank.

Commission of the European Communities (1996), The European Union And The Issues Of Conflicts In Africa: Peace-Building, Conflict Prevention And Beyond (= Communication from the Commission to the Council), Brussels: European Commission.

Duffield, M. (2000), 'Globalization, Transborder Trade, and War Economies', in M. Berdal and D.M. Malone (eds.) *Greed and Grievance. Economic Agendas in Civil Wars*, Boulder/CO, Lynne Rienner, pp. 69–89.

Ellis, S. (1999), *The Mask of Anarchy. The Destruction of Liberia and the Religious Dimension of an African Civil War*, London, Hurst.

Engel, U. (2001), *Whither conflict prevention. International norms and African politics*, Paper prepared for the 44th African Studies Association (ASA) meeting, Houston/TX., 18 November 2001.

Engel, U. and A. Mehler (2000), "Closing the gap' between early warning and early action: Applying political science to violent conflicts in Africa', *University of Leipzig Papers on Africa*, no. 44, Leipzig, University of Leipzig.

Frynas, J.G. (2001), 'Corporate and State Responses to Anti-Oil protests in the Niger delta', *African Affairs*, vol. 100, no. 398, pp. 27–54.

Gagnon, G. and J. Ryle (2001), *Report of an Investigation into Oil Development, Conflict and Displacement in Western Upper Nile, Sudan* (commissioned by several Canadian NGOs)—October 2001.

Hartmann, C. (2001), *Côte d'Ivoire: A Prevention Case for EU Policy* (= CPN Briefing Paper), Berlin, SWP-CPN.

Hear, N. van (no date). *People who stay: migration, development and those left behind*, The Refugee Studies Centre of the University of Oxford; <http://www.qeh.ox.ac.uk/rsp/TextWeb/rerep1.html>.

Heinecken, L. (2001), 'Strategic implicatoins of HIV/AIDS in South Africa', *Journal of Conflict, Security and Development*, vol. 1, no. 1, pp. 101–109.

Herbst, J. (2000a), 'Economic Incentives, Natural Resources and Conflict in Africa', *Journal of African Economies*, vol. 9, no. 3, pp. 270–294.

——. (2000b), *States and Power in Africa. Comparative Lessons in Authority and Control*, Princeton, Princeton University Press.

Holsti, K.J. (1996), *The state, war, and the state of war*, Cambridge, New York, Melbourne, Cambridge University Press

Jean, F. and J.-C. Rufin (eds.) (1996), *Économie des guerres civiles*, Paris, Hachette.

Klingebiel, S. et al. (2000), *Socio-political Impact of Development Cooperation Measures in Tanzania: Analysing Impacts on Local Tensions and Conflicts*, Bonn, German Development Institute.

Korte, W. and R. Kappel (2000), 'Crisis and Intervention: How ECOMOG Brought About Peace in Liberia, but Was Still Unable to Guarantee a Democratic New Beginning', *Liberian Studies Journal*, vol. 25, no. 2, pp. 83–105.

Le Billon, P. (2001), 'Angola's political economy of war: The role of oil and diamonds, 1975–2000', *African Affairs*, vol. 100, no. 398, pp. 55–80.

Lemarchand, R. (2001), *Exclusion, Marginalization and Poltical Mobilization: The Road to Hell in the Great Lakes* (Centre of African Studies, University of Copenhagen Occasional Paper), Copenhagen: Centre of African Studies.

Lund, M. (1998), 'Preventing Violent Conflicts: Progress and Shortfall', in Peter Cross (ed.), *Contributing to Preventive Action* (= CPN Yearbook 1997/98), Baden-Baden, Nomos, pp. 21–63.

Lund, M. and G. Rasamoelina (eds.) (2000), *The Impact of Conflict Prevention Policy. Cases, Measures, Assessments* (= CPN Yearbook 1999/2000), Baden-Baden, Nomos.

Mehler, A. (2002a), 'Der Beitrag regionalwissenschaftlicher Ansätze zur Analyse gewaltsamer Konflikte in Afrika südlich der Sahara', in S. Kurtenbach and A. Mehler (eds.), *Die Vielfalt von Gewaltkonflikten. Analysen aus regionalwissenschaftlicher Perspektive*, Hamburg, Deutsches Übersee-Institut.

——. (2002b), 'Structural stability: meaning, scope and use', Afrika Spectrum, vol. 37, no. 1, pp. 5–23.

Mehler, A. and C. Ribaux (2000), *Crisis Prevention and Conflict Management in Technical Cooperation. An Overview of the National and International Debate*, Wiesbaden, Universum.

Miall, H. (2000), 'Preventing Potential Conflicts. Assessing the Impact of Light and Deep Conflict Prevention in Central and Eastern Europe and the Balkans', in M. Lund and G. Rasamoelina (eds.), *The Impact of Conflict Prevention Policy* (= CPN Yearbook 1999/2000), Baden-Baden, Nomos, pp. 23–45.

Ross, M.L. (2001), 'Does oil hinder democracy?', World Politics, vol. 53, no. 2, pp. 325–361.

Schmitt, S. (2001), *Städter und Bürger. Lebenswelten städtischer Armer in Zeiten politischer Umbrüche in der Côte d'Ivoire. Eine Untersuchung zu politischer Kultur und politischen Handeln*, Hamburg, Lit.

Senghaas, D. (2001), 'The Civilization of Conflict. Constructive Pacifism as a Guiding Notion for Conflict Transformation', in Berghof Research Center for Constructive Conflict Management (ed.), Berghof Handbook for Conflict Transformation, Berlin (<http://www.berghof-center.org/handbook/cf.htm>).

Uvin, P. (1998), *Aiding Violence. The Development Enterprise in Rwanda*, West Hartford/Connecticut, Kumarian Press.

——. (1999), *The Influence of Aid in Situations of Violent Conflict. A synthesis and a commentary on the lessons learned from case studies on the limits and scope for the use of development assistance incentives and disincentives for influencing conflict situations* (= DAC Informal Task Force on Conflict, Peace and Development Co-operation), Paris, DAC.

——. (2001), 'Difficult choices in the new post-conflict agenda: the international community in Rwanda after the genocide', Third World Quarterly, vol. 22, no. 2, pp. 177–189.

Verstegen, S. (2001), *Poverty and Conflict. An Entitlement Perspective* (CPN Briefing Paper), Berlin, SWP-CPN.

Villalón, L.A. and P. Huxtable (eds.) (1998), *The African State at a Critical Juncture. Between Disintegration and Reconfiguration*, Boulder/CO and London, Lynne Rienner.

Walraven, K. van (1999), *Conflict Policy in some Western Countries*, The Hague, Netherlands Institute of International Relations/Clingendael.

Wohlgemuth, L., et al. (eds.) (1999), *Common Security and Civil Society in Africa*, Stockholm, Nordiska Afrikainstitutet.

Zartman, I.W. (ed.) (2000), *Traditional Cures for Modern Conflicts*, Boulder/CO, Lynne Rienner.

——. (1985), *Ripe for Resolution. Conflict and Intervention in Africa*, New York and Oxford, Oxford University Press.

PART TWO

MANAGING CONFLICT AND IMPLEMENTING CONFLICT
RESOLUTION IN AFRICA

CHAPTER SIX

THE SOCIAL COST OF CONFLICT IN THE DEMOCRATIC
REPUBLIC OF CONGO

Theodore Trefon

The latest round of conflict in the Democratic Republic of Congo (DRC) continues to fuel misguided 'heart of darkness' clichés about the country once referred to by Franz Fanon during an earlier spiral of violence as the 'trigger of Africa'. Such clichés portray the Congo as a kind of 'forsaken' black hole characterized by tribal hatred, malicious dictatorship and social cannibalism.[1] Without trying to downplay the pertinence of these atrocious realities, this chapter challenges the 'heart of darkness' mode of representation. It does so by analysing the human implications of what is already a very long history of violence and conflict within and around the Congo.

The social tragedy that we are witnessing there today has complex and historically deep-rooted origins. State failure facilitated Kabila's 'war of liberation' and subsequently the second 'war of aggression', led primarily by Rwanda. State failure conversely has resulted in the creation of dynamic new forms of social organization, constituting order within the broader context of disorder. While I will briefly consider conflict and crisis through a 'top down' political science lens, along with a discussion of the 'failed state' theoretical framework, greater emphasis will be placed on the role and sacrifice of the Congolese people. Despite monumental obstacles, they continue to believe in their Congolese identity and in the need to maintain the geographic area of the Congo as a unified political entity. In so doing, they have proven to be remarkably inventive in finding solutions—not only to ensure physical and collective survival but also to improve their well being.

---

[1] 'Forsaken' is the title of Philip Gourevitch's bleak account of war and its implications for the Congolese (Gourevitch 2000).

Explaining the Crisis

Conflict in post-Mobutu Congo is intimately linked to the failure of the post-colonial nation-state system hastily fabricated by interest groups from within the Belgian political, commercial, industrial and financial ruling coalition. State failure in turn is a result of historical processes. The origins of crisis at least go as far back as the immediate pre-colonial 'Scramble for Africa' and the extractive system put in place by King Leopold II of Belgium. The Congo Free State, circumscribed in Berlin in 1885, was Leopold's personal property. Descriptions of the brutality of his system date from over a century ago and have provided some very powerful and emblematic pieces of literature in English over the intervening years.[2] Paternalism replaced the brutal Leopoldian system of rubber and ivory extraction in 1908. Belgian colonial policy was based on the Missionary-Administration-Commerce triumvirate, and justified itself in terms of a 'civilizing mission'. The obvious limitation of this 'civilizing mission' was the complete absence of political responsibility. No elite leadership had been trained. All-important decisions emanated from Brussels. Even the European expatriate community in the Congo enjoyed no political rights.

The lack of political preparation led to one of the African continent's most chaotic transitions to independence. The Congo-Zaire post-colonial state rapidly abdicated its role as provider of basic social and administrative services, becoming a social predator. Mobutu, like King Leopold, also exploited the Congo and its resources as though they were his personal property. Because of Cold War politics and Western capitalist interests, the West (mainly the US, France and Belgium) supported the Mobutu regime. Until the fall of the Berlin wall, they backed a regime characterized by violence, nepotism, and the personality cult of the 'supreme leader', human rights abuse and absence of freedom of expression.

By the early 1990s, Mobutu had outlived his political usefulness. The erstwhile 'trusted ally' had become a political liability and an embarrassment. On 24 April 1990 he welcomed the period of demo-

---

[2] The obvious examples are Joseph Conrad's *Heart of Darkness* first published at the turn of the century and Mark Twain's *King Leopold's Soliloquy* (1907). Although probably exaggerated and methodologically dubious, Adam Hochschild has charged the despotic Belgian monarch with "a death toll of Holocaust dimensions" (1998: 4).

cratic transition and the end of the Second Republic. During the period of 'intransitive' democratic transition that was to follow, however, he continued to control politics until the mid-1990s. He did so largely by playing opposition groups against each other (de Villers and Omasombo 2002). The presidential movement of Mobutu and associated parties outmanoeuvred the Sacred Union of the opposition that was created in July 1991, headed by Etienne Tshisekedi and the Catholic Church, and politically represented by Mgr Monsengwo, Archbishop of Kisangani. Carefully elaborated economic strategies employed by the ruling elite also succeeded in stifling his political opposition (De Herdt 2002). Eventually, however, the Mobutu regime's patrimonial and predatory networks reached the limit of their effectiveness and this self-destructive system consumed itself, leaving only remnants of a state. This situation was exacerbated by the failing health of the dictator, who eventually died from prostate cancer.

The fact that the end of the Mobutu regime coincided with the seizing of power by Laurent Désiré Kabila has been described more as an 'accident of history' than the result of clear social and political processes (de Villers and Omasombo 2002: 403). In 1994, approximately 1 million Hutus and moderate Tutsis were massacred in Rwanda. Following this episode of 'tit-for-tat ethnic violence' (Lemarchand 2001: 15) in the Great Lakes Region, up to 1.2 million refugees poured into the eastern North and South Kivu provinces of what was then still Zaire. Among them were approximately 100,000 Interahamwe militias. According to Lemarchand, they were armed and violent: "there was no precedent in the history of the region for such a massive eruption of armed refugees into the host country" (ibid.: 15).

In August and September of 1996 Banyamulenge, supported by Rwanda, started a rebellion. This [context] facilitated the creation of the *Alliance des Forces Démocratique pour la Libération du Congo-Zaire* in October 1996. Kabila's Rwandan and Ugandan backers put him in command of the AFDL. Bukavu, Goma, Mbuji-Mayi, Lubumbashi, and eventually Kinshasa, were successively taken by the Alliance forces. Mobutu's *Forces Armées Zairoises* put up surprisingly little resistance. The march to Kinshasa from the east took less than seven months. On 17 May 1997 Laurent Désiré Kabila took Kinshasa and on 29 May he officially— but certainly not democratically—became the country's new leader.

When Kabila fell out with his Rwandan and Ugandan backers after an uneasy year long alliance, Rwanda did in fact evacuate the Congo briefly in late July 1998, but re-emerged in a blitzkrieg operation only a few weeks later. Kabila's Rwandan ex-chief-of-staff, Colonel James Karbarebe, commandeered a Congolese troop carrier in Goma, flew it across the Congo to Kitona on the Atlantic coast—more than 1,900 kilometres—and somehow persuaded several thousand local troops to mutiny and march, once again, towards Kinshasa. Before reaching the capital, however, they took control of the Inga dam that provides Kinshasa with its electricity. In what turned out to be a serious mis-calculation, they cut Kinshasa's power supply. The *Kinois* were con-sequently deprived of electricity and water. People's nerves were stretched to the limit. If it had not been for a well-constructed anti-Tutsi hate campaign that played on the Kinshasa residents' sense of 'patriotism', Karbarebe's invasion might have succeeded. Hundreds of Tutsis—and anyone resembling one—were lynched in Kinshasa in late August and September of 1998. The degree of violence was unprece-dented in Kinshasa according to the local press (see de Villers et al. 2001: 30–31).

Although the Congolese have now reinvented their relations with the state, it also appears they expect relatively little from it (Trefon 2002a). There is clearly no absence of political engagement or ideas in the Congo, but people have failed to develop their political aspi-rations into concrete political initiatives. This could be related to the culture of *la débrouille*: Mobutu kept people preoccupied, both indi-vidually and creatively, with survival to avoid political mobilization. There is also the perception that political mobilization is a long-term investment with little chance of success. People are disillusioned by the political forces they blame for having sabotaged the transition to democracy. The catastrophic relationship between state and society during the Mobutu dictatorship has hardly evolved under the regimes of Laurent Désiré Kabila or his son Joseph Kabila. Although popular discourse is admittedly not useful in measuring leadership capacity, under Mobutu, people often referred to Belgian colonialism with nos-talgia. Today, many Congolese deplore the unfulfilled expectations of new leaders and say that their lives were better under Mobutu.

Congo's War Economy

Mark Duffield's work on 'complex political emergencies' (1994) and 'post-modern conflict' (1998) helps to put the war economy in the DRC into the appropriate theoretical perspective. For Duffield, post-modern conflict is best understood in terms of innovative and long-term adaptations to globalization rather than the conceptually limited failed-state analytical framework. Economic factors have become the driving force of new wars, replacing ideology, culture and identity. With specific reference to the Congo, this translates into what the United Nations refers to as the 'illegal exploitation of natural resources' (United Nations 2002) or what the Congolese in general and the people of Kivu refer to as *pillage*—plunder and looting. Because of the number of actors involved, former U.S. Secretary of State Madeline Albright characterized the 'unresolved turmoil' in the DRC as 'Africa's first world war'.[3]

Despite this 'diplomatic sympathy' discourse, "the U.S. has helped build the arsenals of eight of the nine governments directly involved in the Congo War" (Hartung and Moix 2000: 8—italics in the original). European Union policy has been equally dubious—notably through its support of Rwanda (André and Luzolele 2000).[4] The exploitation of diamonds (Samset 2002), coltan (Jackson 2002), gold, timber and coffee has contributed to prolonging the war. Although extraction is essentially being carried out by force, the way that networks function indicates that the withdrawal of invading forces will not necessarily put an end to current forms of exploitation. Many of these networks need to negotiate with a variety of military and militia and are often involved in criminal activities. The militarization and criminalization of these networks of economic extortion is an extremely dangerous development because it stifles local business and economic initiative and has a negative impact on social relations. Local populations rarely benefit—if at all.

The copper and cobalt exports that in the late 1980s constituted around 70 per cent of the country's major source of revenue are now negligible. A bankrupt state simply cannot afford to operate capital-intensive industries such as copper and cobalt. Zaire's parastatals have consequently been replaced by new networks of diamond, gold and timber smugglers. Conversely, these networks thrive on the dismantled Mobutist system of patrimonial exploitation of natural resources and the absence of a Weberian state system with tax collectors,

---

[3] Welcoming remarks at the UN Security Council Session on the DRC, New York, 24 January 2000.
[4] For a detailed analysis of the sources of arms in the Congo war, see Augusta Muchai 2002, notably pp. 189–191.

a functioning bureaucracy and impartial judicial system. This situation supports William Reno's argument that "[n]atural resource dependent economies appear to be particularly vulnerable to disorder and violent competition among those who lay claim to natural resources. Most African states that currently or have recently hosted major internal strife also are dependent upon petroleum or a single mineral for export earnings" (2001: 3).

'Looting' and 'illegality' are extremely complex concepts that are perceived differently by different actors. The government's 'invited' allies are involved in very similar economic practices to those of the uninvited 'aggressors/rebels'. Moreover, the government itself could be accused of 'looting' because its corrupt and clientelist practices 'ransack' the resources of the population. Angola is 'paid' in petroleum for its war efforts just as Zimbabwe has been granted generous mining concessions in Katanga as well as logging concessions in the country's rich and under-exploited tropical forests. The strategy of the two Kabila regimes seems more designed to gain economic control over profitable networks that operate within the country than to establish authority and administer the entire country.[5]

There is a genuine concern that Western companies are fuelling the conflict with business and trade transactions involving minerals originating from the DRC. The Belgian Senate in this respect conducted a parliamentary enquiry into the involvement of Belgian companies in the war.[6] While such concerns are not misplaced, it can often lead to neo-colonial conspiracy theories of unscrupulous Western conglomerates plundering the Congo. The reality, however, is somewhat different—and far more complex. When there are few laws, and those that exist are seen as either very flexible, little known, or rarely enforced, and violated even by the government, to attempt to limit the study of war-fuelling activities to those deemed illegal is a dubious approach. What legitimate regulatory framework exists in a country where effective rule of law is replaced by tentative rule by presidential decree? Moreover, what relevance does a regulatory framework have in a country where no institution has been able to enforce regulations for years, or even decades?

---

[5] For an excellent analysis of the challenges of establishing administrative control over the country, see Pourtier 1997.

[6] Transcripts can be consulted at the website: <http://www.senate.be>.

While the 'greed versus grievance' analysis is certainly pertinent to central Africa, some versions of it minimize the complex relationship between mineral wealth and other economic assets, economic development and the multiple and overlapping motivations of actors involved in conflict. Analysing the Congo war in terms of 'greed' rather than in terms of more complex historical, social and political factors—'grievances'—had led certain international NGOs to campaign against the purchase of minerals originating from conflict zones. 'No blood on my mobile phone' was one such initiative because coltan from the Kivus in Eastern Congo is used in mobile phones.[7] The intense but short-lived fury over coltan illustrates the fact that international NGOs and institutions condemning the pillage of the Congo's natural resources often fail to recognise that local populations also engage in and benefit from war economies (Jackson 2002). The war economy is firmly rooted in their daily lives because they are the ones who are digging up coltan in Kivu or heterogenite (a copper and cobalt alloy) in Katanga. For many people the only economic alternative to these 'informal' and 'illegal' activities is subsistence agriculture, something that no longer reflects their perceptions or aspirations of well being or modernity.

The goals of the different warring factions have never been really clear and are becoming increasingly nebulous. This can be accounted for by the multiplicity of actors, shifting alliances, the changing nature of economic possibilities, and problems related to decoding official discourses. One thing, however, has remained constant since the beginning of the war: the maintenance of at least low intensity conflict is in the economic interest of the various actors. While Interahamwe groups pose a real threat to Kigali, Rwanda prefers to keep them in check rather than destroy them completely. The same argument has been made for other countries involved in the DRC war, such as Burundi or Uganda. This makes it very difficult to end the conflict, and leads to the question of who really controls policies. Those who currently possess the means to end the violence are paradoxically the protagonists invited to the negotiating table. Without some reassessment and reconstruction of the Congo state system, the country will remain vulnerable to outside intervention. It will be an

---

[7] *Geen bloed aan mijn GSM* was an operation organized by a consortium of Flemish NGOs.

area perceived as a 'free access' zone where resources can be extracted with impunity by the most powerful armed forces.

The Social Cost of War

State failure and crisis due to the processes described above have been, and continue to be, major factors facilitating the outbreak and perpetuation of war. War, nonetheless, is a recurrent tragedy in Zaire/Congo. Since independence in 1960, some form of violent conflict has erupted regularly (Hamuli 2002: 58–61). Although the eastern areas have suffered the most, not one of the country's eleven provinces has been spared. The secessions in the early 1960s caused approximately half a million deaths. The Muleliste insurrection in 1964–65 in eastern Congo also caused considerable loss of life, and further rebellions in the east in 1967 destroyed a large part of the city of Bukavu. Katanga saw two more wars/invasions in 1977 and 1978 when Mobutu was saved by foreign assistance from Morocco and France (Trefon 1989). The Moba war of 1980 served to remind people inside and outside the country that there were still pockets of armed opposition. The 1996–97 war of 'liberation' and the subsequent invasion have had indescribable human consequences. Although probably exaggerated, the International Rescue Committee reported the figure of 2.5 million deaths occurring between August 1998 and March 2001 (IRC 2001).[8] It is also reported that 60 per cent of children die before their 5th birthday from infectious diseases such as cholera and meningitis. Violent and 'non-violent' deaths are inseparable; pregnant women experience unique risks; violence against civilians appears indiscriminate; and adult death from malnutrition has been an almost exclusively female phenomenon.

Human development is inextricably linked to the rich natural heritage of the DRC. Throughout the Congo basin area, people's livelihoods, belief systems and cultures are intimately linked to nature. City dwellers and rural populations alike depend on natural resources such as fuelwood, game and non-timber forest products in order to

---

[8] This report has been widely criticized, mainly on methodological grounds because many of its findings are based on extrapolations. It nonetheless has the merit of bringing the nature of human tragedy to the attention of the international community—even though international peace keeping efforts have been deplorably inadequate.

meet daily needs for survival (Trefon 2000a). It may appear surreal to evoke natural resource management in a war-ravaged country where people are starving, sick and deprived of political participation, but when the environment is threatened, people suffer even more. From the Kinshasa hinterland or the degraded peri-urban halo around Bukavu where hundreds of thousands of Rwandan refugees amassed in 1994, to the emblematic nature reserves such as Virunga, Kahuzi-Biega, Garamba, Okapi or Salonga, environmental degradation translates into human deprivation. The impact of this degradation, moreover, will be felt long after hostilities have ceased.

In the rural areas, where coltan or diamond mining is impossible, people survive thanks to their subsistence skills—hunting, gathering, fishing and farming. Due to the decay of the road infrastructure and the inadequate level of international aid, they live in relative autarchy, especially in war zones. Access to health care, education or administrative services is extremely rare (both before and since the war). Today, in the rebel held areas (approximately two thirds of the country), basic supplies no longer exist. Medicines, batteries, petrol, soap, salt, and food are referred to as 'memories'. The absence of salt, for example, is a serious problem. Without the iodine it provides many children now suffer from goiter, a deficiency that had been nearly eradicated by the end of the colonial period. Clothing is also increasingly hard to find. Consequently, many children do not attend school because they literally have nothing to wear.

Hunger is one of the most terrible consequences of conflict and crisis. Westerners often joke that 'we have watches but Africans have time'. This is a serious misperception because the subsistence activities of rural communities are very carefully planned. Food production adheres to a strict calendar. Surpluses are rarely produced. When communities are displaced or when soldiers steal their food, the risk of starvation is exacerbated. This helps to explain why populations in rebel-controlled areas are slowly dying of hunger. As soldiers are not paid and do not receive food supplies they force the local population—often at gunpoint—to supply them with food. The usual reaction is for people to flee into the forest, thus becoming internal refugees. An estimated two million people have been internally displaced in North and South Kivu and Katanga. The nutritional situation of women and children is particularly appalling. "In rebel-held areas, the rates of global malnutrition among children under five

reported in the past year have reached 41 per cent, with severe malnutrition rates of up to 26 per cent".[9] Displaced peoples living in
forests mainly eat cassava roots and leaves and wild fruits. This con-
stitutes a poorly balanced diet that results in nutritional deficiencies
and increased susceptibility to disease. These populations also lack
simple farming tools, seeds and planting material. They often steal
food and planting material in their flight, further adding to tensions
and conflict.

Lack of food in occupied areas is also one of the main causes of the
cannibalism that was reported in early 2003. Accusations of cannibalism were made against the troops of Jean-Pierre Bemba in the Ituri
forest of north east Congo.[10] It seems that pygmy groups had been
caught between opposing groups supporting the Kinshasa government and Ugandan-backed rebel groups. According to UN sources,
Bemba's troops forced pygmies to hunt for them and if they returned
without game, they were themselves eaten. The ritual aspects of eat-
ing one's enemy, or using body parts as trophies, while atrocious is
far from being unimaginable in the region.

The extreme militarization of eastern Congo, a region where the
status of women has traditionally been low, has had a particularly
catastrophic impact on women (Kadima and Kabemba 2003). Rape and
sexual slavery are now commonplace. Interahamwe militia took tens
of thousands of women with them as human shields and sex slaves
(Brittain 2002). The many foreign armies and indigenous militias
behave similarly. Women risk rape and other forms of humiliation or
aggression when they go to work their fields or collect fuelwood.
Violence against them is arbitrary and systematic. Victoria Brittain
further reports that:

> ... rape is one element in the rapid destruction of the society's life pat-
> terns because of the way it destroys families and communities with the
> rupture of trust and the poison of shame. Family members and neigh-
> bours were often forced to witness the rape of mother or daughter,
> shame overwhelms grief and their families usually, though not always,
> rejected the wives and daughters afterwards. The scale of the victim-
> ization of women in eastern Congo by rape in the last few years may
> even have dwarfed historical precedents for mass rape in war. (...)

[9] Save the Children-Oxfam-Christian Aid 2001: 25, quoted in Tollens (forthcoming).
[10] *The Guardian*, 9 January 2003.

Prostitution has also increased because sex is one of the few economic opportunities available. Women live in military camps for protracted periods of time because the money they earn enables them to feed their children—a situation tragically described as 'survival sex' (Human Rights Watch 2002).

Children are also particularly affected by crisis and the war in the Congo: as in most of Africa, 50 per cent of the population is under fifteen years of age. Some become soldiers like the *kadogos*, who helped Laurent Désiré Kabila come to power. In Kivu, militia youth claim that 'with a gun you can eat'. Others seek their fortune by digging for coltan or diamonds in Angola—the *bana lunda* (Sabakinu 2000, De Boeck 2000). On the streets of Kinshasa or Lubumbashi, some simply live by their wits as *moineaux*, *phaseurs* or *sheges* (local nomenclature for street children). Unschooled, undernourished, disillusioned and separated from their families, these children are part of a lost generation.

Urban Suffering

Conditions in the occupied rural parts of the country are clearly catastrophic. The situation is equally serious in urban areas. In cities throughout the Congo, economic and political crisis exacerbated by war translates into the decline, absence or hijacking of municipal and administrative services. There are public transport problems, inadequate distribution of water and energy and housing shortages. Access to health care and schooling is a major challenge.

In occupied Congo, Kisangani, the country's third largest city is a martyred city—*une ville martyre*. The political and military situation there has been extremely complex because Kisangani has been occupied by both Rwandan and Ugandan forces at the same time—as well as their Congolese allies/proxies. In May, June and August 1999, the residents found themselves in the centre of a confrontation between soldiers from Rwanda and Uganda (and to a lesser extent from Burundi). The area is particularly coveted because of its gold and diamonds. Erstwhile allies became new enemies in the ongoing process of shifting alliances. The city suffered serious material damage and an unconfirmed number of casualties that according to some sources could have been as high as 650 soldiers and 30 civilians (de Villiers et al. 2001: 62). For similar motives less than a year later, in May and June 2000, Rwandan and Ugandan forces began fighting again. This time heavy artillery was used to pound the city. The fighting took place in the heart of civilian areas: people were used both as targets and as human shields. Nearly 400 civilians, the numbers probably underestimated, lost their lives; tens of thousands fled into the forest hinterland (ibid.: 112).

The extract below provides a chilling picture of yet another outbreak of hostilities and brutality.

> In a report to the U.N. Security Council, Human Rights Commissioner Mary Robinson blamed Rwandan-backed rebels from the Congolese Rally for Democracy for carrying out 'summary executions and extrajudicial killings of civilians, soldiers and police' following an uprising in the port city . . . Late last month . . . the RCD rebels who control Kisangani embarked on an 'indefensible massacre' to put down a mutiny, killing at least 150 people . . . [P]eople were shot and stabbed to death—and . . . some were cut open and their bodies filled with stones and thrown into the river to sink . . . 103 civilians and at least 60 soldiers and police officers were massacred by the rebels and reports indicate another 20 unidentified bodies were observed in the Tshopo river in the days after the RCD regained control of the city . . . The killings came after mutineers occupied a radio station in Kisangani, a Congo River port and diamond trading centre, and issued a call for an uprising against the 'Rwandan invaders', the report said . . . Robinson said the rebels had a right to react to the mutiny but their reprisals and crackdown 'were brutally calculated' to silence protests against RCD oppression and its alliance with Rwandan troops in the area . . . Robinson accused the rebels of continuing to exploit the situation by claiming they are protecting the Tutsi population, which has resulted in isolating the Tutsis, polarizing society, and raising fears of ethnic violence initiated by the rebels to silence all opposition.[11]

In Kinshasa, Congo's capital and sub-Saharan Africa's second largest city, 50 per cent of the population have only one meal per day, 25 per cent have one meal every two days (Ministère de la Santé Publique 1999: 47). Throughout the city, 25 per cent of families—and in this case it is children and women—have to walk more than one kilometre per day to fetch water (ibid.: 55). Although population figures for Kinshasa are based on rough estimates, it is widely accepted that the 6,000,000 mark has been exceeded. With the arrival of hundreds of

---

[11] Associated Press wire 17 July 2002—"The U.N. human rights chief is calling for the arrest of Congolese rebels and civilians responsible for a massacre in the city of Kisangani in May that killed over 180 people".

thousands of displaced people from the east, the figure could be much higher—perhaps 7,000,000. Kinshasa's overwhelming preponderance in the Congo in terms of population, infrastructure, employment, industry, trade and public works reflects Mobutu's highly centralized political rule. This preponderance helps to explain the city's inter-action with, and dependence on, the environment. A striking result of this relationship is Kinshasa's relentless gnawing away at peri-urban space. Aerial photographs compared with more recent satellite images testify to this change in land cover. The continuing expansion of Kinshasa is a good example of urbanization without urban plan-ning. It goes hand in hand with two other land use implications that have also seriously altered the region's natural environment. The first and foremost is agricultural expansion; the second is pressure on for-est areas for fuelwood (Trefon 2000b).

Despite the Mobutist rhetoric on the need to prioritize agricultural self-sufficiency, as epitomized by the *retroussons les manches* campaign launched in 1965, the Congo has never had a comprehensive policy integrating production, transportation and commercialization of agri-cultural produce. By the late 1980s, the percentage of the national budget devoted to agriculture dropped to around 2 per cent-3 per cent. Rural communities are handicapped by this lack of policy but urban populations are even more vulnerable. Indeed, it is estimated that a minimum of 50 per cent of household expenditure in Kinshasa is devoted to food: for the very poor this percentage can be as high as 72 per cent (De Herdt and Maryssee, 1996: 23).

For this reason, along with such factors as unemployment, unpaid salaries and the general impoverishment of Kinshasa's inhabitants, the *Kinois* have once again become farmers: all available space within the city has now been converted into farm plots. The juxtaposition of farm plots with a densely urban landscape is striking when flying over the city. Urban agriculture is thus one of many survival strate-gies developed to survive. Produce serves generally to feed the fam-ily but eventual surpluses could be sold in small local markets. The fact that husbands help their wives in the fields is a notable new trend. Men also gather fuelwood—another shift in what was tradi-tionally a strictly gendered activity. As men have lost their salaried jobs over the past twenty years, their status within the family and community has declined significant. Conversely, the status of women and children, who now provide money for food thanks to their small-scale trade efforts, has increased.

Kinshasa is more severely affected by a fuelwood crisis than any other Congo Basin city. This results from the convergence of a large population, overwhelming poverty and a hinterland whose natural environment is relatively poor in woody biomass. It also results from poor policy. Reforestation was never seriously addressed and electricity from the Inga dam, which has the potential to help reduce Kinshasa's reliance on fuelwood and charcoal, was never intended to help the urban poor. Today most of Kinshasa relies almost exclusively on wood or charcoal for cooking fuel. Even those households that have access to electricity (used primarily for lighting) are unable to afford even the most rudimentary type of electric stove. Unlike other cities in the region where fuelwood is preferred to charcoal for cooking, the opposite is the case in Kinshasa. But poor families, caught up in the spiral of poverty, can no longer afford a whole bag of charcoal: increasingly it is purchased in small quantities that in the long run are more expensive. The typical African phenomenon of small-scale retail commerce is pushed to extremes in Kinshasa where the portions of goods packaged and sold are increasingly reduced in size.

Scarcity of fuelwood has thus become a dramatic public health issue. A related but often overlooked problem pertains to water distribution and fuelwood consumption. Despite recommendations by public health officials in Kinshasa to boil drinking water, few people do. They prefer to use their scarce fuel for cooking instead of boiling water. As a result serious diseases such as typhoid fever, cholera, hepatitis A, or diarrhoea are endemic. It is not surprising, therefore, that 30 per cent of all registered medical visits in Kinshasa in 2000 were water related (Oxfam 2001: 31). Despite the efforts of public health officials, mainly from international humanitarian groups, people remain largely unaware of the relationship between unsuitable drinking water and disease.

Sharing in Times of Hardship

Given the precariousness of life in Kinshasa, people are forced to depend on each other. Although there is obviously no uniform social fabric in a city of such magnitude, there are clearly identifiable social patterns with respect to solidarity. Everyone participates in the bargaining system that operates in all sectors of daily life, cutting across the entire social spectrum (Nzeza, forthcoming). This pertains to buying a bag of charcoal, applying for an official document or sharing a seat in a taxi. In any transaction there are a number of intermediaries who expect a commission, tip or bribe, euphemistically referred to as 'motivation'. While the *Kinois* are able and willing to extend psychological support, financial and material constraints limit this to a pragmatic system of exchange. People help each other primarily because they expect something in return. The debt, whether it be in the form of a loan, a service rendered, or a favour, will ultimately have to be redeemed.

Although social pressure to share remains strong, few people can afford to. 'Everyone has become poor' is a litany heard throughout this city where half the population eats only one meal per day. Parents often have to decide which children will eat one day and which the next. Despite this, the neighbourhood unit fulfils an important role at mealtimes. The main meal is usually eaten in late afternoon and is preceded by what *Kinois* tragi-comically refer to as SOPEKA (*SOmbela ngai, PEsa ngai et KAbela ngai*—'buy for me, give me, please give me'). In order to acquire the salt, oil or hot pepper sauce needed to prepare a meal, neighbours are urged to show their solidarity and help out—hence the SOPEKA expression. Death and mourning are other frequent occasions for neighbourhood solidarity. Collections are spontaneously organized to help bereaved families, and children set up roadblocks to ask passers-by for contributions for funeral expenses. This form of neighbourhood bonding is often reinforced by church or prayer groups.

The 'NGOization' of Kinshasa

Another interesting form of coping strategy pertains to the development of Non Governmental Organizations and associations (Trefon 2002b). As elsewhere in Africa, the number of civil associations (NGOs), and community-based solidarity networks exploded in the Congo in the early 1990s (Hamuli Kabarhuza 2002). They have become vital components of the dynamic and multiformed survival strategies invented by the Congolese to replace the state in many areas of public life (Giovannoni, Kasongo and Mwema, forthcoming). The Congolese have been forced to invent their own solutions based primarily on friendship, ethnicity, trade and profession, neighbourhood ties and religious affiliation. The association phenomenon is a clear example of people-based social organization driven by pragmatism and the will to survive.

While the association and NGO phenomenon clearly has a unique meaning in Kinshasa, its mechanisms and dynamics are similar to those in other African cities. Given the particular degree of crisis in Kinshasa, however, it is possible that the association and NGO phenomenon there may result in similar forms of social organization developing in other cities that are increasingly confronted by new political, economic and social challenge. In the absence of public services the need to get things done is the primary reason why *Kinois*, like people living in other ostensibly 'ungoverned' and 'ungovernable' societies, create associations. They form NGOs because of their links with international funding opportunities. This is perceived locally as not only international solidarity but neo-colonialism as well. This obviously simplified dichotomy between association and NGO needs to be clarified because there are a number of other inter-connected and overlapping reasons that motivate *Kinois* to pursue both of these dynamic forms of social organization. Given the overwhelming degree of un- and under-employment, participating in an association or NGO offers the hope that voluntary work will develop into gainful employment. In a society where people are forced to explore every opportunity (to find food, work, psychological sustenance), the NGO is just one more 'card to play'.

Millions of people in Kinshasa are members of at least one of these associations or NGOs. In the spirit of multiplying opportunities, many belong to several at the same time. Because they are so diverse and numerous, *Kinois* joke that if the presidents of every association and NGO in the capital were to meet, the *Palais du Peuple* would not be big enough![12] On a more serious note, many intellectuals in Kinshasa consider that in the years to come, associations will be in a far better position than the state to help them find peace, improved quality of life, and eventually democracy and perhaps alleviation of poverty.

In Lubumbashi, the country's second largest city (approximately one million inhabitants) social conditions are nearly as deplorable as in Kinshasa. The mining capital has undergone steady decline over the past thirty years but, as elsewhere in the Congo, conditions have

---

[12] Although it is impossible to quantify their exact number, Elikia M'Bokola has recently alluded to 1,322 NGOs (2002: 10). The number of solidarity groups is considerably higher.

been made worse because of war. Pierre Petit and a local research team are currently carrying out a systematic study of households as part of a Belgian funded project.[13] They report that "in the past, the town was under the thumb of the Union Minière/GECAMINE, which regulated the lives of the people from birth to death. The enterprise housed them, fed them, sent missions to the countryside to find husbands or wives for the workers, educated their children and planned their leisure." Today with the threat of closure of GECAMINE (which operates at approximately 10 per cent of production capacity) unemployment and poverty are the rule. From near full employment in the early 1970s, today 42 per cent of Petit's sample claim to have salaried work. White- and blue-collar work has been replaced by neo-rural activities such as market gardening and charcoal production. It has also been replaced by a vast array of 'informal' trade and service activities. The study emphasizes that characterizing these activities as informal is misleading because even groups of street children are organized along specific identifiable social patterns. As "[t]he quest for life is not easy: only those who undertake it with energy, cunning and skill escape . . . social and economic death". The urban hero throughout the Congo is no longer the *évolué* or 'White Black' of the late colonial and early independence period. The new hero is someone who is crafty and wily. Being well versed in trickery is a new social asset. Trickery, moreover, is perceived as being a legitimate form of self-defence because it "allows ordinary people to re-balance society. They just retrieve what they have lost with the crisis, whose origins are attributed to the state and the elite" (Petit and Mulumbwa).

In both Kinshasa and Lubumbashi the common denominators are poverty and crisis. Differences result largely from the way the two cities have evolved. People in Kinshasa have put up with hardship for years, but the crisis in Lubumbashi is far more recent. Consequently, Lubumbashi residents have proven to be less resilient in a crisis than their counterparts in Kinshasa, where economic patterns and survival strategies have evolved differently. Crisis discourse is one indicator of this. In Kinshasa, people say 'when you are rock bottom you can still dig deeper', while in Lubumbashi they continue to complain. In both communities, people are trying to pray their way out of difficulties:

---

[13] *Observatoire du Changement Urbain*, University of Lubumbashi, University of Liege, Free University of Brussels. Citations in this paragraph are from Petit and Mulumbwa, unpublished paper. For further details, see Petit 2001.

divine intervention is perceived by millions of Congolese as the only solution to crisis.

Perspectives for Peace and Renewal

The Lusaka Peace Agreement was signed in July 1999 by the governments of Angola, Congo, Namibia, Rwanda, Uganda and Zimbabwe and by the representatives of some rebel movements. Its terms include political agreement between armed belligerents; a cease fire; deployment of a UN peace keeping force; withdrawal of all foreign troops and disarming of rebel groups; support for the Inter-Congolese Dialogue (ICD); establishment of a state administration for the whole Congolese territory and the setting up of a state based on the rule of law, reconstruction and sustainable development. Despite major shortcomings, notably the non-adherence of Burundi and the continued activities of the Mayi-Mayi rebels, this agreement is the only legal instrument available for the moment. Although it establishes the equality of ICD participants (notably the Kinshasa government, rebel movements and the unarmed opposition), Joseph Kabila appears intent on acting as the legitimate head of state.

People have responded to the challenges of daily survival by developing their own personal solutions. Analysis of how people get things done on a daily basis raises the question as to whether or not the distinction between formal and informal economy is of any analytical value. These solutions are based most notably on the 'parallel' economy, innovative use of resources and space, and on a host of social, kinship, community, religious and commercial networks. Diaspora populations also contribute to family needs back home (Sumata 2002). These solutions can be considered as part of the legendary capacity of the Congolese for social innovation and adaptation to economic and political constraints.

One would expect social institutions to fall apart in times of intense social stress and transition from authoritarian rule, but in the Congo they appear to be diversifying and even strengthening. Examples that support this hypothesis pertain to the re-shaping of civil institutions, class and gender formations, access to power and 'voice', and the role of ethnicity and neighbourhood and professional organizations. Although the social cost of the ongoing crisis in the Congo is enormous, war and sacrifice have helped people appropriate the sentiment of 'being Congolese'. There is a Congolese nation—plural yet with a clear sense of collective belonging and destiny. It will take a long time to heal the wounds of poverty, oppression, rebellion and war but perhaps this sentiment of 'being Congolese' can be transformed into the energy needed to reinvent the state and society.

Bibliography

André, C. and L. Luzolele (2000), *Eléments Indicatifs de la Coopération entre l'Union Européenne et les Pays ACP Impliqués dans la Guerre en République Démocratique du Congo (RDC)*. Brussels, Réseau Européen pour le Congo.

Brittain, V. (2002), 'Calvary of the women of eastern Democratic Republic of Congo', *Review of African Political Economy*, no. 93/94, pp. 595–601.

Conrad, J. (1996), *Heart of Darkness*. London, Everyman.

De Boeck, F. (2000), 'Comment Dompter Diamants et Dollars: Dépense, partage et identité au sud-ouest du Zaïre (1980–1997)', in L. Monnier, B. Jewsiewicki and G. de Villers (eds.), 'Chasse au diamant au Congo/Zaïre', *Cahiers Africains*, no. 45–46, Institut African-CEDAF, Tervuren/L'Harmattan, Paris, pp. 171–208.

De Herdt, T. (2002), 'Democracy and the Money Machine: Monetary policy in Zaire before and during the Transition', *Review of African Political Economy*, no. 93/94, pp. 445–462.

De Herdt, T. and S. Marysse (1996), *Comment survivent les Kinois? Quand l'Etat dépérit*. Antwerp, Centre for Development Studies.

de Villers, G. with J.O. Tshonda and E. Kennes (2001), 'Guerre et politique. Les trente derniers mois de Laurent Désiré Kabila (août 1998–janvier 2001)', *Cahiers Africains*, no. 47–48, series 2000. Tervuren-Paris, Institut Africain/CEDAF-L'Harmattan.

de Villers, G. and J. Omasombo (2002), 'An Intransitive Transition', *Review of African Political Economy*, no. 93/94, pp. 399–410.

Duffield, M. (1994), 'The Political Economy of Internal War: Asset Transfer, Complex Emergencies and International Aid', in J. Macrae and A. Zwi (eds.) *War and Hunger: Rethinking International Responses to Complex Emergencies*, London, Zed Press.

——. (1998), 'Post-Modern Conflict: Warlords, Post-Adjustment States and Private Protection', *Civil Wars*, vol. 1, no. 1, pp. 65–102.

Giovannoni, M., J.K. Banga and C. Mwema (forthcoming), 'Acting on Behalf of the State: The Role of NGOs and Civil Society Associations in Kinshasa', in T. Trefon (ed.) *Reinventing Order in Kinshasa*.

Gourevitch, P. (25 September 2000), 'Forsaken', *The New Yorker*.

Hamuli Kabarhuza, B. (2002), *Donner sa chance au peuple congolais: Expériences de développement participatif (1985–2000)*, Paris, Karthala and Brussels, SOS Faim.

Hartung, W.D. and B. Moix (2000), *Deadly Legacy: U.S. Arms to Africa and the Congo War*, New York, Arms Trade Resource Center-World Policy Institute.

Hochschild, A. (1998), *King Leopold's Ghost: A story of Greed, Terror, and Heroism in Colonial Africa*, Boston and New York, Houghton Mifflin Company.

Human Rights Watch (2002), *The War within the War, Sexual Violence against women and girls in Eastern Congo*. New York, Washington, London, Brussels.

International Rescue Committee (2001), *Mortality in Eastern Democratic Republic of Congo: Results From Eleven Mortality Surveys*, Bukavu and New York, International Rescue Committee.

Jackson, S. (2002), 'Making a Killing: Criminality and Coping in the War Economy, Kivus, DR Congo', *Review of African Political Economy*, no. 93/94, 517–536.

Kadima, D. and C. Kabemba (eds.) (2003), *Whither Regional Peace and Security? The Democratic Republic of Congo after the War*, Pretoria, Africa Institute of South Africa.
Lemarchand, R. (2001), *The Democratic Republic of Congo: From Collapse to Potential Reconstruction*, Occasional Paper, Centre of African Studies, University of Copenhagen.
M'bokolo, E. (2002), 'Preface' in B. Hamuli Kabarhuza, *Donner sa chance au peuple congolais: Expériences de développement participatif (1985-2001)*, Paris, Karthala and Brussels, SOS Faim.
Ministère de la Santé Publique (1999), Etat des lieux du secteur de la santé. Profil sanitaire du niveau central, des provinces, des zones de santé et des ménages. Kinshasa.
Muchai, A. (2002), 'Arms Proliferation in the Congo War', in J.F. Clark (ed.) *The African Stakes of the Congo War*. New York, Palgrave, pp. 185–199.
Nzeza, A. (forthcoming), 'The Kinshasa 'Bargain'', in T. Trefon (ed.) *Reinventing Order in Kinshasa*.
Oxfam/Great Britain (2001), Aucune Perspective en Vue: La Tragedie Humaine du Conflit en Republique Democratique du Congo. Unpublished report. Kinshasa.
Petit, P. (ed.) (2001), *Lubumbashi 2000. La situation des ménages dans une économie de précarité*. Unpublished report from the Observatory of Urban Change, University of Lubumbashi, University of Liege, University of Brussels.
Petit, P. and G. Mulumbwa, *Poverty and wealth—life and death: Ethos and dynamics of the Lubumbashi lexicon*, Unpublished paper.
Reno, W. (2001), *Foreign Firms, Natural Resources and Violent Political Economies*, no. 46, University of Leipzig Papers on Africa.
Sabakinu, K. (2000), 'A la Recherche du Paradis Terrestre: Le Bana Luunda entre le diamant et le Dollar', in L. Monnier, B. Jewsiewicki and G. de Villers (eds.), *Chasse au Diament au Congo/Zaïre*. Tervuren, Institut Africain-CEDAF/Paris, L'Harmattan, pp. 127–169.
Samset, I. (2002), 'Conflict of Interests or Interests in Conflict? Diamonds and War in the DRC', *Review of African Political Economy*, no. 93/94, pp. 463–480.
Save the Children-Oxfam-Christian Aid (2001), *No End in Sight-The human tragedy of the conflict in the Democratic Republic of Congo*. Unpublished report. Kinshasa.
Sumata, C. (2002), 'Migradollars and Poverty Alleviation in the Congo', *Review of African Political Economy*, no. 93/94, pp. 619–628.
Tollens, E. (forthcoming), 'Food Security in Kinshasa: Coping with Adversity', in T. Trefon (ed.), *Re-inventing Order in Kinshasa*.
Trefon, T. (1989), *French Policy Toward Zaïre During the Giscard d'Estaing Presidenc*, Brussels, CEDAF.
———. (2000a), 'Forest-City Relations', in S. Bahuchet (ed.), *Les Peuples des Forêts Tropicales Aujourd'hui, Vol. II. Une approche thématique*. APFT-ULB, Bruxelles, pp. 305–330.
———. (2000b), 'Population et pauvreté à Kinshasa', *Afrique Contemporaine*, no. 194, pp. 82–89.
———. (2002a), 'The Political Economy of Sacrifice: The Kinois and the State', *Review of African Political Economy*, no. 93/94, pp. 481–498.
———. (2002b), 'Changing Patterns of Solidarity in Kinshasa', *Cadernos de Estudos Africanos*, no. 3, pp. 93–109.
Twain, M. (1907), *King Leopold's Soliloquy: A Defence of his Congo Rule*. London, T. Fisher Unwin.
United Nations Panel of Experts. Interim Report of the Panel of Experts on the Illegal Exploitation of Natural Resources and Other Forms of Wealth of the Democratic Republic of the Congo. UN Security Council Document S/2002/565, 22 May 2002.

CHAPTER SEVEN

ASSESSING AFRICA'S TWO-PHASE PEACE IMPLEMENTATION
PROCESS: POWER-SHARING AND DEMOCRATIZATION*

Donald Rothchild

How can the design and initial establishment of political institutions
sometimes contribute to the collapse of peace agreements or to the
shift from power-sharing regimes to more centralized institutional
arrangements? Negotiations have frequently led to power-sharing
arrangements that seek to balance power among the main adversaries. Unable to win a military victory on the battlefield, they agree,
sometimes reluctantly, upon compromise formulas providing for the
inclusion of major groups in executive, legislative or party organs or
for partitioned power on a territorial basis by means of regional autonomy or federalism. But the implementation record of Africa's peace
accords has proved problematic in a number of cases. Thus, in such
countries as Angola (1992, 1994), Burundi (1993), Rwanda (1994), the
Democratic Republic of the Congo (DRC) (1999) and Sierra Leone (1999),
carefully negotiated post-civil war peace agreements have proved
fragile during the implementation process—and then collapsed. Clearly,
implementation is a dynamic process. Conditions change from the
point at which bargains are reached at the negotiating table and have
led to consequences not anticipated by negotiators at the end of the
war.

This chapter concentrates on a specific aspect of the implementation puzzle—the problem of institutional design after civil war. It con-
tends that peace implementation is most appropriately viewed as a
two-phase process—the short-term confidence-building phase and

* This is an expanded and revised version of a chapter that appeared in Volume
27 of *Africa Contemporary Record* (2004). The present iteration also draws heavily on
work I have done with both Philip G. Roeder and David A. Lake in our various co-
authored chapters for a volume edited by Philip G. Roeder and Donald Rothchild
entitled: "Sustainable Peace: Democracy and Power-Dividing Institutions After Civil
Wars." I am indebted to Caroline Hartzell, Mathew Hoddie, and Edith Rothchild for
their helpful comments.

the long-term security-building phase. In many cases, these phases involve very different expectations and dynamics. The expectations of inclusion and autonomy that the parties (most often, the weaker parties) have at the time a peace agreement is signed and in the initial implementation phase that follows may be disappointed later on, for the dominant elite's political priorities may shift during the consolidation phase. To show how this change of priorities can lead to peace collapse or to a decisive shift of regimes, this chapter begins by examining the different sets of challenges facing the rival parties in both the short- and long-term. It then attempts to indicate how these different challenges create strains and affect the types of commitment that the negotiating parties can credibly make to accept and maintain agreements. In the concluding sections, the chapter discusses the different implications of this two-step implementation process for long-term institutional design. After indicating some of the main reasons for the instability of power-sharing arrangements, the chapter will explore the possibilities for group inclusion and autonomy that are present within majoritarian systems.

The Confidence Building Phase

It is important to discuss the issues that preoccupy the external and internal actors involved in implementing peace accords, because they indicate the reasons for the lack of careful attention given to political institution-building during the initial phase. Confidence building efforts in the aftermath of civil war occur under extremely tense and hazardous conditions. The mistrust and animosity surrounding military encounters are carried over into post-conflict relations. Viewing their adversaries in 'zero-sum' terms, leaders of the various political groups are extremely uncertain about the transition to peace, fearing that it will result in their vulnerability and possible elimination—either as a political force or as a physical entity. Insurgent leaders perceive demobilization and the integration of their trained soldiers into the new army to be threatening to their political survival. Thus in 1996, former UNITA (the National Union for the Total Independence of Angola) leader Jonas Savimbi, considering the implications of disarmament, demobilization and the reintegration of forces for himself and his movement, expressed his fears of the consequences of implementation as follows: "No leader in history that I have known disarmed and stayed in power" (Rothchild 1997: 140). This fear of the future contributed mightily to Savimbi's subsequent decision to desist from the peace accord and reignite the civil war.

If fears of vulnerability following civil war limit what can be achieved through bargaining, what can third-party actors, working with local leaders, do to help design institutions and promote processes to reassure adversaries about their security and well-being in the post-conflict phase? Statistical data indicate the presence or prospect of a third-party enforcer is important in reducing the risk of the collapse of a peace agreement during its first five years, a period that often corresponds with the confidence-building phase (Hartzell, Hoddie, Rothchild 2001: 199). In reassuring the negotiating parties during the treacherous transition period, the third party must play an active role in a number of interrelated military/security aspects of the peace accord agreed at the bargaining table: monitoring the cease-fire, verifying the quartering of troops, setting realizable goals on disarmament and demobilization, overseeing the integration (or re-integration) of the new army, and emphasizing police reform and professionalism (Stedman and Rothchild 1996: 18). A successful effort by the third-party actor to verify and enforce these measures will likely encourage the parties to commit to an agreement, carry through with general elections, and begin the process of designing political institutions for effective governance.

In facilitating the transition process, the third party, supported in most cases by a relatively small peacekeeping force, inevitably relies upon the goodwill and backing of the rival leaders and their force commanders to control the troops in the field and adhere to the spirit and provisions of the peace accord. Where the state and its institutions are weak and key military and political elites lack commitment to the agreement, as in the DRC or Sierra Leone, the third party's ability to guide the transition process from a cease-fire to general elections is marked by uncertainty. When the third party is prepared and able to oversee the military/security-building phase and the rival parties act in a cooperative manner, as in Namibia and Mozambique, it contributes significantly to stabilizing the peace during the transition to elections. In these cases, third parties played an active role in dealing with local misunderstandings and in reassuring the local parties about the protection of their interests in the years to come.

However, in many of Africa's post-conflict experiences, the UN and its member states have not always been willing or able to make a sustained commitment. In Angola under the 1991 settlement, with only $132 million allocated to the UN observer team and only 480 monitors deployed to oversee the demobilization of troops and the reintegration of Angola's armies, the international force was unable to rise to the challenge of implementation (Rothchild 1997: 134). And in the DRC following the 1999 Lusaka Agreement, the Security Council only authorized a 5,537 member force of military observers and support troops (later increased) to monitor the cease-fire in that large and poorly integrated country.

When those responsible for implementation deal effectively with the short-term, military-related challenges, they help to create a structure of incentives that increases the prospect of a safe outcome. Institutions of governance cannot gain stability and predictability unless the irregularity of civil war is replaced by regular social interactions (Huntington 1968: 24). Hence, those involved in implementing peace agreements have to focus much of their attention on the military-related aspects in the early phases of stabilizing the peace, often giving short shrift to establishing the institutions of governance initially agreed upon during the bargaining stage of the settlement.

The military-related processes are interconnected; nevertheless, I will separate them out to discuss them more effectively. First, the task of monitoring the cease-fire to prevent violent encounters tests the credibility of the parties' commitment to the agreement. Although cease-fires are a necessary beginning of the peace process after civil wars, they are often a cause of uncertainty for both the parties to the conflict and the peacekeepers. The parties themselves sometimes have reason to fear that the insurgent leaders or their military commanders in the field will contemplate the momentary advantages and attack their opponents. As for the peacekeepers, they usually operate with limited military forces at their disposal and imprecise guidelines regarding their role in the event that controversies arise. When preventive diplomacy fails to bring an easing of tensions, the peacekeepers face difficult choices with respect to the use of force. If they utilize too much capacity (as was contended with respect to the Economic Community of West African States Monitoring Group's [ECOMOG's] bombing of insurgent positions in Liberia), they open themselves up to charges of bias and the violation of sovereignty. However, if they fail to act decisively or are unable to send sufficient forces to achieve their mission, they are viewed as weak and dismissed contemptuously, as happened with the Revolutionary United Front (RUF) insurgents' capture of some 500 lightly-armed UN peacekeepers in Sierra Leone in May 2000. The result is to make commitments to cease-fires extremely hard to maintain, complicating the transition to the next stage of confidence building.

Second, intermediaries and peacekeepers promote confidence during the transition by separating the different military units and quartering them at specified assembly points. This is a most perilous phase in the peace process, for the opposing forces fear that the quartering of troops will leave them vulnerable to attack. After the negotiations on Zimbabwe's independence, Patriotic Front leaders expressed extreme uncertainty over possible collusion between the Rhodesian Security Forces and the Commonwealth peacekeeping force. In this context, quartering appeared threatening, for it held out the prospect of entrapment and the loss of everything that the insurgents had achieved on the battlefield (Ginifer 1996: 29–34). The third party can play a critical confidence-building role under these circumstances, assuring both sides that it will protect the agreement and prevent a surprise attack. In the end, however, it is the parties themselves who have to be prepared to cooperate with the mediator. Where, as in Angola, one of the contending forces failed to send its best trained troops and advanced equipment to the assembly points, there was little the third party could do to stabilize the agreement (Hare 1998: 97).

Third, once the quartering of troops is under way, the third party can build confidence in the agreement by overseeing the disarmament and demobilization processes. The third party's role in achieving these tasks is critical, because the insurgents, fearing the consequences of reduced military capacity during the transition period, seek an intermediary's protection as these efforts proceed. The third party's role in observing, verifying, and supervising the disarming and demobilization of forces and in assisting the ex-combatants to reintegrate into society is likely to prove critical for stabilizing the peace. A peace agreement that is precise about the role of the intermediary in enforcing an agreement, clear about the guidelines on disarming the combatants and disposing of illegal arms, and definite regarding the procedures for demobilization seems likely to promote initial commitment to the agreement. Unfortunately, however, external support for the demobilization programmes in Liberia (in 1995) and in Mozambique was inadequate in terms of planning and funding the return of soldiers to a beneficial and self-supporting civilian life. They also failed to reduce or limit the weapons available to discharged ex-combatants, criminal elements or militia, increasing societal insecurity as a consequence (Marley 1997–98: 142; Clark 1996: 27).

Fourth, in many, but not all, cases (e.g. Bosnia and Chechnya), it is important for the third party to begin the process of integrating (or re-integrating) the rival armies. Where this has occurred, it has proved a risky undertaking for insurgents. This is because the uniting of their military wing with the government army leaves the opposition force potentially exposed and vulnerable. It was the insurgents' reliance on a separate military arm that provided them with an element of political leverage in the bargaining process. Now, with their soldiers included in the government army, they are left with little choice but to work within the established political system to secure their demands. A third party, when dealing with the challenge of military reintegration, can help to allay the uncertainties of the various parties. It sets timetables, verifies the integration process, proposes formulas for the size and composition of the new armed forces, and advises the international community of any failures to meet commitments. If the challenge is surmounted effectively, as in Namibia and Mozambique, it is likely to prove instrumental in enabling the peace process to move ahead. In Angola, however, the failure to unify armies led to an unravelling of the agreement itself and a renewal of the civil war (Rothchild 1997: 140).

In brief, it is never easy for a third party to convince former adversaries to accept a cease-fire following a civil war, or to quarter their troops, disarm and demobilize their forces, and reintegrate their armies. They must also begin the process of re-training and professionalizing their police arms (Stanley and Call 1997). With distrust of an opponent's intentions extremely high, the rivals are likely to attempt to protect themselves by taking a variety of dubious measures (including the hiding of arms caches and communications equipment and the withholding of well-trained units from the demobilization process). The third party plays an indispensable role in overcoming the mutual uncertainty of the ex-combatants by upholding the terms of the agreement and by helping the parties (especially the weaker ones) to commit themselves to what seemed to them to be a potentially hazardous political relationship with their ex-enemy. If the third party is prepared to invest heavily in the implementation process, and if the former enemies and their supporters are prepared to act in a cooperative manner, it is possible to surmount the uncertainties leading to a founding election. Then, if this challenge is overcome, it will be possible to move on to tasks of security-building—the establishment of institutions and rules that will enhance regular patterns of inter-group reciprocity and political exchange.

The Security-Building Phase

Ideally, both the negotiators and those involved in the initial military/security phase of the transition to stable relations should be concerned with the long-term aspects of institution-building; in practice, however, much of the effort that goes into dealing with these complex tasks is left for later consideration. Those dealing with the military-related features of implementation during the transition may have little additional energy left for institution building during the hectic period after the signing of a peace agreement. An effective peace process requires a long-term commitment on the part of leaders and their followers to engage in an ongoing bargaining encounter over the institutions of governance, negotiating unanticipated issues as they arise. While most leaders clearly wish to avoid the uncertainty of a breakdown in the implementation process and are prepared to take part in protracted negotiations to resolve critical institutional design, security, and resource allocation questions, the possibility always exists that some spokespersons will not negotiate sincerely (Stedman 1997).

The long-term process of implementing an enduring peace agreement inevitably involves uncertainty and insecurity at every stage, and problems of post-conflict design are complicated by the difficult political circumstances of negotiation and institution building. Most importantly in terms of a durable agreement, the provisions that send reassuring signals to weaker parties and cause them to accept peace agreements in the negotiating phase will not necessarily survive the long-term implementation phase. In principle, negotiation and implementation should be coextensive; where that happens, the effects are likely to reduce dilemmas of credible commitment and information. In practice, however, the processes of negotiation and implementation often diverge—at times, noticeably—because the circumstances of negotiating an end to a war and the institutionalization of a sustained peace are very different. As Manuel Tome, the secretary-general of Mozambique's ruling party (Frelimo), put it so clearly, "the peace accord was a means to an end, and not an end [in] itself. It was an exceptional regime for a predetermined length of time, after which we return to the full norms of the constitution" (Manning 2002: 71). It is because these dynamics tend to be distinct that frustrations (particularly on the part of losers) can surface and lead to political instability, even to the breakdown of well-conceived peace accords.

Let me now examine the dynamics of negotiation and implementation as they affect institution-building more closely. During the peace negotiations and the initial phases of implementation, a country's dominant coalition must take pains to build minority confidence in the peace agreement. To do this, the ruling coalition must indicate that it will credibly commit not to threaten or exploit the weaker parties during and after the peace process. This is not easy to achieve, because subordinate (usually minority) elements fear that when the third party withdraws and the local actors are left to their own devices, the dominant (usually majority) groups will use their power to threaten the security and cultural traditions of the weaker ones. To overcome this diffuse sense of risk, it is necessary for the dominant coalition to reassure its rivals that in the future they will not be victimized or excluded from the political process. In light of this pervasive uncertainty, the range of credible options is limited. A critical first step in signalling restraint and goodwill is often the ruling coalition's preparedness to accept a third-party enforcer's supervision of the demobilization, disarmament, and military reintegration of the armed forces. An external protector proved indispensable in upholding the peace bargain in Namibia and Mozambique and its ineffectiveness explains much about the failures of Angola's negotiated agreements.

Once the founding election is held and the third party withdraws its troops, a new situation prevails. At this point, the rules and institutions previously insisted upon by the weaker parties in an effort to reduce minority uncertainty about their future role in the country's political life might no longer seem binding. Certainly democratic institutions that provide for regular elections, divided powers at the political centre, government transparency and accountability, as well as individual rights are likely to have a reassuring effect. They are perceived as offering credible promises of institutional stability over time. In a rather general way, then, the adoption of a democratic regime can have a calming effect. Currently available statistical data do give some indication of the link between democracy and stable ethnic relations. Zeric Smith's data, for example, show an inverse relationship between ethnic conflict and civil liberties (Smith 2000: 32). Democracy's ability to channel demands along predetermined lines and the political stability that is likely to follow from this can produce incentives for development that lower the levels of ethnic conflict (Ibid.: 35).

Even so, it is important to stress how narrow the scope for credible accommodations is in the context of post-conflict relations. Although attitudes and perceptions may undergo some change during and after negotiations, political memories and continuing uncertainty over the intentions of rivals can lead to ongoing credibility problems. Not only are some of the provisions in a peace agreement likely to be viewed as disadvantageous to minority interests, but doubts persist that the dominant ruling coalition will actually deliver on its bargains. Third-party mediators and enforcers can soften these anxieties for a time, but weaker parties know that in the end external actors will want to withdraw their forces and concentrate on pressing issues closer to home (Hartzell, Hoddie and Rothchild 2001: 197, 203). Over time, an ongoing bargaining relationship can lead to an easing of suspicions and uncertainty. In Namibia and South Africa, cooperation in coping with joint problems did lead to a learning process regarding each other's habits, insecurities, aspirations, and shortcomings. Even so, Rwanda, Burundi and Angola stand as sobering reminders of the risks involved in implementing peace accords. Where leaders manipulate ethnic loyalties and mobilize their members for destructive encounters, liberal centrist mechanisms of reconciliation can prove extremely fragile, especially in the period after the external protector begins to disengage.

In order to prevent destructive interactions among identity groups and between these groups and the state, it is important to focus on available state institutions that can engender trust between post-civil war rivals (Rothchild 2000: 246). Some of the main confidence building measures provided for in peace accords include provisions that facilitate civil liberties, wide-ranging coalitions, election systems based on proportional representation, the inclusion of minority interests, and formal arrangements for political decentralization that assure minority group leaders a measure of autonomous control over budgets and policymaking. These measures can be very heartening to minority interests because they signal respect and goodwill; they promote confidence in the intentions of the dominant political coalition, at least in the short term. Hence, such signals can be critically important in terms of gaining the commitment of weaker parties to the post-conflict bargain. For example, current data indicate that the insertion of a provision in an agreement on territorial autonomy (although not its implementation) stabilizes the peace significantly in the period after implementation is under way, greatly reducing the likelihood of failure *at this stage* (Hartzell, Hoddie and Rothchild 2001: 199).

Not only can mechanisms of inclusion, proportionality, individual (and possibly group) rights, and decentralization encourage credible commitment to peace agreements in the short run, but they can also contribute to the development of long-term democratization by allaying ethnic group fears of vulnerability and possible victimization. Where weaker parties feel that they can afford to lose an election because they can compete for office again in the future, or where smaller group interests are assured representation in power-sharing executives or are convinced that they will be in a position to protect their group's cultural traditions and special interests through measures of political autonomy, they will be more likely to evince confidence in a peace agreement that links their fate to that of their adversaries (Walter 2002: 86).

Nevertheless, these assurances on minority inclusion made at the time peace agreements are negotiated may not be sufficient to overcome the long-term hazards of political consolidation. Not only is it difficult for those negotiating an agreement to bind their successors, but political issues can change significantly over time. As peace becomes accepted, the concerns of politicians shift from reconciliation to governance and to the unending political struggle for power and the maximization of interest. Now the military-related threats to peace are behind the negotiating parties and the initial post-civil war election has been held. Party leaders and those engaged in peace implementation must therefore enter the second phase of implementation—that of institution building.

During the security-building phase, the pressures on political leaders to establish an enduring peace may be less apparent, but the tasks are no less challenging. Unless those involved can maintain a long-term commitment and can establish a self-enforcing regime, the possibilities of a return to internal war are still present. What is necessary at this stage is to implement an acceptable institutional framework that includes rules on future elections, legislative-executive relations, intergovernmental practices, police and military professionalism, autonomous space for civil society, reform of the civil service, and economic rejuvenation. Lacking the urgency that surrounded the civil war settlement, it may be extremely difficult to overcome the resistance of entrenched political and economic interests to political change. Therefore, concessions made by the dominant coalition to secure a peace agreement in the heat of war may become difficult to put into effect after the insurgents are disarmed and demobilized and a return to 'normality' appears to be in place.

Clearly, variations in institutional priorities between the earlier and later phases of the peace implementation process reflect different political imperatives at distinguishable times. Shifts in goals may represent a logical adjustment to a changing political environment, notably altered concerns regarding the urgency of maintaining past concessions to secure agreement at the bargaining table. Some evidence of a trend toward institutional redesign in the later post-conflict period can be seen in the modifications that have been proposed or have occurred for changing political rules with respect to three power-sharing institutions: inclusive executives, electoral institutions designed to promote power-sharing outcomes, and such decentralized political arrangements as regional autonomy and federalism.

Executive Power Sharing

Provisions on executive power sharing represent an important incentive to encourage minority spokespersons to sign on to peace accords (Rothchild 1997: 13–15). Participation by the leaders of the main minority ethnic interests in the cabinet and other central government institutions has generally been perceived as helpful in reducing the threat of possible future victimization. Executive power sharing normally builds confidence in the agreement because ethnic group representatives are included at the very heart of the decision-making process. In deeply divided Burundi, for example, some leaders in both major communities viewed executive power sharing as critical to stable political relations in 1994 (Ould-Abdallah 2000: 73–80). Burundi's power-sharing approach reappeared in 2000–01, when former South African President Nelson Mandela, acting as mediator, launched a new peace initiative there and proposed a three-year power-sharing government leading to democratic elections. Under this transitional power-sharing agreement, signed in 2001, a Tutsi president and a

Hutu vice-president would hold office in the first period and would then exchange roles in the second period. National institutions, including the army and the National Assembly, would also be shared between the two rival ethnic groups, with 14 out of 26 portfolios going to Hutus and 60 per cent of the National Assembly seats reserved for Hutu representatives (*BBC News* 2001: 2). However, any assumptions that the Burundi arrangement could survive intact after democratic elections had taken place seem problematic.

Because executive power-sharing arrangements involve the continuing costs of negotiation and because they open up possibilities for pressure from extremist leaders dissatisfied with the compromise politics these institutions promote, they have frequently encountered problems in establishing the peace. Following the signing of the Arusha agreement, Rwanda's hard-line Hutu leadership, viewing the power-sharing arrangement as shifting the balance of group power in a highly disadvantageous manner during the transition, became increasingly determined "to derail it by means of a coup and mass murder" (Suhrke and Jones 2000: 244). In this case, an agreement on power sharing had a destabilizing impact and failed to survive the turbulent implementation process. The instability of executive power sharing is sometimes also evident after elections have been held and political leaders concentrate on the challenges of governance. Not only can power-sharing institutions give rise to 'outbidding' politics, where extremist politicians within a group make radical demands on moderate leaders of their own party who are active participants in the ruling coalition and communal members in the diaspora who may make radical demands on group representatives in the ruling coalition. Consequently, as fears for the survival of the peace agreement ease, the dominant majority may come to regard the formal provisions on executive power balancing to be a less urgent matter and therefore open to change. When this occurs, formal power-sharing arrangements may give way to informal power-sharing practices (Sisk and Stefes, forthcoming).

The experience of South Africa is instructive in this respect, for the consensus democracy of the 1993 interim constitution was quickly overtaken in 1996 by a majoritarian democratic formula (Rothchild 1997: 54). Under South Africa's 1993 constitution, any party that won over five per cent of the seats in the National Assembly would be included in the cabinet on a proportional basis for a five-year period. After the 1994 general election, this resulted in a 27-member coalition government composed of 18 members from the African National Congress (ANC), 6 from the National Party (NP), and 3 from the Inkatha Freedom Party (IFP). With a trend toward majoritarian governance emerging in the period that followed, the NP withdrew from the cabinet. Although the ANC remained aligned in the cabinet with the Zulu-based IFP and subsequently, with the New National Party, the public was left with few doubts about the preponderance of ANC influence on the country's affairs. Power-sharing institutions may well have been useful as an incentive encouraging the weaker parties to sign on to the agreement and in reducing ethnic and racial minority fears during the transition from the old apartheid state; however, it was soon to prove a fragile protection in the new environment of full democracy.

Electoral Institutions to Promote Power-sharing Outcomes

Elections are clearly a critical part of the transition from civil war to peaceful interactions. Provided that the competing parties act with moderation and play by the rules of the game, electoral systems hold out the prospect of legitimate governance over time. Electoral systems have been adapted to local circumstances, as Africa's states have passed through round two of the implementation process. Thus, President Robert Mugabe, seeking to consolidate central government power in Zimbabwe, ended the practice (designed by the Lancaster House Conference on Zimbabwe's independence) of reserving 20 of 100 seats in the House of Assembly for whites elected on a separate voter roll prior to the general elections. Mugabe also encouraged parliament to amend the constitution to allow the president to nominate 30 additional members to the legislature. Just how significant this amendment was became clear following the 2000 parliamentary election, for Mugabe's Zimbabwe African National Union-Patriotic Front (ZANU-PF) won a narrow victory over the opposition Movement for Democratic Change and the presidential nominations swelled the ZANU-PF's margin of influence to a decisive 92–57 majority.

A post-conflict shift in preferences on electoral institutions is also becoming apparent in South Africa regarding the use of the list system of proportional representation (PR). For minority groups in such countries as Namibia, Mozambique, Angola, South Africa and Zimbabwe (1980), the adoption of a PR system was reassuring, because party lists are likely to be ethnically balanced in an effort to attract as many voters as possible. Moreover, where negotiators sought to further the inclusion of minority interests in the decision making process, as in Namibia, South Africa, and Zimbabwe (for the common roll seats in the 1980 election), the negotiators made use of formulas based on the largest remainder that largely reflected the prevailing configurations of power at the time of the transition (Mozaffar 1998: 90).

However, as political elites and scholars examined the effects of PR in the years that followed, they sometimes questioned whether, in ethnically heterogeneous societies, the large district form of PR is any more likely to produce proportional outcomes (and therefore be the basis for more inclusive executives) than majoritarian/single member district electoral systems (Reilly forthcoming). Others contended that it would be useful to improvise on the initial PR arrangement. Not only was PR less of a protection for ethnic minority interests than previously assumed (because of the spatially separate nature of ethnic interests), but PR, with its large, multimember districts, appeared to contribute to a lack of contact between the constituents and their representatives (Barkan 1995: 109). Given the advantages of a single member district system in terms of encouraging political accountability and blocking the emergence of extremist parties, constitution makers in South Africa have begun to consider experimenting with customized arrangements that will link PR with single member districts (Reilly 2000).

Political Decentralization

Measures of political decentralization such as regional autonomy and federalism are included in peace agreements to reassure ethnic and regional minorities regarding their possible vulnerability in the future (Deng and Morrison 2001: 2). Unlike executive power sharing which *includes* spokespersons of the main ethnic and party interests in organs of state at the political centre, political decentralization seeks to protect weaker parties by *partitioning* state power between the centre and the regions (Rothchild and Roeder forthcoming). Regional and ethnic leaders view institutions of territorial autonomy as a means of group protection and empowerment, because these institutions provide them with some political and administrative autonomy in their region in one or more fields.

As ethnic leaders gain a limited autonomy to deal with such issues as language, education, social welfare, and cultural and social matters, they may become less anxious about their security and well being in the post-conflict environment (Rothchild and Hartzell 1999: 259). Of course, this autonomy can come at a price in terms of stable governance, because smaller minorities remaining in the region may find their situation threatening. Also, central governments, intent on enlarging their power and capacity for action, may perceive a region's autonomous control to involve efficiency costs that are deemed unacceptable, and they therefore seek to take back some of the autonomous powers granted to the regions under the peace agreement.

The ruling coalition, when negotiating a peace agreement and shortly afterwards, may be prepared to make concessions on political decentralization to overcome the minority's reluctance to commit to the peace bargain. Although this promise of autonomy may in principle seem genuine, it may nevertheless be difficult for the weaker party to accept the commitment at face value. How can weaker actors be certain that the dominant coalition will deliver on its promises after the insurgents have disarmed and demobilized their forces? What incentive does the majority have to abide by the peace agreement? Such problems of credible commitment become acute when one party (usually the dominant majority) cannot reassure its rivals that it will remain dedicated to the bargain during the later, consolidation phase of the implementation process (Lake and Rothchild forthcoming).

Difficulties of implementation are most likely to emerge in the second, institution-building, phase of consolidating a peace agreement, because it is at this juncture that the military-related issues of implementation have been dealt with and the majority has declining incentives to remain true to its commitments to the weaker actors. As James Fearon (1998: 118) observes, the majority's "bargaining power [in the new state] will have increased due to the consolidation of police and army capabilities". Since one set of leaders cannot bind their successors, the next set of leaders may not feel committed to the peace arrangement. Consequently, should the balance of power between the negotiating parties shift, previously enforceable contracts may become unenforceable. The prospect of such a change in strategic relations among group interests creates fears of vulnerability and manipulation, making agreements fragile. And should a reinterpretation of the terms of agreement occur or should the agreement fail to be carried out as anticipated, a breakdown in the basic bargain—even a return to war—is possible.

Preliminary data on territorial autonomy do in fact suggest some-thing of a commitment problem over the long-term. Recent data on territorial decentralization and civil war outcomes, which groups together negotiated and non-negotiated experiences, found no cases of fully decentralized states in the post-civil war period, 45 cases of centralized states, and 9 cases of semi-centralized states (Lake and Rothchild, forthcoming: Table 2.1). The experience of South Africa with political decentralization illustrates a trajectory of political con-solidation at work once the implementation process is under way (Lake and Rothchild, forthcoming). During the negotiations on South Africa's transition to a non-racial democracy, ANC negotiators made concessions on granting limited legislative responsibilities to provin-cial authorities under the 1993 draft constitution to gain minority support for the agreement. Although a number of responsibilities were in fact transferred to provincial authorities, the ANC-led cen-tral government, determined to consolidate its control over the polit-ical process, played down the extent of sub-unit autonomy. The ANC leadership was careful to maintain central dominance in such areas as taxation and grant disbursement. Opposition leaders, spearheaded by Inkatha's Chief Mangosuthu Buthelezi, recognized the centraliz-ing trends at work in post-apartheid South Africa and insisted that the final constitution give the provincial governments significant leg-islative and fiscal powers. However, the Constitutional Court ruled largely in favour of central government leadership. Buthelezi's calls for international mediation on this issue proved unproductive and the trend toward central hegemony remained intact.

Conclusion: Implications for Power Sharing and Democratization

The implementation of agreements after a civil war involves a two-phase process—a short term confidence building phase that deals mainly with the military-related aspects spilling over from the armed struggle, and the longer term security-building phase relating to the building of institutions. To some extent, these phases overlap. The processes of disarmament and demobilization must be dealt with effectively if the complex tasks of winning support for the institu-tions of governance are to show positive results. Nevertheless, these phases are marked by distinct logics, and these differences increase the precariousness of designing policies and programmes at the initial phase that do not undermine the task of effective governance at a later stage. Countries such as Namibia, South Africa, and Mozambique have managed to navigate their way through these difficult channels, but their efforts required exemplary leadership and, in some cases, considerable international support.

The promise of power sharing contributed importantly to successful confidence building by signalling the preponderant majority's goodwill and empathy toward minority interests. A dramatic indicator of the importance of this signal can be seen in the hazard rate statistics compiled by Mathew Hoddie and Caroline Hartzell (forthcoming) which suggest that agreements providing for territorial power sharing reduce the probability of settlement failure by 90 per cent in the first five years following the settlement. The dominant coalition's preparedness to hold out the prospect of power sharing is a positive inducement because it creates the expectation that minority leaders will be included directly in the decision-making process. Such backing for confidence building measures is also essential for maintaining an agreement after it is negotiated, for the power-sharing pledge reassures minorities regarding their future security and well-being. By providing evidence that minority security will be respected over time, the power-sharing promise can contribute substantially to the preparedness of weaker parties to commit to common institutions.

In addition to signals of good intent, an agreement on power sharing can contribute to effective consolidation in two ways. First, power sharing can be a basis for sustained rule, particularly in situations where a majoritarian regime is viewed as an unacceptable alternative. In Lebanon, for example, there have been four power-sharing regimes since 1861, buttressed in two of the cases by the presence of an external protector. As Marie-Joëlle Zahar (forthcoming) comments about the continuity of this regime-type in the Lebanese context, the choice of regimes is not explained by the preferences of the political actors but by the structure of inter-group relations in the country. Article 95 of the current constitution makes the long-term penchant for an integral solution very clear, for it specifically expresses a preference for ending political confessionalism as a basis for representation in the executive and legislative branches in the long term (*Beirut Review* 1991). Lebanese power sharing therefore represents a prudent adjustment to the local balance of forces.

Second, power sharing can be the basis for a transition to a majoritarian regime. Because the adoption of power sharing at the time of negotiations is reassuring to minority interests, it facilitates a stable transition from civil war to peace. In South Africa, for example, the institutionalization of power sharing not only sought to hearten local whites about their prospects after the shift to non-racial democracy but also to inspire hope among white investors abroad. However, once the interim constitution came into force and the balance of power shifted decisively toward the ANC, power sharing proved to be a brittle basis for mutual adjustment. Consequently, two years later, the interim South African constitution was amended, and a second phase transition to a majoritarian regime occurred. The encounter with power sharing no doubt proved to be a constructive one, contributing to the ease with which the second phase transition process took place. Even so, the public's demand for greater empowerment during the period that the interim constitution was in place left the government with little choice but to support a majoritarian constitutional system.

Nevertheless, even these relatively positive experiences with power sharing underline the general instability associated with such regimes over time. Even in the best of circumstances power sharing has proven difficult to sustain, in part because it requires a minimum of 'convergent expectations' among the main participants regarding the reliability and goodwill of their rivals and their ability to deliver on their bargains (Wagner 1993: 259). These uncertainties are increased as extremist politicians place pressure on inter-elite relationships by acting to scapegoat minorities or by seeking to outbid moderate leaders within their own group. Such problems can be further exacerbated when hard-line elements in the diaspora who, because of their generous contributions to local causes, exert enormous pressure on their co-ethnics in key political positions in their country of origin.

But if these problems are not enough, power-sharing compromises are also tested by the basic challenges of reliable information and credible commitment. Because power-sharing systems are elitist in nature, information tends to be privately shared among a small coterie of participants within the ruling coalition. Such low information systems sometimes make it difficult for group leaders to negotiate their differences and to evaluate their rivals' intentions. Where suspicions arise that members of the ruling elite fail to reveal vital information or misrepresent their position, it can cause grave doubts and even exacerbate inter-group tensions (Lake and Rothchild 1998: 11–13).

Problems of credible commitment can arise when the promises made at the time of the negotiations do not converge with the predilections of the ruling elite during the later phases of implementation. Thus, the dominant coalition (usually the government) may make a credible commitment to institutionalize power-sharing measures when negotiations take place, but their preferences may change as the contract comes into force and new leaders face unanticipated challenges. Because the new leadership may not feel bound by the promises made by its predecessors at the time of the negotiations, it may not be able to assure its rivals that it will remain committed to the power-sharing bargain. This is particularly the case where the balance of power shifts, causing the leaders of weaker parties to fear that the state elite will renege on its promises. In these circumstances, previously enforceable contracts become unenforceable and bargaining failure may become evident. The distrust of commitments made by adversaries helps to explain the early decision by some leaders, such as Jonas Savimbi, to defect from agreements; such leaders may perceive the structure of incentives under the agreement in a negative light, leaving them better off fighting than compromising. The prospect of such a change in strategic relations may make concessions on institutions of power sharing appear risky in terms of protecting vulnerable groups.

Power-sharing safeguards built into peace agreements therefore often represent unstable compromises that may require external protectors for survival. If an external actor is prepared to undertake the potentially costly assignment of protecting an agreement, new uncertainties may arise. For one thing, the external protector will want to disengage at some point; for another, the external protector may well have interests in the conflict (for example, Syria in Lebanon), leading it to favour one of the parties against the others (Zahar forthcoming). However, if no external protector is prepared to uphold the agreement, the power sharing arrangement must depend upon the maintenance of a balance of forces. As armies are merged and political centralization follows, a new situation is created on the ground. The dominant coalition at the political centre, may reorganize the institutions of state to increase its capacity for governance and this, in turn, may cause minority leaders to suspect that the concessions made by the ruling coalition at the time the agreement was negotiated lacked credibility. In this context of suspicion and increasing uncertainty, moderate, centrist institutions such as power sharing may be difficult to sustain. In the worst cases, such as Rwanda and Cyprus, moderate institutions designed to ensure inclusive executives, not only proved fragile but even conflict-creating.

In those political contexts where power sharing appears potentially unstable, the main options seem limited. There is insufficient space here to examine the alternatives in depth, but three main variants deserve comment—some variant of majority democracy with civil liberties, majority concessions, and partition. Majority democracy has much unexplored potential for stabilizing a peace after civil war, as shown by the experiences of South Africa, Mozambique and Namibia. Certainly, there are legitimate grounds in certain circumstances to fear that majorities will misuse their power and repress and exploit their minorities. Nevertheless, the generalizations made by some writers using the consociational democracy approach seem overdone at times. Thus, contentions that "majoritarianism will inevitably lead to the violation of the rights of minorities" may be an accurate warning in some circumstances but not in others (Lijphart 1985: 5). Provided that the state leadership remains committed to civil liberties and to the rules of the game on regular elections, majoritarian frameworks can embrace provisions on an autonomous judiciary and governmental accountability and transparency. In addition, majority governments may decide to embrace practices that take account of what could be deemed the rights of ethnic groups with the state (Van Dyke 1977). Such practices as balanced recruitment into public institutions, proportional representation, proportional systems for distributing central revenues, and autonomous rights for religious or ethnic groups can have power sharing consequences (Rothchild 2002: 130–134). Thus, despite the weakening of formal institutions of power sharing in South Africa, Timothy Sisk's comments on the carry over of informal power sharing arrangements in that country in the period after the transition to a fully democratic regime are quite apt (Sisk and Stefes, forthcoming).

Although these governmental policies may contribute to power-sharing outcomes, their survival is largely dependent upon the continuing goodwill of the ruling coalition. Because majority governments are not likely to feel threatened by limited concessions to minority groups, they may be prepared to respect these special arrangements in an effort to avoid possible resistance and instability. Yet it must be remembered that no set of elites will necessarily feel bound by special arrangements or concessions granted by its predecessor, and therefore can rescind any such provisions at the point they seem irksome.

In an effort to provide a more sustained regime that will protect the rights of minorities within a majoritarian system, Philip G. Roeder (forthcoming) argues cogently for a power dividing strategy as an alternative to power sharing in ethnically heterogeneous societies. In essence, a power dividing strategy rests on three interrelated principles—limited governmental responsibilities, a proliferation of interests that cross cut ethnic groups, and the empowerment of different majorities in multiple institutions. Power dividing seeks to limit and disperse government, while preserving the majoritarian principle, regular elections, and protections for civil liberties. By dividing power between the centre and the regions, and by separating the branches at the political centre between an executive and legislature (or legislatures) elected by different majority principles, it multiplies the arenas in which decisions are taken and encourages cross-cutting links among ethnic interests intent upon bridging the institutional chasm. Such thinking seems constructive because it points us toward a new way of linking majoritarian democracy with the inclusion of ethnic interests in key governmental institutions.

Such proposed variants on majoritarian democracy and concessions by ruling coalitions to minority interests may possibly represent healthy alternatives to power sharing that avoid the perils of the two-step implementation process. Nevertheless, the possibilities of political instability that marked power sharing schemes in the post-conflict stage can also exist for majoritarian regimes, especially where the minority continues to suspect the credibility of the majority's commitment to the new rules of the political game. Should the government renege on promises to respect diversity and individual rights or should its pledges and practices on informal or formal inclusion prove to be nonviable, either regime—power sharing or majoritarian democratic—may collapse and the country become deeply polarized, and even return to civil war. In that event, a non-negotiating process might lead to authoritarian governance, partition or state collapse, with all the costs and risks associated with these alternatives.

Bibliography

Barkan, J.D. (1995), 'Elections in Agrarian Societies', *Journal of Democracy*, vol. 6, no. 4, pp. 106–116.

BBC News (2001, November 1).

Beirut Review (1991), vol. 1, no. 1.

Clark, K.M. (1996), 'Mozambique's Transition from War to Peace: USAID's Lessons Learned', *PN-ABY-278*, Washington, D.C., U.S. Agency for International Development, Africa Bureau Information Center Research and Reference Services.

Deng, F.M. and S. Morrison (2001), *U.S. Policy to End Sudan's War: Report of the CSIS Task Force on U.S.-Sudan Policy*. Washington, D.C., Center for Strategic and International Studies.

Fearon, J. (1998), 'Commitment Problems and the Spread of Ethnic Conflict', in D.A. Lake and D. Rothchild (eds.), *The International Spread of Ethnic Conflict: Fear, Diffusion, and Escalation*, Princeton, Princeton University Press.

Ginifer, J. (1995), *Managing Arms in Peace Processes: Rhodesia/Zimbabwe*, Geneva, United Nations Institute for Disarmament Research.

Hare, P. (1998), *Angola's Last Best Chance for Peace: An Insider's Account of the Peace Process*, Washington, D.C., U.S. Institute of Peace Press.

Hartzell, C., M. Hoddie and D. Rothchild (2001), 'Stabilizing the Peace After Civil War: An Investigation of Some Key Variables', *International Organization*, vol. 55, no. 1, pp. 183–208.

Hoddie, M. and C. Hartzell (forthcoming), 'The Role of Powersharing in Post-Civil War Settlements: Initiating the Transition From Civil War', in P.G. Roeder and D. Rothchild (eds.), *Sustainable Peace: Democracy and Power-Dividing Institutions After Civil Wars*.

Huntington, S.P. (1968), *Political Order and Changing Societies*, New Haven, Yale University Press.

Lake, D.A. and D. Rothchild (1998), 'Spreading Fear: The Genesis of Transnational Ethnic Conflict', in A. Lake and D. Rothchild (eds.), *The International Spread of Ethnic Conflict: Fear, Diffusion, and Escalation*, D. Princeton, Princeton University Press.

——. (forthcoming), 'Territorial Decentralization and Civil War Settlements', in P.G. Roeder and D. Rothchild (eds.), *Sustainable Peace: Democracy and Power-Dividing Institutions After Civil Wars*.

Lijphart, A. (1985), *Power-Sharing in South Africa*, Berkeley, University of California, Institute of International Studies.

Manning, C. (2002), 'Conflict Management and Elite Habituation in Postwar Democracy: The Case of Mozambique', *Comparative Politics*, vol. 35, no. 1, pp. 63–84.

Marley, A.D. (1997–98), 'Military Downsizing in the Developing World: Process, Problems, and Possibilities', *Parameters*, vol. 27, no. 4, pp. 137–144.

Mozaffar, S. (1998), 'Electoral Systems and Conflict Management in Africa: A Twenty-Eight State Comparison', in T.D. Sisk and A. Reynolds, *Elections and Conflict Management in Africa*, Washington, D.C., U.S. Institute of Peace Press.

Ould-Abdallah, A. (2000), *Burundi on the Brink 1993-95*, Washington, D.C., U.S. Institute of Peace Press.

Reilly, B. (2000), Electoral Systems. Paper presented at the Institute on Global Conflict and Cooperation Conference on "power Sharing and Peacemaking." La Jolla, California, December 8–9.

——. (forthcoming), 'Governmental Inclusiveness in Ethnically Divided Democracies: Do Electoral Systems Promote Power Sharing Outcomes?', in P.G. Roeder and D. Rothchild (eds.), *Sustainable Peace: Democracy and Power-Dividing Institutions After Civil Wars*.

Roeder, P.G. (forthcoming), 'Power Dividing as an Alternative to Ethnic Power Sharing', in P.G. Roeder and D. Rothchild (eds.), *Sustainable Peace: Democracy and Power-Dividing Institutions After Civil Wars*.

Rothchild, D. (1997), *Managing Ethnic Conflict in Africa: Pressures and Incentives for Cooperation*, Washington, D.C., Brookings Institution Press.

Rothchild, D. and C.A. Hartzell (1999), 'Security in Deeply Divided Societies: The Role of Territorial Autonomy', *Nationalism and Ethnic Politics*, vol. 5, nos. 3 and 4, pp. 254–271.

Rothchild, D. (2000), 'Ethnic Fears and Security Dilemmas: Managing Uncertainty in Africa', in M. Nincic and J. Lepgold (eds.), *Being Useful: Policy Relevance and International Relations Theory*, Ann Arbor, University of Michigan Press.

———. (2002), 'Settlement Terms and Postagreement Stability', in S.J. Stedman, D. Rothchild and E. Cousens (eds.), *Ending Civil Wars: The Implementation of Peace Agreements*, Boulder, Lynne Rienner.

Rothchild, D. and P.G. Roeder (forthcoming), 'The Dilemma of Power Sharing After Civil Wars', in P.G. Roeder and D. Rothchild (eds.), *Sustainable Peace: Democracy and Power-Dividing After Civil Wars*.

Sisk, T.D. and C. Stefes (forthcoming), 'Power Sharing as an Interim Step in Peace Building: Lessons from South Africa for Other Divided Societies', in P.G. Roeder and D. Rothchild (eds.), *Sustainable Peace: Democracy and Power-Dividing After Civil Wars*.

Smith, Z.K. (2000), 'The Impact of Political Liberalisation and Democratisation on Ethnic Conflict in Africa: An Empirical Test of Common Assumptions', *Journal of Modern African Studies*, vol. 38, no. 1, pp. 21–39.

Stanley, W. and C.T. Call (1997), 'Building a New Civilian Police Force in El Matthew Salvador', in K. Kumar (ed.), *Rebuilding Societies After Civil War: Critical Roles for International Assistance*, Boulder, Lynne Rienner.

Stedman, S.J. (1997), 'Spoiler Problems in Peace Processes', *International Security*, vol. 22, no. 2, pp. 5–53.

Stedman, S.J. and D. Rothchild (1996), 'Peace Operations: From Short Term to Long Term Commitment', *International Peacekeeping*, vol. 3, no. 2, pp. 17–35.

Suhrke, A. and B. Jones (2000), 'Preventive Diplomacy in Rwanda: Failure to Act or Failure of Actions?', in B.W. Jentleson (ed.), *Opportunities Missed, Opportunities Seized*, Lanham, Maryland, Rowman and Littlefield.

Van Dyke, V. (1977), 'The Individual, the State, and Ethnic Communities in Political Theory', *World Politics*, vol. 29, no. 3, pp. 350–377.

Wagner, H. (1993), 'The Causes of Peace', in R. Licklider (ed.), *Stopping the Killing: How Civil Wars End*, New York: New York University Press.

Walter, B.F. (2002), *Committing to Peace: The Successful Settlement of Civil War*, Princeton, Princeton University Press.

Zahar, M.-J. (forthcoming), 'Power Sharing in Lebanon: Foreign Protectors, Domestic Robert Peace, and Democratic Failure', in P.G. Roeder and D. Rothchild, *Sustainable Peace: Democracy and Power-Dividing Institutions After Civil Wars*.

CHAPTER EIGHT

ADMINISTRATIVE DECENTRALIZATION AND
POLITICAL CONFLICT IN MALI

Gerti Hesseling and Han van Dijk

Introduction

Since the early 1990s, decentralization has generally been regarded as an important instrument in improving the interaction between civilians and government, and an important prerequisite to establishing a healthy democracy.

In this article, we will mainly concentrate on the relationship between decentralization and conflicts at local level. One of the objectives of decentralization can be the "reduction of the consequences of ethnic/social and economic diversity and geographical heterogeneity" (Frerks and Otto 1996: 17). This would entail a contribution to the diminution of conflict. However, the most important conclusion reached in recent studies on the process of decentralization in developing countries is that, in general, results are very disappointing (Frerks and Otto 1996, Otto 1999), and the question must be posed as to whether decentralization does indeed contribute to the prevention of conflict or on the contrary whether it promotes conflict. In this paper, therefore, we will address the dangers accompanying decentralization and in particular the risk of inadequate preparation and implementation of decentralization which could result in new (ethnic) conflicts or a revival of old ones. We will do this on the basis of a concrete example, Mali.

The most important reason for choosing Mali as a case study is that it wholeheartedly embraced the process of decentralization, a process we have been able to observe closely from the outset. Another reason is that the current Mali administration is considered to be one of the success stories of democratization and decentralization in Africa. However, as we will be showing, upon closer examination a number of flaws appear in this success story.

We will first deal with some general views of decentralization. After a short analysis of the effects of the colonial regime on the African state we will give a more detailed description of Mali. Subsequently, we will describe how the Malian government prepared for and implemented decentralization in the 1990s. Finally, we will state our conclusions on the basis of a number of concrete examples.

Decentralization and Conflicts: Is There any Relationship?

Before we discuss the possible relationship between decentralization and development, the increase or hardening of conflicts, we need to establish what is understood by decentralization. Indeed, it seems to be a fashionable word, especially in the developing world, and, as is often the case with fashions, the word is not always used judiciously. In general, decentralization is defined as the transfer, from central government to bodies outside the central core, of duties, powers, resources and decision-making powers. However, it is often used as an umbrella term, comprising various types of decentralization (Otto 1999). In practice, though, there will usually be a combination of different forms of decentralization and of an incomplete transfer of powers, duties, resources and decision-making powers.

However, such formal definitions provide little insight into questions such as what decentralized should be, how, to what extent and within what framework. Governments and policy-making bodies in general have an instrumental and positive view of law and government. They assume that laws and regulations change people's conduct, bringing it in line with the law. But nothing is further from the truth: human conduct is determined by a large complex of social and political relationships, only one of which is the law (Griffiths 1996: 477; Hesseling 1996: 121). In order for decentralization to succeed, local communities need to be properly functioning organizations already, based on equality and mutual cooperation. Knowing what the results of a certain form of decentralization will be further requires an understanding of the political processes that have dominated Africa's political landscape for many years.

Although, after independence in most countries, democracy and popular participation were set as the standard, these objectives were soon abandoned under the influence of socialist experiments and the transformation of many regimes into *de facto* or *de jure* single-party states. This transformation occurred under the guise of promoting national cohesion and overcoming regional, ethnic and class differences within these newly independent countries (Wunsch 1990).

Moreover, it soon became clear that any modernization of under-developed economies and local political structures would be con-fronted by a number of fundamental obstacles. A centralist state seemed an effective way of implementing the solutions to these prob-lems. Poor and incompetent implementation, recalcitrant civil ser-vants, and the awkward realities of underdeveloped economies frustrated many efforts in the seventies and eighties to bridge the gap between the government and the population (Olowu 1990). There never was any true decentralization in those years.

After the fall of communism in Russia and Eastern Europe, and under the influence of internal protest movements (Bratton and Van der Walle 1994; Huntington 1991), a new democratic movement was born in a large number of African countries in the early 1990s. Decentralization was regarded as one of the most important compo-nents in a package of measures for initiating effective democratiza-tion. It was hoped that it would, at the same time, trigger sustainable development. Finally, it was assumed that in a decentralized system it would be easier to resolve divergent local interests by negotiation, thereby reducing the risk of these problems escalating into conflicts. But, as the political unrest in large parts of Africa shows, it is cer-tainly not inconceivable that ethnic differences can be accentuated by politicians who regard decentralization of state powers as a wel-come opportunity to claim a privileged position for their own ethnic group.

To our knowledge, studies on decentralization in Africa do not make a direct link between the some processes of decentralization and the emergence of conflict, but they point to some inherent dangers if the transfer of power to the local level is not based on a sound under-standing of past and current socio-political processes.

In the first place, national governments and donors supporting de-centralization reforms are too easily inclined to conceive of local com-munities as homogeneous, idealizing collective interests, shared norms and solidarity of purpose. In order to turn decentralization into a suc-cess, local communities need to be properly functioning organizations, based on equality and mutual cooperation. This is, however, rarely the case, particularly in Sahel communities that are highly stratified. For a number of historical and more recently established reasons, local communities are differentiated by social status, gender, age, reli-gion, origin (especially autochthonous people and 'strangers') and ethnicity (Gentili in this book). And as Ribot (2002b: 13) rightly states,

> It is due to this diversity that questions of community representation
> arise. Since chiefs or 'customary authorities' are very popular as local
> authorities, especially among donors and NGOs (but also among the
> local communities themselves, as they are often elected), it is more
> likely that decentralization reforms tend to reproduce relations of
> unequal power and authority. Customary authorities are notorious for
> (...) favoring divisive ethnic-based membership over the residency-
> based forms of citizenship so fundamental to most democratic systems.
> (Vijayalakshmi 2002, quoted by Ribot 2002a: 12).

The question is whether decentralization might also contribute to
devolution or reinforce systems of political patronage. In his review
of the literature on the experience of decentralization in Africa, Jesse
Ribot (2002b: 46–48) addresses this question by linking the phenomena of elite capture and patronage. Local elites tend to use the resources
channelled in the process of decentralization for their own benefit
and for patrimonial or clientelist purposes. At the same time, the central government allocates state resources at the local level "along
lines of political economic alliances between central state actors and
the patronage networks they need to maintain their political base".
He warns however that more empirical research is needed to measure the effects of what he calls 'elite capture' at the local level. But
according to one of the prominent World Bank researchers on decentralization, comparative analysis has confirmed that many politicians
see decentralization not as an alternative to a system of patronage
but a device to extend and renew those systems (Manor 1999).

An additional difficulty here is that local government officials and
politicians are often only accountable to central government and not
to the local population that they are deemed to represent (see also
Silverman 1992). The result is that the local population can no longer
rely on the intermediate level of government for protection and turns
to its own groups, which are organized along ethnic lines.

It is generally accepted that 'ethnicity' is a complicated concept,
and that conflicts are often labelled 'ethnic' by international donors,
sometimes with the compliance of traditional leaders. The construction of ethnic identities is a dialectical process and often occurs around
newly established borders. The imposition of borders by colonial governments for administrative purposes can lead to a process of artic-
ulation of ethnic identities (e.g. Amselle 1991). It follows from the
interaction of internal dynamics that a balance needs to be found
between internal relations of power and the need to relate to the outside world in one way or another (De Bruijn and Van Dijk 1997).

Administrative decentralization creates such new borders (and some-times physical frontiers) between groups that they may lead to a renewed relevance of ethnicity.

Decentralization, if implemented correctly, will not automatically lead to (more) conflict or to the emergence or accentuation of eth-nicity. It may even contribute to the strengthening of local govern-ments and to more equity in the use of (local and national) resources and thus to a decrease in conflict. In practice, however, decentral-ization appears to be quite a complex process with the occasional unexpected, unfortunate, outcome. The following examples from Mali will show that the standard view of decentralization is an inadequate way of understanding the true problems involved. In particular, as regards the management of natural resources at a local level, it is important to have, along with the transfer of power to a local body, local procedures to ensure that minorities also have access to land, water and forest, and that they can exploit these and enjoy the fruits of their labour. And the development of such procedures requires an understanding of the past and of present political processes.

Mali

Like the other Sahel countries and other 'French-speaking' African countries, Mali has a tradition of centralized government. After inde-pendence in 1960, president Modibo Keita quickly took control. Once he had consolidated his position, he began a socialist experiment, which by 1968 had almost led the country to bankruptcy. At that stage a group of young army officers led by Lieutenant Moussa Traoré suc-cessfully seized power.

During the period from 1968 to 1991, when the country was still governed by Moussa Traoré, Mali not only experienced two severe droughts (1970–73, 1980–85) but also suffered at the hands of its own rulers. Food aid during the first drought did not reach its destination. Aid funds disappeared into the pockets of military officers, high-rank-ing civil servants and politicians, the president first and foremost. The country was rife with corruption.

When Moussa Traoré's system of patronage could no longer be financed, his regime collapsed. In particular, the youth of Bamako and other large cities acted as the driving force behind the protests that brought about a popular revolt, while at the same time the

Touareg in the north caused much unrest. On 26 March 1991, Moussa Traoré was removed from office by the army after a wave of violence. Power passed into the hands of General Amadu Tumani Touré, who, within a short period, organized elections to approve a new constitution, parliament and president, and then left the political arena.

His successor, Alpha Oumar Konaré, was elected in June 1992. He not only based his election campaign on decentralization, but also promised many other improvements. It was under his leadership that Mali became the showcase of international development and an example of economic and political success. Nevertheless, there were a number of serious problems, which undermine the image of the success story.

During the regime of Alpha Konaré (1992–2002), the governing party dominated despite the existence of many political parties—in November 2001 the 78th political party was officially registered (Boilley 2002). Effectively a kind of one-party system still existed. Mali has hardly any institutions or networks capable of working out compromises. Every party develops its own vertical hierarchy of patronage networks. This process still obstructs political modernization even today.

The political picture was still problematic after the presidential and general election in 2002. Amadu Tumani Touré made a successful comeback as (now elected) president, ten years after handing over power to the civilian Konaré. Before the elections Konaré's party (ADEMA) had split into various factions, because they had been unable to agree upon a common candidate to succeed Konaré who had to step down at the end of his two constitutional mandates. It is rumoured that Konaré secretly supported the independent Touré as a result of a covert deal between the two politicians in 1992 (Boilley 2002). At present, 14 political parties divided into 5 alliances are represented in the General Assembly, and it is not always clear who the opposition is and who is supporting the president. This does not mean that there is no opposition, but neither is it an indication of a strong political organization.

The turnout at the most recent elections was at a disconcertingly low level: in 1997 only 21.6 per cent and 28.4 per cent at the general and presidential elections (Lange 1999: 126) and at the presidential elections of 2002 less than 30 per cent (Boilley 2002). In rural areas participation was particularly low, which was partly due to the poor organization (although they were not necessarily unfair) and partly an indication of the depth of popular disinterest in national politics (Lange 1997; Bratton *et al.* 2002). One of the factors to which this can be attributed is that, despite decentralization, people still do not feel they are participating in an open political process. The low literacy rate of about 25 per cent may be another factor (UNDP 2003).[1]

Another reason for popular disinterest in politics is that by and large the civil service has remained unchanged. With few exceptions, those who were guilty of corruption and abuse of power were neither punished nor transferred (Fay 1995). Rent seeking and corruption within the civil service are on the increase, stimulated by attempts to elude public regulations, since there is no sense of the public good (Lange 1999: 127). On the contrary, pressure groups, such as student organizations, try to get a piece of the cake by means of strikes and violence. As a result, 50 per cent of the budget for education disappears into fellowships for pupils and students who now have incomes largely exceeding those of workers.

A further reason for disinterest in politics may be that little has been done to recover the funds that were misappropriated under the former regime. According to persistent rumours some of these spoils have disappeared into the pockets of prominent politicians or into the coffers of the governing party, ADEMA, in exchange for immunity from prosecution. Also, a number of leading politicians from the former regime have returned under the new government. Former president Moussa Traore has been released from prison, his death sentence having previously been reduced to life imprisonment. At the local level, political networks are still operational (Fay 1995). Alliances between local politicians and civil servants can still block development initiatives, if these pose a threat to their political power or their 'informal' income (Bouju 1998, 2000; Dorrier-Apprill 2002).

However, the most important reason for disinterest may be that little progress can be seen in an economic sense, except in the cotton regions in the south of Mali.[2] The contrast between the capital Bamako, the scene of a real estate *boom*, and smaller cities is perplexing. At village level there are some visible signs of change in the form of new

---

[1] According to the Prime Minister of the day, Mandé Sidibé, the number of school-age children had increased from 29 per cent to 50 per cent between 1990 and 1999.

[2] Cotton is the main export product of Mali. Mali is one of Africa's main producers of cotton and a substantial proportion of government income comes from the cotton company, 50 per cent of which is owned by the Malian state.

school buildings and new dispensaries, but there is no qualified personnel to teach or provide basic health care. There has certainly been no change in the economic situation for the majority of the rural population. There are still no funds for the development of local economic initiatives, except for the Touareg, who fought their way into the governmental system.[3] During the 1990s the percentage of Malian living below the poverty line stuck at around 60–70 per cent. After twelve years of democracy and in spite of substantial donor funds, Mali is still at the bottom of the list of poor countries (172 out of 175), even below countries such as Angola, Chad, Rwanda and Liberia that have been ravaged by dictatorial regimes and civil wars (UNDP 2003).

Poverty in itself is a factor contributing to conflict. The lack of income and the lack of prospects for millions of young people in Mali may be a cause of civil unrest. Most of the rural areas are still as poor as they were at the beginning of the 1990s. Decentralization brought hope of economic progress to young ambitious people at the local level. When local administration and economic growth are not able to address these ambitions there is a risk of political and social unrest.

The drop in the price of cotton on the world market gave rise to a serious economic crisis in the cotton regions of Mali; contributory factors were also the embezzlement of resources by employees of the cotton company and the over-indebtedness of the upper strata of farmers. Discontent, as well as refusal to cultivate cotton at such low prices, triggered a genuine peasants' revolt in the summer of 2000.[4]

Finally, at present there is still no powerful civil society. This has only begun to be developed since the fall of the Moussa Traoré regime and what independent organizations do exist depend to a large extent on foreign aid and have little standing at the grassroots level where they could support local initiatives (cf. De Bruijn et al. 2001).

---

[3] There are initiatives to make means available for local municipalities. An example of this is the ANICT (Agence nationale d'investissement des collectivités territoriales). However, these sources of funding are not always known about at local level or rural municipalities have great difficulty in meeting the technical and administrative criteria of these agencies.

[4] The cotton harvest in 2000 was half of that in 1999 (250,000 ton instead of 500,000). Production is now back to normal, thanks to an injection of 58 thousand million FCFA (€ 88,5 million) into the cotton company (Marchés tropicaux 2002).

Decentralization in Mali

Decentralization could resolve some of these issues and has figured prominently on the agenda of the Malian government. Former president Konaré lived up to his promise in the area of decentralization, not only in words (in speeches, decentralization was characterized as a priority of his policy),[5] but also in deeds.

In 1993, an Act was passed setting out the general guidelines for the decentralization process.[6] In it, four equal levels of government are distinguished: the regions, the district of Bamako, the districts and the municipalities. These territorial units are governed by elected councils that appoint an executive board from among their members. According to this Act, not only powers but also (financial) resources are transferred to the local governments. Finally, the Act provides that supervision of the central government is limited to reviewing local resolutions retrospectively, and then only to ensure that they are in accordance with the law, not that they are effective.

In the same year, 1993, a *Mission de Décentralisation* was also set up to prepare for and support the process of decentralization. In the ensuing five years, hundreds of meetings were held throughout the country, where proposed policies and bills were put before various groups. In this way, informal networks were created, consisting of men and women who were deemed to be representative of the various ethnic, political and socio-cultural levels in the region. These groups organized numerous meetings in Mali's rural areas where discussions were held in the various local languages because, as was said by the head of the Mission Ousmane Sy: "The concept of 'décentralisation', in French, means nothing to the Bambara".[7] To this end, a list of the most important words and phrases used had been trans-

---

[5] In March 1992: "Je proposerai l'adoption de grandes lois de liberté portant sur la libre administration ou la décentralisation (. . .)"; when accepting office in 1992: "Les moyens de cette réconciliation seront aussi (. . .) la décentralisation des pouvoirs qui formera les cadres vivants de la participation du plus grand nombre aux affaires de la cité (. . .)"; in 1997, after he had been elected president for the second time: "Le meilleur passeport du Mali pour son entrée au troisième millénaire se trouve être ce vaste chantier de la décentralisation qu'en 1992 j'ai inscrit au rang de priorité."

[6] Act 93–008 of 11 February 1993 relating to the conditions for the free administration of local communities.

[7] Mission de Décentralisation et des Réformes Institutionnelles: *Le cadre d'une nouvelle dynamique de démocratisation et de développement*, Bamako: September 1998: 21.

lated, while the texts of the statutes were also translated into five local languages.

The *Mission de Décentralisation* explicitly presented the process of decentralization as a spearhead of government policy. Decentralization was not only regarded as a necessary step within the context of globalization, but also as a condition of the process of democratization—an important strategy within the context of the war against poverty and a solution to the conflicts that had for many years been raging in the north of Mali due to the revolt of the Touaregs.[8] In addition, Mali's history was used to explain the concept. Certain forms of decentralization had already been in existence since the third century. For example, certain principles of government from the old empire of Wagadou are described, that show that the separate kingdoms within Wagadou were governed according to local custom. The decentralization of Mali as it originated in the early 1990s was therefore certainly no isolated process, according to those who had taken the initiative, but a development that was embedded in history and in the processes of globalization, democratization, development and internal pacification.

It has been argued that Konaré actually had no other choice than to decentralize. His predecessors, Moussa Traoré and Amadu Tumani Touré, had made various concessions to the Touareg insurgents in the north that were deeply resented in the south. In order to live up to these concessions, to keep the north within the national state and to contain the unrest in the south, the only way out was to engage in a process of administrative decentralization encompassing the whole country. In this way it would be possible to control the political aspirations of regional politicians and prevent an increase in regional unrest (Seely 2002).

---

[8] For example, Ousmane Sy says, in the preface to a document in which he explains the process of democratization: "La réforme de décentralisation semble être le 'visa d'entrée' des acteurs du futur village planétaire que sera le monde dans le troisième millénaire." and he quotes a comment made by the president: "(. . .) pour le Mali la dernière grande réforme de cette fin de siècle est la décentralisation qui demeure la plus grande justification politique de la démocratisation (. . .)". Elsewhere in the same document (p. 6), he writes: "La réforme de décentralisation est envisagée comme un facteur direct et incontournable de faisabilité de cette stratégie (la stratégie nationale de lutte contre la pauvreté proposée par le Gouvernement en Juin 1998)". Finally, on p. 12: "La décentralisation administrative apparaît vite dans ce contexte comme la voie d'une solution politique au problème du Nord (. . .)". Mission de Décentralisation et des Réformes Institutionnelles: *Le cadre d'une nouvelle dynamique de démocratisation et de développement*, Bamako: September 1998.

One of the sensitive issues facing the *Mission de Décentralisation* was the demarcation of the borders of the new rural municipalities. A rural municipality had to meet the following three criteria: there had to be a desire among the residents to form a municipality together, the future municipality had to exhibit 'bonds of solidarity', and it had to be economically viable.[9] In order to support this process, *Commissions de Découpage* were set up throughout the country in which, besides (local) civil servants, two representatives of the population and five representatives of NGOs had a seat. After many palavers in the villages, these committees eventually prepared a proposal for the demarcation of the rural municipalities that was adopted by parliament in 1996—following three months of meetings and numerous amendments.[10] Accordingly, the most important and most noticeable result of decentralization to date is the formation of 684 new (rural) municipalities that, together with the already existing nineteen city municipalities, form the first new decentralized institutions of Mali. The rural municipalities take the place of the districts, which had formed the lowest governmental unit in Mali up to that time and have since been dismantled. They consist of a number of villages and/or 'fractions' (groups of nomads).

In March 1998, the duties of the *Mission de Décentralisation* were extended with the execution of *Réformes Institutionnelles* and became the responsibility of the President, with new instructions to improve the institutional development of the municipalities.[11] In this context, a network was set up in every region to support the municipalities in which NGOs, donors, development projects, the private sector and local leaders were represented. Finally, in 1999, there were elections for the 703 municipal (684 rural and 19 urban) councils and almost 10,000 new council members were elected. Shortly thereafter, the policy of decentralization became the responsibility of a ministry and thus integrated into normal governmental policy.

It is clear that Mali did not make light of setting up new decentralized local institutions. Neither expense nor effort was spared to involve the population as much as was possible in the preparations: many impressive information folders and booklets were distributed

---

[9] See section 3 of the Code des Collectivités territoriales: "la volonté de vivre ensemble", "l'existence de liens de solidarité"; "La viabilité économique".

[10] Act 96–059 of 4 November 1996 creating 682 new 'communes'.

[11] Decree no. 98–083/P-RM.

throughout the country. Even in the smallest villages, meetings were convened at which the idea behind decentralization was explained in the native language. The press was mobilized on a large scale. In this respect, the process pursued from 1993 onwards was certainly exemplary.

Decentralization in Practice

Despite this expensive, careful preparation and strong commitment to the process of decentralization, there are signs that in practice the new rural municipalities will be faced with tremendous, possibly insurmountable, problems. These problems will no doubt occur in all kinds of service sectors such as education and health care, as a result of, among other things, the lack of finance and qualified professionals at the local level. But with financial and technical support from outside and much patience, such obstacles can be overcome in time.

The scope for such solutions, however, is quite limited. The difficulties for small rural municipalities are enormous. Income consists of the head tax, levied on each adult between 15 and 55 years of age. In one such municipality, Dalla in the Douentza district, the income of the *commune* is around € 3,200. With this sum only the salaries of the mayor and the secretary can be paid, as well as some of the expenses of the members of the municipal council. The mayor earns € 23 per month—just enough to buy a 100 kg bag of millet, whereas he actually needs three to feed his family.

Some of the more intractable problems generated by the process of decentralization are the new kinds of ethnicity that have surfaced when establishing new administrative borders, and arrangements for the local management of land, water and forest. Villages that once competed with each other for use of space and exploitation of resources in the form of land, pasture and forest, now all of a sudden had to cooperate. Borders that had been disputed in the past now had to be set without the original border dispute having been resolved. Things were even more complicated when villagers were of different ethnic origins. Among other things this led to a situation where municipalities were usually dominated by a single ethnic group (see Fay 2000). In some cases inhabitants belonging to one municipality and to a specific ethnic group have settled in the territory of another *commune* or ethnic group. Administratively they have been attached to their municipality of origin, whereas they may have been settled elsewhere for decades. There they live on land borrowed from the original inhabitants, but have become second-class citizens. The position of nomadic groups in areas dominated by sedentary populations has also not been considered.

In many cases the local legitimacy for a division into municipalities dates back to pre-colonial and colonial territorial divisions, and incorporates everything that has been added and accumulated since by way of changes and conflicts in the colonial and post-colonial period. This combination of old and new power centres has created a new reference point in the form of political principles and arenas, within which actors and groups have developed new strategies in order to appropriate a larger portion of the total available resource. This has led to an increase in conflicts, negotiations and fragile compromises between various groups (Koné and Fay 1998: 2).

In legislation relating to decentralization and its implementation, the position of minorities at the municipal level was not taken into account in any way, nor was the history of such groups in this context. There are indications that the position of minorities is deteriorating as a result of an increase in the population and the lack of good land (Nijenhuis, forthcoming). In the districts of Nioro and Diéma conflict between various groups (salary demands of Fulbe herdsmen towards their employees, conflicts between sedentary farmers and nomadic herdsmen, banditry) is on the increase. The newly elected communal authorities confirmed that, in spite of a long tradition permitting cattle to graze on fields after the harvest, they now refuse the herders in transhumance access to 'their' territory. Conflicts between farmers and cattle-breeders in Mali are common and not new, but this time the conflicts were explicitly labeled 'ethnic' by the international agency involved in mediation. The UNDP invited the customary chiefs of the different ethnic groups in the area—Fulfude, Bambara and Soninké—to act as official mediators in the conflict but reported it later as a "conflict between Peul, on the one side, and Soninké and Bambara on the other" (Leclerc-Olivee 2001: 40). Experts report that more than 300 deaths had to be attributed to disputes over resources in 1999–2000 (Ribot 2002a). At the Bandiagara escarpment there were clashes between villages resulting in the death of a number of men when ancient conflicts over land ownership were stirred up.

Another development is that Malian intellectuals have begun to align themselves with the decentralization process on the basis of ethnic affinity. For a number of years the movement N'Ko, a Malinké organization, has been active in the south. This movement opposes both Arab and European influences on Mali. The present process of decentralization is regarded as a way of restoring the old structure of Soundjata Keita's 13th-century Mali empire (Amselle 1996). This association can boast some prominent members, including a number of ministers and top-ranking officials of the cotton company. Other Malian intellectuals and administrators also refer to the decentralized character of the 'original African-Malian' political structure of the Mandé society as a primordial model for political organization.[12] They are increasingly associating the Malian nation with the Malinké ethnic group and other related groups, rejecting other solutions to the political problems of Mali.[13] The Peul intelligentsia, too, has set up a similar opposition movement called Tabital Pulaaku. The struggle at local level thus has its counterpart at the national level.

Apart from these problems involving villages and ethnic groups, it seems that true decentralization, the encouragement of local development and the peaceful resolution of conflicts, will require the delegation at the local level of at least control over the primary means of existence of the rural population: in other words control over land and its natural resources. Indeed, the problems surrounding the right to land reflect many of the issues relating to the structures, expression and exercise of power (Koné and Fay 1998: 2). A number of studies have been made on these problems, which conclude that this is one of the most explosive issues on the political agenda. According to observers, decentralization is bound to fail if land issues are not included. However, on account of its explosive nature, the government has removed land rights from the agenda. Under the present Land Ordnance, replacing the Land Act of 1986, the state remains the owner of all vacant land and land that has been left fallow for more than 10 years—though this ordnance provides for the possibility of

---

[12] Amselle (1998: 19fn) lists a whole series of ministers, presidential advisors and influential intellectuals. This view of the original African structure was set out in writing by important colonial administrators such as Delafosse (1912).

[13] It is interesting to see how Western (American) intellectuals have associated themselves uncritically with this political project by organizing seminars on democracy in Mali with the former president Konaré and his wife as guest of honour and the champions of democracy and intellectual and economic progress in Africa (see Bingen et al. 2000, notably the contributions of Wiley, Adama Ba Konaré, Robinson.

title to land for collective units.[14] However, with these land titles the problem will re-appear: who is supposed to belong to the collective units and who is not.

Land Conflicts in the Inner Delta of the Niger

The complexity of the land rights problem becomes clear if we turn to the situation in the inner delta of the Niger. For thousands of years, fishermen, cattle farmers, rice farmers and traders have been trying to make a living on this flood plain of the Niger delta, the largest in West Africa.[15] And for just as long, these groups have been disputing hegemony over the region. In the course of time domination has moved back and forth between groups. Immigrants have also tried to divide a portion of its resources amongst themselves. This has led to a multi-layered system of rights to resources, which has created much interdependence between the various groups, and also created conflicts that continue to this day (see Fay 1997). This mosaic of interests was reorganized in the 19th century by an Islamic empire, founded by the Fulbe (Peul) in order to ensure that fishing, rice cultivation and cattle breeding could all take place at the same time or in succession. One of the objects of this was to strengthen the economic foundation of the empire, but it also established the dominion of the Fulbe elite, as the overseers of this land use scheme (Gallais 1967). The entire inner delta was divided into a number of territories under a *dioro*, who was responsible for the organization of land use. He represented the 'owners' of the land. Often, a political leader worked alongside him. Unwilling groups and their leaders were removed. Conflicts were resolved by recourse to Islamic law.

Under the French colonial government, this system was basically left intact. However, the French did intervene in conflicts and this led to changes. Some groups managed considerably to extend their control over natural resources by manipulating the government. Others lost power. At the same time, due to the increase in population, more and more land began to be used for rice farming. The French administration gave these kinds of developments a formal character by granting official approval for the cultivation of wild

---

[14] With a discouragingly complicated and costly procedure.
[15] The extent of the flood area varies between 5,000 and 30,000 km^2, depending on rainfall in the river basin.

grazing land, determining the borders of wild grazing land or by establishing routes for passing cattle, in order to preserve the mobility of the herds (Moorehead 1991; Vedeld 1997).

These changes continued after independence. In addition, population growth and periods of drought in the 1970s and 80s led to increasing pressure on natural resources. Cattle farmers and arable farmers from both within and outside the delta area attempted to settle in those parts, which were still being flooded. With the political mayhem under the Moussa Traoré regime and the unreliability of the legal system, what was left was a system that virtually defies analysis (Cissé 1991; Turner 1992; Moorehead 1991).

A study by Vedeld (1997) of village politics in the inner delta contains a number of case studies of land conflicts. These show that most conflicts (> 50 per cent) are still resolved informally, i.e. without the intervention of a government administrator. This is not necessarily an indication that local institutions work well. According to Vedeld, the parties prefer to leave government out of a conflict. It is also noticeable that there is little certainty about access to resources in the long term. Local political leaders were able to use party networks to persuade civil servants to rule in their favour in conflicts about historically disputed rights. In this way, some cattle farming villages saw their pastureland being converted into rice fields by arable-land farmers from neighbouring villages who also believed that they had an historical claim (Vedeld 1997). Another important finding was that a large number of decisions made at government level with respect to conflicts over land are not respected at all, and that some are only partially observed. Conflicts are generally between different groups: sedentary arable-land farmers, nomadic cattle farmers, fishermen etc. Another aggravating factor is that these groups often have different ethnic origins.

The government's call for the private settlement of conflicts wherever possible, stating as reason that it (the government) was temporarily incapable of stepping in, was in fact giving entirely the wrong message. Given the local views of the state, it was precisely its 'omnipotence', the threat of violence and its unpredictable nature, that created the sole motivation for solving problems amongst disputing parties. The removal of this pressure created the fear that conflicts would become more severe. As one old man said: "See the lies they tell us so that we will kill each other" (Fay 1995: 46). This was also an open invitation to make completely ludicrous claims on another person's land and to revive claims that had already been dismissed. In this way, an administrative vacuum emerged in the farming community in the inner delta of the Niger, in which all kinds of conflicts that had evolved over many centuries of dictatorial power structures were heightened, now threatened to blow up into open conflicts between villages, ethnic groups, natives and the 'settler' population, elites and the population at large.

Local Level Democratization

One of the reasons for increasing conflict is the competition for political positions at local level. During the years of political stagnation local political elites had been in a position to dominate local politics and to control and manipulate monetary flow in their direction. Democratization and decentralization were, among other things, meant to bring an end to these practices. This supposed that local politics was transparent and based on equality. It appears, however, that in most municipalities and towns, people close to the former circles of power have been elected, and that these local officials have consolidated their grip on the management of public funds to the detriment of the public good.

An evaluation of investments in water infrastructure in a number of small towns in the region of Mopti shows that these local networks are able to prevent action being taken to the advantage of public health and the regular provisioning of clean water, when it is against their interest. In the town of Bandiagara investment in a new water network was blocked by the intervention of local elites, who saw their position threatened as managers of the old dysfunctional system of water provision (Bouju 1998).

Local politics in the regional capital of Mopti in Central Mali may serve as another example of the ambiguous and contradictory effects of decentralization. Local politics is still dominated by political patronage. Within the city this predominantly centres on control over land and the distribution of land by the founding families of the city and their clients. Originally the distribution of land was in the hands of the founding families. Newcomers, who obtained land from these families, were obliged to render political service to them indefinitely. While the one-party system was in operation, they formed a political network of politicians attempting to gain prominence within the single party, the UDPM. Now, in the era of multi-party politics, each party is constituted of a (number of) founding family(ies), who depend for their prominence in local politics on the number of clients they can mobilize (Bouju 2000).

Surrounded by rivers and floodplain, space for expansion in Mopti is extremely limited. Often land to build houses is created by land-fill—dumping human and solid waste at the borders of existing areas—a situation very undesirable from the point of view of hygiene and public health.[16] The founding families of the town have always claimed a privileged position in activities to extend the town borders. Although the distribution of land is the prerogative of the municipality these days, originally much of the land was illegally appropriated by the founding families, who settled there with their clients and descendants.

However, the new municipality wants to change this situation. It is undesirable from a public health perspective, and because there is donor money involved that could be used to improve public hygiene in Mopti, the new municipality has come into conflict with the representatives of the founding families over control of land distribution. As a result the distribution of land and the allocation of land for the processing of human and solid waste have been suspended. In this way the improvement of public health has become secondary to the struggle for power between, on the one hand, newly elected municipal officers and their modern bureaucrats working on the basis of a legalistic interpretation of land tenure regulations and, on the other, traditional authorities who employ systems of patronage to serve their own interests and those of their political clients (Dorrier-Aprill 2002). Members of ethnic groups and founding families are now opposed to each other in this process.

Of course this does not serve to make politics and the management of the public good any more transparent or democratic. The poor and particularly the newcomers among them, still do not have any influence on politics since they remain locked in their position as political clients. With some reason one could argue that they have become even more vulnerable, because the risk that they may be ousted from the land they inhabit now is considerable as the political struggle between the elites intensifies.

---

[16] Mopti is regularly struck by cholera epidemics, the latest dating from 1995.

Conclusion

In part as the result of increased pressure from the international donor community, Mali began a process of decentralization in the early 1990s. On the basis of a few examples, it has become clear that in practice matters can be awkward to resolve.

1. Drawing new administrative borders has meant that in a country in which ethnic differences (with the exception of the Touareg problem) are not yet salient, the ethnic problem could well become much more prominent in the near future.
2. In part as the result of decentralization, certain groups (ethnic and otherwise)—and nomadic cattle farmers in particular—are at an increasing risk of losing access to natural resources and the possibility of establishing a reasonable level of subsistence. Since the local institutions' dysfunction, there is much uncertainty in Mali's rural regions.
3. Finally, the resources (particularly financial) of the new rural municipalities prove to be so limited that new and old patronage networks and corrupt practices on a local level may well expand. The key to understanding these processes is not in the laws and regulations applying to these rural municipalities, but in an analysis of the networks of patronage and the political hierarchies that use these laws and regulations to acquire or retain power.
4. Even in urban municipalities, systems of patronage are very much alive and are able to block development initiatives and a more rational and modern management of public affairs.

Research shows that the Malian population may be more interest in local government than in national politics, at least when the turnout at the polls is examined. Decentralization is bound to fail if certain issues are not resolved, especially the issue of social inequality and the position of minorities. The first factor negatively affects the degree of transparency and accountability of the decentralized authorities. The second factor increases the potential for violent conflict. Conflicts threaten to paralyze any initiative, especially if these municipalities are founded on an ethnic basis. Further, there has to be scope for real governance at local level in the form of funding for development activities. Not only do political and legal powers have to be transferred to rural and urban municipalities, but so do the financial means to organize communal activities.

As it stands now, it is unlikely that administrative decentralization will contribute to a decrease in conflict. On the contrary it has the potential to increase conflict, as it has already done in the context of interethnic and land tenure relations. All in all, decentralization is not a quick fix for conflict prevention, even in a situation such as Mali, where a real start has been made with democratization, transparency and accountability. The results of these efforts are still quite modest, in the sense that levels of corruption remain high, poverty does not decrease and political participation is still low. As long as efforts to decentralize are not based on a thorough analysis of local political processes as well as social and political contradictions, expectations and objectives will be phrased in unrealistic terms, both at the level of policy and at the grassroots.

Decentralized structures of government in contemporary states do not only require political choices to be made by political elites and activists. They also require social scientists to make crucial choices of method, approach and underlying assumptions about power and the state (Smith 1985: 206).

Bibliography

Amselle, J.-L. (1991), *Logiques métisses. Anthropologue de l'identité en Afrique et ailleurs*, Paris, Payot.
——. (1996), 'Le N'Ko au Mali', *Cahiers d'Études africaines*, 144, XXXVI-4, 1996, pp. 823–826.
——. (1998), 'Une source majeure de l'idéologie de la decentralization au Mali: le N'Ko', in *Pouvoirs locaux, pouvoir d'État, démocratie et décentralisation au Mali, rapport d'étape*, Bamako, ISH-EHESS-Ministère de la Coopération, 7–23.
Bingen, R.J., D. Robinson and J.M. Staatz (eds.) (2000), *Democracy and Development in Mali*, East Lansing, Michigan State University Press.
Boilley, P. (2002), 'Presidentielles maliennes: l'enracinement démocratique', *Politique africaine*, no. 86, pp. 171–182.
Bouju, J. (1998), Approche anthropologique des stratégies d'acteurs et des jeux de pouvoirs autour du service de l'eau à Bandiagara, Koro, et Mopti (Mali), Paris, Ministère de la coopération, Projet PS/eau FAC/IG no. 94017700, "Eau et assainissement urbain dans les quartiers peri-urbains et les petits centres" Action de recherche no. 10, Rapport Final, Marseille, SHADYC.
——. (2000), 'Clientélisme, corruption et gouvernance locale à Mopti (Mali)', *Autrepart*, no. 14, 2000, pp. 143–163.
Bratton, N.M. and N. Van Der Walle (1994), 'Neo-patrimonial Regimes and Political Transitions in Africa', *World Politics*, vol. 46, no. 4, pp. 453–489.
Bratton, M., M. Coulibaly and F. Machado (2002), 'Popular Vierws of the Legitimacy of the State in Mali', *Canadian Journal of African Studies*, vol. 36, no. 2, pp. 197–238.
Cissé, S. (1991), *Concurrences spatiales et nouvelles cohabitations foncières en 5e région: La dynamique des leyde*, Observatoire du Foncier au Mali, ESPR/ODEM, Sevaré, Mali
Delafosse, M. (1972 (1912)), *Haut-Sénégal Niger*, Paris, Maisonneuve et Larose, 3 vols.

De Bruijn, M., K. Sidibé and H. van Dijk (2001), *Évaluation des appuis des OCF néerlandaises à la construction de la société civile au Mali*, Ede, Stuurgroep Evaluatie Medefinancieringsprogramma, Leiden Afrika-studiecentrum, Bamako, Koni-expertise.

Dorrier-Apprill, E. (2002), 'Gestion de l'environnement urbain et municipalisation en Afrique de l'Ouest: le cas de Mopti (Mali)', *Autrepart*, no. 21, (2002), pp. 119–134.

Fay, C. (1995), 'La démocratie au Mali ou le pouvoir en pâture', in J. Schmitz and M.E. Gruénais (eds.), 'La démocratie déclinée', *Cahiers d'études africaines*, vol. XXXV(1), no. 137, pp. 19–55.

——. (1997), 'Les derniers seront les premiers: peuplements et pouvoirs mandingues et peuls au Maasina (Mali)', in M. de Bruijn and H. van Dijk (eds.), *Peuls et Mandingues. Dialectique des constructions identitaires*, Paris, Karthala, Leiden, Africa-studiecentrum, pp. 165–192.

——. (2000), 'La décentralisation dans un cercle (Tenenkou, Mali)', *Autrepart*, no. 14, 2000, pp. 121–142.

Frerks, G. and J.M. Otto (1996), 'Decentralization and development: A Review of Development Administration Literature', Leiden, Van Vollenhoven Institute.

Gallais, J. (1967), *Le Delta Intérieur du Niger: Étude de géographie régionale*, Mémoires de l'IFAN, 78, 2 tomes, Dakar, IFAN.

Griffiths, J. (1996), 'De sociale werking van het recht', in J. Griffiths (red.), *De sociale werking van het recht. Een kennismaking met de rechtssociologie en de rechtsantropologie*, Nijmgen, Ars equilibri, pp. 469–513.

Hesseling, G. (1996), 'Legal and Institutional Incentives for Local Environmental Management', in H.S. Marcussen (ed.), *Improved Natural Resource Management—The Role of Formal Organisations and Informal Networks and Institutions*, Roskilde University, International Development Studies, Occasional Paper no. 17, pp. 98–134.

Huntington, S. (1991), *The Third Wave. Democratisation in the late 20th Century*, Oklahoma, Oklahoma Press.

Kone, Y.F. and Claude Fay, 1998, 'Introduction', in *Pouvoirs locaux, pouvoir d'État, démocratie et décentralisation au Mali, rapport d'étape*, Bamako, ISH-EHESS-Ministère de la Coopération, pp. 1–5.

Lange, M.-F. (1997), 'Elections in Mali (1992–1997): Civil society confronted with the rules of democracy', in J. Abbink and G. Hesseling (eds.), *Election observation and democratization in Africa*, London, Macmillan, pp. 228–254.

——. (1999), 'Insoumission civile et défaillance étatique: les contradictions du processus démoratique malien', *Autrepart*, no. 10, 1999, pp. 117–134.

Leclerc-Olive, M. (2001), 'Décentraliser, enjeux théoriques et politiques', in M. Leclerc-Olive and A. Rochegude, *Décentralisations: entre dynamiques locales et modialisations*, Cahier du GEMDEV no. 27, pp. 29–43, Paris, GEMDEV.

Manor, J. (1999), *The Political Economy of Democratic Decentralization*, Directions in Development Series, World Bank, Washington DC.

Marchés Tropicaux (2002), 57e année, 19 April 2002, *Spécial Mali*.

Moorehead, R.M. (1991), *Structural Chaos: Community and State Management of Common Property in Mali*, Brighton, University of Sussex, Ph.D. thesis.

Olowu, D. (1990), 'The Failure of Current Decentralization Programs in Africa', in J.S. Wunsch and D. Olowu (eds.), *The Failure of the Centralized State. Institutions and Self-Governance in Africa*. Boulder Co., Westview, pp. 74–99.

Otto, J.M. (1999), *Lokaal bestuur in ontwikkelingslanden*, Bussum, Uitg. Coutinho.

Ribot, J. (2002a), *Democratic Decentralization of Natural Resources. Institutionalzing Popular Participation*. Washington, DC, World Resources Institute.

——. (2002b), *African decentralisation: Local Actors, Powers and Accountability*, Democracy, Governance and Human Rights—Paper no 8, Geneva, United Nations Research Institute for Social Development.

Seely, J.C. (2001), 'A political analysis of decentralization: co-opting the Tuareg threat in Mali', *Journal of Modern African Studies*, vol. 39, no. 3, pp. 499–524.

Silverman, J.M. (1992), *Decentralization. Structures of Authority: A Checklist.* Unpublished paper.

Turner, M.D. (1992), *Life on the Margin. Fulbe Herding Practices and the Relationship Between Economy and Ecology in the Inland Niger Delta in Mali,* Berkely, University of California, Ph.D. Thesis.

UNDP (2003), *World Development Report,* Washington DC, United Nations Development Program.

Vedeld, T. (1997), *Village Politics. Heterogeneity, Leadership, and Collective Action Among Fulani of Mali,* Ås, Agricultural University of Norway, Dept. of Land Use and Landscape Planning, Ph.D. Thesis.

Wunsch, J.S. (1990), 'Centralization and Development in Post-Independence Africa', in J.S. Wunsch and D. Olowu (eds.), *The Failure of the Centralized State. Institutions and Self-Governance in Africa,* Boulder Co., Westview, pp. 43–73.

CHAPTER NINE

PRINCIPLES FOR CONFLICT TRANSFORMATION
PRACTITIONERS IN AFRICA

Shamil Idriss

Not long ago, I was in a bare, concrete room in a slum called 'Bone Suffer' in the capital city of Freetown, Sierra Leone. Surrounded by overcrowded shacks built along the banks of exposed sewage drains, I sat in a circle of thirty young men and women in desperate circumstances. Some had been forcibly recruited into the war between the Revolutionary United Front (RUF) and the government. All had suffered from it, but they had devised a number of schemes to generate and pool income, such as washing clothes and raising pigs on the surrounding steep banks.

Among them was Ambrose James, a young man who worked with youth leaders in Bone Suffer and other impoverished districts to organize the biggest event in Sierra Leone's recent history. In less than a month, national elections would mark the final transition between Sierra Leone's vicious war and its hopeful future.

Many of these youths, once feared as the potential cause of disruption during the elections, gained recognition for having ensured that they took place without a single violent incident. They were officially accredited as domestic monitors and posted at polling stations to ensure proper election procedures were carried out. They were linked to an unprecedented national network of Sierra Leone's community radio stations, which enabled election results to be reported and updated as they occurred in each district. Government officials and Sierra Leoneans applauded the efforts of the monitors and participating radio stations everywhere. They had introduced transparency to the electoral process, reduced tensions, raised confidence in election results because of the immediacy of their reporting, and pioneered a new way of engaging at-risk youth and the media for the stability of Sierra Leone.

The creativity and optimism of people such as Ambrose and the young Sierra Leonean election monitors in the face of overwhelming

odds form the basis of this paper, which considers the operating principles for conflict transformation practitioners, citing examples of
those principles in action.

Those principles, and examples thereof, are drawn from twenty
years of applied work by two organizations and countless local and
international partners, donors and supporters. Search for Common
Ground (SFCG) and the European Centre for Common Ground (ECCG)
are international non-governmental organizations based in Washington
DC and Brussels respectively that work in partnership to transform
how the world deals with conflict, removed from the adversarial 'win-
lose' approaches toward collaborative problem solving. The principles presented here form the core of our work.

Two disclaimers are necessary at the outset:

1. By presenting principles drawn from experience we do not seek
   to establish strict or rigid blueprints for action. The principles are
   meant to add to current thinking in this field as it continues to
   evolve and expand. Lessons drawn from this work can best be
   viewed as 'learning to inspire', rather than restricting creativity
   or narrowing thinking in a field that is as much art as it is science.
2. This paper is not the result of extensive academic study with
   the inherent rigours and research procedures that such a study
   would entail. It is written from a practitioner's viewpoint in the
   hope that other practitioners and those seeking lessons learned
   through experience would find it useful. It is based on the reflections of current and former Common Ground staff, practitioners
   and partners, as well as on the results of internal and independent
   evaluations of our Africa programmes and the reflections of other
   practitioners.[1]

Defining the Issue: Conflict Transformation

A debate exists within the field of conflict studies concerning which
term best describes the field itself: conflict resolution, conflict pre-

---

[1] For those interested in more theoretical or academic research-based resources
in the field of conflict transformation, there are several sources, including the extensive
web-based directories of the Co-Existence Resource Center <http://www.coexistence.
net/resource_center> and the Conflict Resource Information site <http://www.crinfo.org>.

vention, conflict management, etc. Rather than enter into this debate here, we shall simply explain why Common Ground has chosen the term 'conflict transformation'.

We do not equate 'conflict' with violence or view it as something negative that should be avoided, prevented or ended. Rather, we understand conflict to be the unavoidable friction resulting from differences in human affairs, whether ethnic, religious, ideological, racial or otherwise. Our work is based on the premise that the existence of conflict is natural, and that it is as much at the root of progress and innovation as it is of polarization and violence, depending on how those engaged in conflict understand and deal with it.

By viewing conflict in this way, we believe the perceptions and decisions of those engaged in conflict are central to whether it leads to progress or disaster. The term 'transformation' reflects the goal of our work. Transformation encompasses efforts that aim to resolve specific crises or problems as they arise, but its compass is broader, placing such problem solving within a wider sphere—trying to change how communities view, and therefore deal with, their differences.

Our experience is that through processes by which traditionally divided stakeholders engage in collaborative problem solving, their views and the dynamics of the conflict itself may alter to make possible what may have been at first unimaginable. This is the broader conflict transformation toward which we attempt to apply the principles noted below.

Principles of Conflict Transformation

These are the five principles:

1. Make Long-Term Commitments with the Goal of Social Transformation
2. Seek Profound Cross-Cultural Immersion
3. Work Within the System as a Social Entrepreneur
4. Model What You Aim to Bring About
5. Seek and Appreciate Catalytic Impact (Accepting the Limitations of Linear Thinking)

While this chapter focuses on work in Africa, these five principles are drawn from Common Ground's efforts worldwide to help traditional adversaries collaborate in solving shared problems, be they Hutus and Tutsis in Burundi, former RUF fighters or non-combatants in Sierra Leone, or Republicans and Democrats in the United States.

Principle 1: Make Long-Term Commitments With the Goal of Social Transformation

To many, 'conflict resolution' describes the structured approaches used to resolve specific disputes; that is, one-to-one or group mediation, arbitration or negotiation processes.

Although we apply these processes in some of our work, we view such finite, facilitated problem solving as part of a much broader societal transformation that requires a carefully considered and sustained presence over time.

The goal of our engagement is not so much the resolution of a specific dispute or even a set of disputes. Rather, our goal is to affect an attitudinal shift so that traditional adversaries begin to view their differences in perspective and address them in a way that respects the human dignity of all stakeholders.

A shift in attitudes and behaviour within the context of a long-standing, ongoing conflict can be achieved incrementally at best. It cannot be done through intermittent problem solving. Such inconsistent intervention poses serious hazards if attempted without sufficient knowledge of the context, without gaining the trust and full engagement of local stakeholders, adequate follow-up, and other prerequisites.

For these reasons, we make long-term commitments and try to minimize 'parachuting,' or short-term, in-and-out interventions. This allows us to develop focused approaches that support local peacebuilders instead of imposing results-focused solutions from outside, or trying to introduce sudden changes in often-volatile situations.[2]

In Africa, Common Ground offices have been in Burundi since 1995, in Liberia since 1997, in Angola since 1996, in Sierra Leone since 2000, and in the Democratic Republic of Congo (DRC) since 2001. But long-

---

[2] Andries Odendaal's article, 'The Rules of the Game: When Outsiders are Offsides in Peacemaking', published in the April 1997 edition of *Track Two*, draws similar conclusions from the lessons of outside agencies that intervened in South Africa during that country's transition from apartheid to democracy.

term Common Ground engagement on the ground does not always mean establishing an office—in Nigeria and Uganda, for example, we work with local organizations that promote reconciliation and conflict transformation through targeted training-upon-request, fundraising support and information sharing. Similarly, London-based International Alert has effectively supported peace-building and reconciliation in the Great Lakes region of Africa through consistent engagement of staff, based mainly in London, who have been visiting and working with local partners for nearly a decade.

The commitment to remain engaged throughout the ups and downs of the peace process and fluctuations in donor interest is a first and necessary step to supporting and accompanying local peace-builders. Ultimately, they are the only ones who can effect a sustained transformation in their societies' attitudes and behaviour.

EXAMPLE: Burundi

In 1995, Common Ground launched Burundi's first independent radio outlet, *Studio Ijambo*. Burundi was still in the midst of 'The Crisis'— the three-year period of intense bloodshed and instability between the assassination of the country's first Hutu president in 1993, and the coup that returned Tutsi Colonel Pierre Buyoya to power in 1996. Employing a multi-ethnic staff of journalists, producers and technicians, *Studio Ijambo* produced accurate news programmes to counter the rumours that fed inter-ethnic fear and violence, and soon expanded to include documentaries, roundtable discussions and dramatic programmes, all of which promote reconciliation and present balanced approaches to Burundi's problems.

In 1996, when a number of international agencies were forced to leave Burundi following the coup that returned Colonel Buyoya to power, *Studio Ijambo* not only remained on air but also sparked the development of a second Common Ground project, the *Women's Peace Centre (WPC)*. Initially, the *WPC* provided a safe space for Burundian women of all backgrounds to gather and generate cooperative solutions to their shared problems. Eventually, the *WPC* became a resource and training centre for what has become a dynamic women's movement.

Burundi is still in the midst of a precarious transitional phase with continuing clashes between the government and rebel groups. While ethnicity is no longer a taboo subject for public debate, the concentration of political and economic power within a small clique of elite is still not discussed. Nevertheless, over the past seven years independent evaluations, including interviews and focus groups with Burundians at all levels of society, and assessments by donors and other practitioners, have reflected a steadily increasing rejection by Burundians of the 'ethnicization' of politics in their country. The professionalization of radio broadcasting and the proliferation of locally organized inter-ethnic organizations and events are among the factors that have contributed to this development.

We believe that the insistence of the Burundian staff of *Studio Ijambo* and the *Women's Peace Centre* on continuing to work in 1996, coupled with the willingness of our main donor, USAID, to support them, has allowed staff to play an important role in these developments. The process is incremental, to be sure, but it appears that, with each year of sustained effort by local organizations and international supporters, Burundians are less likely to be manipulated into participating en masse in ethnically motivated violence, and they are determined to keep the fragile peace process on track.

Principle 2: Seek Profound Cross-Cultural Immersion

A glance at Common Ground programmes gives the impression that the organization is 'all over the map', in terms of geography (stretching from the United States to Indonesia), and content. Common Ground programmes include exchanges of professional wrestlers between the U.S. and Iran; congressional policy debates in the U.S.; bilingual, inter-ethnic kindergartens in Macedonia; multi-ethnic staffed radio studios in Burundi, Liberia and Sierra Leone; conflict resolution capacity building in Internally Displaced Persons (IDP) camps in Angola.

The diversity of programmes reflects an acknowledgement that the dynamics of every conflict are different, as are the cultures within which different conflicts develop. Consistent throughout all programmes are the principles described here and the core mission of Common Ground is to transform traditional adversarial behaviour from a win-lose to win-win approach, to help in an *understanding of their differences* and *act on their commonalities*. How to achieve this varies widely from situation to situation and from culture to culture.

While parallels sometimes exist between different conflict situations, every conflict presents different challenges and a highly complex and

unique set of inter-related causes and effects that can make it difficult—if not impossible—to predict outcomes or identify single factors
that could effect widespread change. In addition, every culture has
unique attributes and sensitivities.

As a result, Common Ground seeks *intense immersion into the cultures
in which we work*, relying heavily on local partners and staff to guide
approaches and develop and implement strategies for conflict transformation. We have found that expatriate programme directors often
bring a fresh perspective that inspires creative thinking and enthusiasm, but this is only effective when accompanied by genuine humil-
ity and the skill to facilitate dialogue between local actors to create
the best synthesis of ideas for project implementation.

We also realize that the most significant breakthroughs are often
not achieved by using traditional methods of conflict resolution, but
through creative problem solving combined with a profound knowledge of local cultures. Such approaches only arise out of a commitment to engage local actors from the outset and to explore with them
creative and culturally appropriate ways of exploiting opportunities
for reconciliation and conflict transformation. In some cases it is necessary to hire expatriates although it is difficult to recruit people who
are willing to commit for the long-term. Maintaining this consistent
cross-cultural immersion is particularly challenging when there is a
turn over of programme directors on average every three years. We
have tried to minimize the use of expatriate staff—some of our programmes employ no expatriates at all, while none employ more than
three (and only then in an office with a total of over 100 staff).
Regardless of staff composition, we have learned that wherever we
work, local staff and partners are the guides by which any substantial shift in programmes or strategy must be judged.

EXAMPLE: Sierra Leone

In late September/early October 2001, the RUF appeared close to capit-
ulating in Sierra Leone, yet the media and most international organizations were prevented from entering RUF-held territories. Common
Ground's Sierra Leone Director, Frances Fortune, a Canadian who has
lived in the country for 15 years, devised a scheme for gaining access
to RUF commanders and civilians in RUF-held territory. She hoped
to play a role in facilitating an end to hostilities and creating a catalyst

for the process of reintegration that would be necessary for the country to return to normalcy. Together with Steady Bongo, a popular musician from what had long been the RUF stronghold of Kailahun, she made a tour of RUF-held territory. At each stop, RUF soldiers welcomed Bongo. As someone of similar age to many of those from his home district who had chosen to fight and were now commanders, he was a model for offering an alternative approach. Throughout the tour, Bongo performed while Ms. Fortune established a rapport with and interviewed RUF commanders and civilians.

These interviews led to the first publicly aired radio broadcasts by RUF commanders and some of the first broadcasts giving the opinions of Sierra Leoneans suffering under RUF rule in the east of the country. The radio programmes established a link between the two sides of the country, which would grow and expand as the peace process progressed, the war was declared over, and the demobilization process began. Judging when and how to venture into RUF-held territory in a way that would be accepted and welcomed is not something that headquarters staff in Brussels or Washington DC could have known—it had to come from the sort of local knowledge creatively developed by Ms. Fortune and Steady Bongo.

EXAMPLE: Angola

In Angola, where a third of the population is made of internally displaced persons (IDP), much of our work has been concentrated in IDP camps. As with all camps that arise out of humanitarian crises, the international community is wary of establishing permanent structures that would create a disincentive for IDP to return to their homes in the future. But the war in Angola has been raging for so many years that some Angolans have been living in temporary camps for over a decade. In seeking a venue where IDP could gather to discuss problems arising in the camps and present and view cultural events, IDP representatives working with Angolan Common Ground staff came up with the idea of establishing jangos, round huts that have for generations served as central meeting places within the community. Jangos have since been erected by IDP in camps throughout Angola and serve as meeting places, venues for educational theatrical performances and, as necessary, makeshift classrooms.

Principle 3: Work Within the System as a Social Entrepreneur

Conflicts in Africa, from the Great Lakes to the Mano River Union, are often described as endless or intractable, giving the impression that little changes. Yet anyone engaged in countries such as Burundi, Sierra Leone, Angola, and the DRC knows that the situation in these countries and in the region at large is very unstable.

We are often asked how we are able to broadcast radio programmes in Burundi or Liberia, on the assumption that the media in those countries is so controlled by the central government that airing anything that hints at change or development is likely to be censored. While taboo and off-limit topics do exist in these countries, we have also found that there are few immovables in the world. A radio programme presented to the national station in Burundi might be rejected today but accepted tomorrow, the only difference being that today a new employee might perceive it as too risky to air, while tomorrow a veteran staff member at the station who has a pre-existing relationship with a particular journalist is willing to broadcast the programme without hesitation. Similarly, today a local military commander will not allow a women's association to demonstrate; tomorrow his replacement may be more flexible—either because he is personally more open-minded or because he happens to be the cousin of one of the directors of the women's association.

Viewed from within, and often only from within, all situations present cracks of light—opportunities that open and close and then open again somewhere else at a later time.

We believe a long-term commitment to engage on the ground and a consistent effort to immerse ourselves in local culture allow these relationships to develop and provide us with the familiarity necessary to recognize opportunities as they arise. Taking advantage of those opportunities requires a social entrepreneur—someone who is opportunistic in the best possible sense.[3] Frances Fortune's initiative entering RUF-held territory with Steady Bongo is an excellent example, but there are others, including one of many inspirational stories about Nelson Mandela during the South African peace process.

---

[3] Clearly our use of the term 'social entrepreneur' has nothing to do with making money. While an entrepreneur in the traditional sense may see the profit-making opportunity in every situation, a *social* entrepreneur views every situation with an eye toward the opportunities it might present for promoting social cohesion and positive, inclusive change in society.

EXAMPLE: South Africa

On 10 April 1993, as South Africa was at one of its most critical junctures in the transition from apartheid to democracy, Chris Hani, secretary general of the South African Communist Party, was assassinated
by a white man while walking home with his daughter. Hani was influential among the most politicized and militant youth within the African
National Congress and his murder could easily have derailed South
Africa's move toward peaceful elections and an end to apartheid.

As tensions mounted and sporadic violence began to erupt, Nelson
Mandela made a public announcement: Hani had been murdered by
a white man, but the license plate of the man's car had been taken
down and reported to police by a white woman. The division in the
country was now clear: one either stood for peace or for war. Mandela's
stance helped shift the dynamic from one of white vs. black to one
of peace vs. war, and it was clear on which side he stood. Together
with the efforts of grassroots peace activists throughout the country,
this intervention helped turn what could otherwise have been a disaster into one of South Africa's many turning points toward peace.[4]
The Chinese character for 'crisis' consists of two characters that represent 'danger' and 'opportunity'. While many only see the danger
and become debilitated by it, social entrepreneurs see the opportunity and take advantage of it. Mandela saw and took the opportunity
created by Hani's death to re-define the opponents in South Africa's
conflict.

Social entrepreneurship need not be so dramatic, of course, nor
depend on the stature of a figure such as Nelson Mandela. Social entrepreneurs can be ordinary people working tirelessly for years to prepare themselves for the right moment, and then they seize it when
it arises.

EXAMPLE: Burundi

After several years during which *Studio Ijambo* developed an excellent reputation, the Burundian team of journalists and producers were
eager to launch their own private radio station. Unlike a production

---

[4] A moving description of the efforts taken by community peace activists to stem
the tide of violence triggered by Hani's assassination is included in chapter three of
Susan Collin Marks's *Watching the Wind: Conflict Resolution During South Africa's Transition
to Democracy*. United States Institute of Peace, 2000.

company such as *Studio Ijambo*, which makes programmes and sells them to a station for broadcast, a radio station broadcasts direct. The result is more available airtime for in-house productions and greater editorial control. For a while their dream seemed unattainable as the Ministry of Defence, which oversees authorization of radio outlets, was led by a colonel who was particularly suspicious of the independent media. In 2000, a minister who had a well-established relationship with many of the *Studio* journalists, and who was much less restrictive of the media in general, replaced the colonel. Shortly thereafter, the *Studio* team applied and received authorization to launch a station, *Radio Isanganiro*, which recently began production. The initiative to launch *Radio Isanganiro* might have been impossible without their years of steady and committed work building *Ijambo* and establishing their reputation as responsible professionals. In an independent evaluation conducted in 2000, the director of Burundi's government-run radio station acknowledged that the quality and balance of *Ijambo's* programmes had inspired his own staff at the national radio station to be more professional.

Admittedly, some countries are more restrictive than others. Of all the places we work, Liberia presents one of the greatest challenges to promoting reconciliation and risking reprisal. Nevertheless, even in Liberia we have found that people and cultivated relationships are the key to opening and closing opportunities.

EXAMPLE: Liberia

In February 1999, a property dispute between Mandingo and Lorma tribesmen led to the killing of two Mandingos. The violence spread to other parts of Lofa County resulting in further injuries and looting of houses. The Lofa-based reporter from Common Ground's *Talking Drum Studio* (*TDS*), John Gayflor, contacted the head office in Monrovia with news of the violence. At that time, the government was unaware of the incident, and the media had not covered it. *TDS* staff, who had been reporting on the situation in Lofa County for months and had established a good reputation with both tribes, decided not to air news of the violence. Given the recent history of violence and atrocities between the Mandingo and Lorma tribes, they feared publicity would enflame passions and lead to further polarization and violence nation-wide. Instead they informed the Ministers of Justice and State, as well as the Lofa County representatives in parliament, and expressed a willingness to work with the government to help resolve the situation peacefully.

TDS staff were soon invited to accompany government representatives to Lofa to help reconcile the tribes. At an initial meeting tribal leaders were asked to begin by discussing their shared history of over 300 years and to explain what they felt had gone wrong. They established a committee of 24, consisting of members from each tribe, which listened to witness testimonies about past incidents of violence, determined responsibility for them, and set ground rules for future interaction. An inter-tribal agreement was brokered with TDS staff serving as witnesses and signatories. When asked, *TDS* staff explained that notifying the government was the proper course of action because the need at that time was to re-establish security in the county and prevent violence from spreading. Informing the government while remaining engaged seemed the best way to do that.

Two months later, interviews with Lofa County citizens and government officials confirmed how much they appreciated how *TDS* staff had handled the information they had gathered. Many journalists may find it difficult to accept the role TDS staff journalists played. Nevertheless, because they viewed themselves as agents for peaceful change, working creatively within the system, rather than as journalists with a story to tell, they were able to help contain an otherwise volatile situation. Although impossible to prove, one could argue that, by approaching the situation in this way, the journalists also played a role in tempering what might otherwise have been a more aggressive approach by President Charles Taylor's regime.

A Non-Adversarial Approach to Social Change

This entrepreneurial approach reflects a philosophy of social change: one that is non-adversarial and works within local cultures and parameters yet takes advantage of every possible opportunity to expand what those local parameters allow in terms of inclusive, progressive social change. This stands in contrast to adversarial approaches: naming-and-shaming campaigns, that seek to effect change through direct pressure on governments. As opposed to an adversarial approach that promotes press freedom and criticises the government of Burundi's, we believe the future work of *Radio Isanganiro* and other independent stations that succeed *Studio Ijambo* will do much to expand freedom of expression and offer a model for inter-ethnic cooperation in Burundi.

Of course, there are times when confrontation is useful and may even appear to be the only moral approach to take. Nevertheless, engaging over the long-term, immersing in local cultures and working within the system to create and seize opportunities for advancement are all part of the non-adversarial approach to social change to which we at Common Ground are committed. This is an approach that requires tremendous patience, with gratification coming in incremental advances, yet we believe it engages the broadest sector of society and, therefore, ensures the greatest sustainability in the long run.

Principle 4: Model What You Aim to Bring About

We believe that in our work the process is, in many ways, the product. While the projects we implement seek to promote reconciliation and peace-building in their own right (through radio programmes, support and training women's associations, promoting peace, theatrical and artistic events, facilitating Track II diplomacy, etc.), the way these projects are carried out is as important as the events and outcomes themselves.

When a multi-ethnic and otherwise diverse team of women in Burundi develops a Women's Peace Centre that is open to women of all backgrounds, or a pair of former RUF combatants produce and air radio programmes that facilitate and promote further demobilization in Sierra Leone, or when leaders in Angolan IDP camps, who are themselves from a variety of towns, work together to establish a system for handling intra-camp disputes, or radio producers in Liberia trains children as cub reporters to raise and discuss the rights of children and the role they could play in reconstructing that country, they are all reflecting the aims of the community at large. At Common Ground, we see our role as helping to provide a space for them to do this— for natural peace-builders to develop ideas and implement projects they know can have an impact on their communities and connect with one another to help turn their distinct projects into wider movements.

The diversity of staff and partners is particularly important in societies where communities have been physically divided or otherwise torn apart by conflict. In each of the countries in which we work, we

seek to hire and join with local activists who represent diverse interests, whether divided along ethnic, religious, gender, geographic, or
other demographic lines.

Implications for Hiring Staff and Selecting Partners:

We deliberately try to develop strong and diverse teams; this goal
guides our decisions on whom to hire and with whom to partner.
Most often, our primary criterion is to seek creative problem solvers
who approach conflict from a holistic perspective, seeking innovative ways to draw traditional adversaries together, rather than taking sides. While we often work with those who have training and
experience in conflict resolution skills, this is not as central to our
hiring and partnering process as finding partners and staff with inclusive, innovative and action-oriented approaches to social change. We
view teams and partners with these skills, regardless of training or
experience as natural agents for change. If technical training (in radio
production, for instance) is needed this can usually be done on the
job or as part of a partnership. We believe that this sort of team offers
the greatest potential for generating projects and approaches that
are modelled on the inclusive, holistic approach to the societies they
promote.

   For example, the 'reconciliation' radio programming produced by
Studio Ijambo (25 hours per week) in Burundi has had a significant
impact there, as evidenced by independent evaluations and listener
surveys. But *Ijambo* itself, an established organization with a staff of
both Hutu and Tutsi, all unified by loyalty to both *Ijambo* and the new
station they are launching, is a model that others have noted, appreciated and even tried to emulate. We believe their achievement in
building this model is as important as the programmes they air.

Principle 5: Seek and Appreciate Catalytic Impact
(Accepting the Limitations of Linear Thinking)

It is said that Napoleon was once asked whether the key to success
in battle was extensive planning—anticipating and preparing for any
contingency prior to engagement. Although it may seem strange for
a conflict transformation organization to emulate a warrior, Napoleon's
reply has become a motto within Common Ground: 'On s'engage et
après on voit' ('one engages and then one sees' what the possibilities

are). The key to success in dynamic situations lies not so much in trying to plan for all possible contingencies, but in making the commitment to enter what may appear to be a chaotic situation, and then
seizing the opportunity as it arises. While we do not throw ourselves
haphazardly into conflict situations, we have learned that once a situation has been assessed and a plan developed, the key is to identify
or place entrepreneurial, creative problem-solvers on the ground
ready to act in the event of changing circumstances.

In the field of international conflict transformation there is an increasing emphasis on assessment and planning, as well as on out-
come-focused evaluation. These are useful trends as they reflect a
serious approach by international organizations to understand situations before acting and to be accountable for the impact of their
actions. At the same time, context assessments and evaluation method-
ologies tend to reflect a kind of Newtonian logic—linear thinking,
which posits that if you can identify the cause or set of causes for a
conflict and address it, you can change the outcome in some predictable way. Whether linear cause-and-effect logic is used to assess
conflict situations and then set a plan of action, or linear activity-to-
outcome logic is used to judge the impact of a particular project, such
thinking has severe limitations when applied to complex and dynamic
situations.[5]

Our experience has been that most conflicts involve a complicated
and constantly shifting set of interrelated causes and effects. Seemingly
unrelated events can significantly shift the dynamics of a conflict by

---

[5] Carole Frampton in an unpublished paper written in December 2000, 'The Principles
of Quantum Physic: A Framework for Conflict Resolution. Lessons from an Experience
of Intervening in Burundi', compares the need to understand and evaluate conflicts
with linear models while operating in a non-linear world with the tension that exists
in physics between chaos theory and Newtonian theory. She points out that Newtonian
theory seeks to identify laws of cause and effect that govern how the world around
us works, while chaos theory posits that although cause and effect do exist, in complex systems there are so many causes and effects that identifying a single prime
cause or predicting the end effect of a single intervention is practically impossible—
that the only real constant in the world is change. Drawing on her personal experiences working in conflict transformation in Burundi, she points out that just as some
physicists have come to accept that both Newtonian theory and chaos theory are
relevant to understanding the world around us, so too can conflict transformation
practitioners reconcile and have a perspective on the seeming contradictions between
how we plan or evaluate our work and how we actually experience the doing of it.
The paper draws additional parallels and conclusions that are inspiring for practitioners and insightful for researchers. As it is unpublished, it can only be obtained
by contacting the author at cframpton@sfcg.org.

opening or closing possible areas of intervention and impact. As an example, consider Angola. In the 1960s, the U.S. supported Jonas Savimbi and his National Union for the Total Independence of Angola (UNITA) rebel movement against President José Eduardo dos Santos. Shortly after the events on 11 September 2001, the dos Santos regime used American intelligence equipment to locate Savimbi, who was assassinated in February 2002.[6] While there is no proof that the U.S. supported the assassination in any way other than by supplying equipment, the history of American support for Savimbi and the timing of the assassination have raised the question of whether there was a shift in American allegiance. One of the alleged reasons for such a shift was the American government's desire to increase influence in oil-rich countries outside the Middle East, where the U.S. was seeking a freer hand in reacting to September 11 and preparing to invade Iraq.[7] Whatever the rationale for American assistance to the dos Santos forces, few predicted the assassination of Savimbi, and that single event has set into motion an entirely new set of dynamics that affects Angola's prospects for peace in ways that are still being played out.

In fact, the entire post-September 11 global context, within which governments everywhere re-labelled opposition movements and rebel groups as terrorists to justify increased repression or to gain the sympathy of the U.S., is an example of a wholly unpredictable event affecting seemingly unrelated parts of the world. Far less dramatic, yet equally unpredictable, shifts such as the appointment of someone new to a key ministerial post or a severe drought that brings down a country's economy at the same time as a peace accord is signed, can also have major implications for peace prospects in a country or region.

At Common Ground, we acknowledge the unpredictability and interconnectedness of events in conflict zones, which are usually impossible to control and often difficult fully to understand. This does not mean we dismiss the importance of researching trends, seeking primary causes of conflict or evaluating programme impact based on

---

[6] The 2 March 2002 edition of *The Economist* reported, 'Without surveillance equipment from America and its ally, Israel, the Angolan army could probably not have tracked down and killed Mr. Savimbi'.

[7] Further to this hypothesis, these events in Angola were soon followed in April by a failed coup in oil-rich Venezuela against President Hugo Chavez. Chavez later claimed he had evidence that the U.S. had supported the coup attempt, although the U.S. State Department has consistently denied any American involvement.

linear models. On the contrary, as we have grown, we have been able to increase the assessment and evaluation elements in our programme planning. It does mean, however, that we recognize the limitations of those models for telling the whole story.

Implications for Donor Relations

Accepting the limitations of pre-planning and the need for maintaining a long-term presence on the ground raises the problem of dependence on funding. Ideally, we would like to attract grants that allow for an extended commitment with a six-month lead time during which creative staff could be hired to assess situations, engage local personnel and partners, and then develop a plan of action that would be open to constant revision and review. Of course donors are accountable to their boards or governments and are expected to fund projects that achieve results, so this type of funding is not always available. In addition, organizations such as Common Ground are expected to produce proposals outlining expected output and outcome in often changeable and volatile situations where the approach may need to be flexible.

EXAMPLE: Democratic Republic of Congo

In 2001, we began work in the DRC to support the Inter-Congolese Dialogue (ICD). The ICD was meant to educate the Congolese people and initiate public dialogue among Congolese citizens regarding the principles of the Lusaka Accord signed in 1999 by all belligerents in the Congo conflict. It was also intended to lay the groundwork for the implementation of the peace and reconciliation processes. Former Botswana president, Ketumile Masire, was designated the Facilitator of the ICD, and his office sought support for the huge task ahead. In response, our strategy was two-fold: to work with local radio stations, theatre troupes and musicians to inform the public and invite their input regarding the content and ramifications of the Lusaka Accord; and to provide support and training for local civil organizations promoting practical approaches to peace-building and reconciliation throughout the country. Initially we were based in Bukavu and Kinshasa.

Within six months, the Sun City negotiations were underway between the government and the two Congolese rebel groups backed respectively by Uganda and Rwanda. As the negotiations seemed destined to end without agreement, the people within and beyond Kinshasa began to coalesce around a menacing proposition: if the political leadership returned to the DRC without an accord, they would be met and killed at the airport.

Along with several other international and local organizations we scrambled to address the situation. Our approach was again two-fold: to provide a way for the threatening message to reach the negotiators in Sun City; and to facilitate a roundtable dialogue with DRC civil leaders for radio broadcast in the DRC, in order to explore the likely ramifications of such an action and introduce other potential responses to a failure at Sun City that might promote progress in future peace overtures.

Word of the threat eventually reached the delegates in Sun City through the efforts of international and local organizations, and the negotiations were extended long enough for President Kabila's government and the Uganda-backed Congo Liberation Movement (MLC) to sign an accord. This immediately reduced tensions in and around Kinshasa, but raised anxieties in the east, where the Congolese feared that the rapid formation of a government that excluded the Rwanda-backed Congolese Rally for Democracy (RCD) would crystallize the divisions in the country and prevent progress. Our tactic was to shift focus to promoting the almost 40 points of agreement reached by all parties in Sun City, while providing the means, again through radio, by which the Congolese in the east could voice their fears and their message that the government's job was only half completed.

These changes of programme occurred within the space of one week. Our goals and objectives had not changed. We were still there to support the peace process primarily through radio broadcasts in partnership with existing stations, and through support of civil groups. The tactics, however, had shifted considerably to respond to the rapidly changing situation.

Establishing logical frameworks to predict outputs and outcomes in situations requiring constant readjustment are important, as they force international interveners to be explicit about their approach and plans, but they are limited in how they reflect conflict transformation work in reality.

Making long-term commitments while dependent on international donors for funding support can be a difficult. At Common Ground, we work hard to cultivate open relationships with many donors in each of the countries and regions in which we work to enable us to survive those periods when donor interest shifts to crises elsewhere in the world. Ideally, donors and programme staff view themselves as partners in effecting change. We have found that donor representatives based 'in-country' often appreciate the flexibility of conflict settings and thus understand the need regularly to adjust their approach; they also appreciate being engaged in discussions on such approaches.

Just as we sometimes struggle to translate our 'on s'engage et après on voit' approach into proposals that require measurable outputs and indicators, we have found that donor representatives on the ground often struggle with the linear structure within their own agencies from where funds are disbursed. It is not unusual for donor representatives to voice frustration when they are told that the country in which they are based is no longer considered to be in a humanitarian crisis: it is now in a development phase, or out of a development phase and into a democratization or rule of law phase, and so their allocation of funds must be adjusted accordingly. We have often found that both donors and our staff on the ground agree that situations rarely shift neatly from one phase to another, and that most dynamic conflict situations fluctuate between what appear to be several phases at once. The result is that we and our donors may work together to present projects and proposals in ways that satisfy bureaucratic necessities for donor accountability while acknowledging that the work and context on the ground will very likely not follow the same linear progression or fit neatly into the same category. We have been fortunate to have donor-partners who are sympathetic to our approach.

Conclusion: Remember the Human Element and Choose to Hope

There is a welcome effort from many quarters to identify, share and, where possible, replicate best practices in the field of conflict transformation. The Reflecting on Peace Practices (RPP) project set up by Dr. Mary Anderson's Collaborative for Development Action, as well as the efforts of donors including USAID and the Swedish Foreign Ministry to identify and disseminate best practices and lessons learned, and are all advancing the field. At best, these efforts reinforce the human element at the centre of this work. In the end, all our work at Common Ground can be described as an attempt to transform and empower individuals (and organizations made up of individuals) to make possible what may seem impossible.

To do this with integrity we believe there is no choice about whether or not to be optimistic—it is imperative. Anyone who has worked as an expatriate in a conflict zone in Africa is well acquainted with the dynamic of the cynical expatriate community that meets for drinks in the evenings and on weekends to bemoan the corruption of a government or the hopelessness of the situation in which they find themselves. Notwithstanding the desire to air frustrations from time to time, the last thing that Burundi, Angola, or any community struggling to cope with prolonged violent conflict needs is more cynicism.

At Common Ground we try to embrace and reinforce the hope of others. We do not strive for naïve idealism, but we do seek windows of opportunity and try to support those individuals and groups that bring hope into what might otherwise appear to be hopeless situations. More to the point, we believe that in many of the places in which we work, if we do not view the situation from a perspective of hope, we will never recognize it around us. No matter how impossible situations appear from the outside, experience tells us that once we have committed ourselves and have established a presence on the ground, we have ample reason for hope, be it in the efforts of local individuals, civil activists, religious leaders, government officials, or military officers. At our best, we consolidate their efforts so that their discrete initiatives, however insignificant, may together build a broader movement for social change in their communities.

CONCLUSION

VIOLENT CONFLICT AND CONFLICT PREVENTION IN AFRICA:
AN ALTERNATIVE RESEARCH AGENDA

Ulf Engel

The contributions to this volume have sought to reflect on the complex discourse on violent conflict and conflict prevention in sub-Saharan Africa which has developed since the early 1990s. This discourse deals with at least two separate, but closely interconnected questions. Firstly, it is about the perceived knowledge of violent conflict in Africa.[1] Secondly, it is about the practical conclusions one could draw from these insights and their translation into conflict prevention, management and resolution. Those participating in the debate are both academics and practitioners—scholars, activists, bureaucrats, politicians, etc. During the past decade dialogue at the interface between academia and practice has increased tremendously. Since then the debate has produced its own orthodoxy. As regards observation and interpretation it is characterized by a search for causation and effect; theory building is either dominated by rational-choice inspired approaches and 'modified rational actor models' (the 'greed' argument) or by a variety of identity-oriented approaches (the 'grievance' school). And in practice it is preoccupied with various post-conflict efforts at reconstruction.

The actual results of both academic debate and practice are, however, sobering. With regard to the former, Cramer maintains that 'the empirical evidence for grand claims about the predictive success of models based on [specific] variables is weak, affected by data imperfection and sample selection bias' (chap. 1 of this volume, p. 24). According to this line of argument, social science simply has too little to offer politics. In contrast, Collier and Sambanis (2003: 3) claim that 'many policies towards conflict have been guided by little more than rules of thumb derived by practitioners from their experience.

---

[1] For an overview see World Bank 2003.

Policy has not rested on a solid foundation of research-driven knowledge'. According to this view the 'knowledge' acquired from the social sciences has in practice been ignored. Finally, and quite irritatingly, practice is to a large extent dominated by conflict *management* and *resolution*—rather than genuine conflict *prevention* (see van Walraven, chap. 4 in this volume).[2] Very few interventions are designed from a genuine perspective of conflict prevention, and even fewer are implemented in this way.

Leaving aside questions of policy formulation and implementation (or whether 'solid' information translates into 'good' policy), what sort of information is needed for a policy which is not reactive, but preventive? My argument is that, in spite of the empirical and practical merits of the debate on violent conflict in Africa, orthodoxy obscures the social dynamics and agency of violence. By focusing on questions of causation rather than on dynamics and agency orthodoxy has *de facto* aided and abetted concentration on post-conflict reconstruction. In order to be able to generate information with practical relevance to conflict prevention, however, different sorts of questions need to be asked and a different method conceptualized.

In this final chapter I will outline such an alternative research agenda. I will develop my argument, firstly, by discussing the main weaknesses of the current orthodoxy on the discussion on violent conflict and conflict prevention in sub-Saharan Africa (this cannot be separated from the complex history of discourse formation which, therefore, will be briefly reviewed); and, secondly, by reflecting the major challenges that conflict prevention in Africa is facing today. I conclude that a focus on violence and agency rather than conflict and causation is necessary, arguing that the search for a different methodological approach should be inspired by 'cultural studies' and the insights of 'post-modern' sociology.

What Do We Know about Conflict in Africa?

To understand the merits and constraints of current research on conflict in Africa (excluding the more general history of peace and con-

---

[2] For a general review, Lund 2000; Mehler and Ribaux 2000; on Germany Debiel and Matthies 2000; Engel 2001.

flict studies), I need to trace the genesis of this debate.[3] This section will concentrate on the post-Cold War era and the emergence of a different perspective on 'new wars' in Africa and conflict prevention as a discourse. I will briefly introduce the contributions of some of the leading analysts—advocates, practitioners and academics—and highlight the conventional wisdom on the subject. This orthodoxy is typically expressed within the parameters of an academic debate and is commonly referred to as the 'greed or grievance' argument. On this basis, I offer below a critique of the orthodox approach.

Discovering 'the Dark Side of Globalization'

The debate on violent conflict and conflict prevention in Africa did not issue from a void. The very notion of 'new wars' (cf. Kaldor 1999) implies that there have been 'old wars'. Indeed, there is a strong element of the historicity of violent conflict in Africa, a *longue durée* of conflict (Ellis 2003a; Govea and Holm 1998). And, of course, this has also been addressed by African Studies. There is a tradition of research into the inter-state wars of Africa's post-colonial period (as there has been research on pre-colonial and colonial violence), and there is research on the large number of military coups. One particular strand has dealt with wars of liberation, primarily in Africa's settler regimes. The early 1980s heralded a fresh approach to post-colonial studies. Historians, for example, began to look at peasant violence in the context of anti-colonial struggles and anti-state rebellions. There was debate on apartheid-related violence in South Africa. Underclass, 'lumpen' and peasant violence continued to be analysed, the latter often in terms of conflicts over land rights. However, during the Cold War all these debates were very much rooted in area studies and somewhat detached from general conflict studies (or the more pragmatic research on conflict resolution).

---

[3] Conflict in Africa was established as a mainstream discipline, from a sociology of science perspective, in the USA between 1945 and 1965 and comprised psychology, comparative politics and international relations. Conflict studies was mainly concerned with inter-state wars which were perceived as a threat to the precarious stability the West enjoyed under the hegemonic US-USSR world order (see Miall et al. 1999: 39–64). In addition a European, mainly Scandinavian, school of peace studies was developed in the 1960s. It was inspired by neo-Marxism and critical of the existing empiricist nature of the field (cf. Jabri 1996: 11). From both perspectives Africa hardly qualified as an object of research.

It was only after the end of the Cold War that the new discourse on conflict prevention in Africa emerged. 1992 was a symbolic watershed: conflicts in Sierra Leone, Somalia and Bosnia reinforced the new image of conflict in general and of conflict in Africa in particular. These developments were seen as markers for another trend, the arrival of an era of 'new wars', characterized by the erosion of territorially based state authority or, as Kaldor (1999) argues, the erosion of state monopolies of violence and in particular state sovereignty. Accordingly, both globalization from above and privatization from below led to a crisis in the 'nation state'. Inter-state wars were replaced by intra-state wars. Identity politics was said to take the place of the geo-political or ideological goals of earlier wars. The mode of denationalized and privatized warfare changed, the actors involved increased and the dynamics became more complex. According to Allen (1999: 369 ff.), Africa's 'new wars' are characterized by violence, targeted directly at civilians rather than armed groups, extreme brutality and barbarity, state initiation or sponsorship of violence, opportunistic looting, and warlordism.

Framing Conflict Prevention

But what from a distance appears to be a focused academic discourse, again lacks cohesion. Not only did the boundaries between disciplines become increasingly blurred (this proved to be rather productive), but the role played by those who could be labelled 'discourse brokers' (i.e. advocates, practitioners or academics) became uncertain as well. Depending on the context, academics contributed to the debate as consultants, advocates became practitioners and—on occasion—vice versa.

Initially, the 'new wars' were addressed by international advocacy NGOs and think tanks. Actors such as International Alert, Saferworld, Global Witness, the Dutch National Committee for International Cooperation and Sustainable Development or the European Platform for Conflict Prevention and Transformation, a network of European NGOs working on peace-building initiatives, took the lead as classic 'norm entrepreneurs' who commanded organizational platforms (Finnemore & Sikkink 1998: 898). They organized workshops, networked practitioners and scholars, and attempted to influence public opinion on issues such as the principles of conflict prevention, the need for early warning and early action, gender and conflict, resources and conflict, etc. In addition, US-based think tanks such as the Carnegie Endowment for International Peace (which in 1994 established the Carnegie Commission on Preventing Deadly Conflict), the US Institute for Peace, the UN-sponsored International Peace Academy and the Clingendael Institute, a think tank of the Dutch Foreign Ministry, played a key role in introducing African conflict to the international agenda and framing policy responses.

Early on, these efforts were mirrored by practitioners who operated in two separate spheres that rarely overlapped. Debate was divided between politicians, diplomats and the military—the securocrats—and other politicians, development agencies and NGOs—the developmentalists (for detailed references see Engel 2001). At the beginning of the 1990s the securocrats dominated the debate. After 1994, the developmentalists got the upper hand, at least up to 1999/2000 when the pendulum swung back again in the aftermath of the NATO intervention in Kosovo. Since 9/11 the debate has been hijacked by securocrats, with developmentalists desperately trying to sell their 'portfolio assets' (e.g. poverty alleviation and institution building) as a contribution to the 'war against terrorism' (cf. Rotberg 2002).

The classic securocrat school of thought was highlighted in the UN Secretary General's 'Agenda for Peace' (UNSG 1992), which was informed by the West's experience that military peace-making became more of an option when both preventive and track-two diplomacy (i.e. interaction outside official negotiations) had failed. Subsequently, the OAU Mechanism for Conflict Prevention, Management and Resolution (established in 1993) as well as African initiatives in the field of early warning, preventive diplomacy and peace keeping featured prominently in this discussion.

In contrast, developmentalists not only focused on non-military means, but also developed a strong sense of preventive action. Initial input came from the 1994 annual UNDP report that highlighted the human and material costs of violent conflict and called for the establishment of an early warning system. The EU Commission soon took a leading role in consolidating this position (Landgraf 1998), with the most comprehensive documents being developed by the EU Commission and the EU Council, the OECD DAC and, again, the UN Secretary General. The focus was now on prevention, coherence, early and targeted action, and the co-ordination of international efforts in this direction.

National development agencies followed suit and tried to link their traditional instruments (development assistance) to what they perceived as new challenges. Currently, the question of 'failed states' or 'states at risk' is at the fore (see below). In these debates, academics-cum-consultants often played a crucial role in framing simple principles of action (such as 'do no harm', cf. Anderson 1996, 1999).[4]

The role played by academics in the debate on conflict and conflict prevention is somewhat difficult to gauge, the functions are too confused and the network of research, debate, and policy advice too intertwined. Nevertheless, one might differentiate between explicit contributions to practical debates, academic discussions with a practical relevance (cf. Gurr 2002, note 14), area study-based chronicles or narratives of specific conflicts, and an academic discourse of a more general nature.

Firstly, most practical contributions, often in the form of consultants' reports, aim to develop instruments and project management tools for the different phases of a putative conflict cycle. This includes the controversial debate on early warning systems (both the method and final use of which were highly contentious). Ambitious projects include the Swiss Peace Foundation's FAST, the network Forum for Early Warning and Early Response (FEWER), and the Dutch PIOOM (Interdisciplinary Research of Root Causes of Human Rights Violations). More recently very practical contributions have aimed at placing the concept into the mainstream of conflict prevention in development aid. This includes the design of Strategic Conflict Analysis as well as Peace and Conflict Impact Assessments (for an overview Ropers and Fischer 2001). The latter is a fine example of how an aid agency, the British Department for International Development, successfully managed to set the agenda and gain international discourse hegemony by generously sourcing out research to British institutions (cf. Goodhand 2001; Hulme and Goodhand 2000).

Secondly, a more indirect contribution to the debate, written from an academic perspective and primarily for an academic audience, is the body of research that deals with institutions of conflict management and resolution. First and foremost, this refers to works on power

---

[4] Some of them were old hands at conflict studies (e.g. Gurr 1995; Lederach 1997 or Lund 1997, 2000).

sharing and the practicalities of implementing peace accords—both of which are increasingly of interest to practitioners (for an overview cf. Engel 2003). On the borderline between academic debate and policy advice are critical contributions that call for dialogue between academics and practitioners, for instance on the relationship between development aid and conflict (see Uvin 1999 and Klingebiel 1999 on the 'unintended consequences of aid'), and the role of the international system in 'best practice' in post-conflict reconstruction and humanitarian interventions.

Thirdly, country specialists have contributed to the acquisition of knowledge. The Great Lakes, Somalia, Sierra Leone and Liberia feature very prominently in empirical studies. A learning exercise on the 1994 genocide in Rwanda (Joint Evaluation 1996) has had a particularly powerful impact. Finally, academics with specialized knowledge have focused on the question of causation and on 'new' actors, such as warlords or urban youth movements. Two different arguments in particular have emerged about the 'root causes' of conflict— one concentrating on ethnicity (and identity), the other on the political economy of conflict. Generally speaking the debate on the relative importance of economic factors in fuelling violent conflict has been reduced to a simple 'greed vs. grievance' dichotomy.[5]

---

[5] For a general overview see Berdal and Malone 2000; Cilliers and Mason 1999; for a critique, see Marchal and Messiant 2002. For an overview of major theoretical contributions to the 'grievance' debate see Anna-Maria Gentili's contribution in this volume (chap. 2), for the 'greed' school see Christopher Cramer's contribution (chap. 1). The econometric modelling of conflict is most closely associated with the World Bank's research programme on 'The Economics of Civil War, Crime and Violence' (headed by the bank's then research director, Paul Collier, and Ibrahim Elbadawi; see http://econ.worldbank.org/programs/conflict/). For an interesting critique see Fearon and Laitin (2003). This tradition of research is based on the rational choice 'logic of consequentialism' which relates to the *homo oeconomicus* (most consultants associate prevailing tool-box approaches with structure-functionalism and universal claims). Jackson (2003: 6f.) associates this line of argument with structuralist or bounded rationality approaches. According to Jabri (1996: 11 f.) this research tradition reflects the positivist inheritance of mainstream peace and conflict studies. In contrast, identity arguments are usually influenced by cultural studies and/or sociological (neo)-institutionalism. They tend to be informed by a 'logic of appropriateness' (March and Olsen 1989) which emphasizes the role of identities, rules and institutions in shaping the behaviour of an assumed *homo sociologicus* (March and Olsen 1998: 951). In addition Mkandawire (2002: 183–191)—who partly follows Allen (1999: 373 f.)—identifies an apocalyptic and culturalist perspective in current explanations of violent conflict in Africa. However, from an epistemological angle this differentiation does not add extra value.

Critique of Orthodoxy

Far from being able adequately to summarize the whole debate, I have limited my remarks to three basic observations on the types of conflict analysed, on what appears to constitute the major research interest and state of methodological debate.

Firstly, mainstream research is only concerned with a specific type of conflict that, I maintain, is certainly important but is not the most relevant form of conflict in Africa—both in terms of frequency and from the perspective of conflict *prevention*. The bias of the orthodox view is illustrated by a recent critique by Collier and Hoeffler (2002) of a publication of the Stockholm International Peace Research Institute (Wallensteen and Sollenberg 2001): a discussion between academics who deal with the quantitative side of conflict in Africa. The issue at stake is whether the frequency and intensity of violent conflict has increased in the 1990s (SIPRI) or not (Collier and Hoeffler).[6] Irrespective of who is right, the arguments demonstrate a preoccupation with a specific form of conflict. Both models, that of the SIPRI and Collier and Hoeffler, are based on a standard definition of conflict derived from Cold War conflict studies: that is, conflict defined by 1,000 combat-related deaths. Similarly, advocates of the 'grievance' argument tend to focus on major conflicts in which identity discourses play a major role—the Rwandan genocide, for example, or the subsequent war in the DR Congo or the internal war in the Sudan.

Some of Africa's armed conflicts fall into this category, but quite a few do not. There are the myriad small-scale violent conflicts which are characteristic of many places in Africa and which are highly relevant to any conflict *preventive* action that deserves the name. Neither the current political crisis in Zimbabwe (to take an obvious case), in Uganda (to quote a neglected case) nor in Malawi (to name a less obvious candidate for potential conflict) would qualify as orthodox subjects for that kind of research, nor would they provide the required

---

[6] Collier and Hoeffler (2003c) claim, firstly, that the incidence of conflict in Africa is similar to that in other developing regions. Secondly, they found that non-African countries have become less conflict-prone over the past 35 years. Thirdly, Africa has indeed experienced a rising trend of conflict. However, they state, 'this is fully accounted for by divergent trends in African and non-African economic conditions' (ibid.: 14). Poor economic performance, thus, has been identified as the key variable. On the general problems associated with comparing violence related data see Eberwein and Chojnacki 2001.

data. Most of these conflicts are not part of mainstream research and, to some extend, they are also outside its methodological competence (of course, Collier and Hoeffler do not pretend to be able to address these conflicts).

Issues of low-level, small-scale, day-to-day experience and routine violence hardly come into the ambit of orthodox research. From the perspective of conflict *prevention*—that is, from the perspective of engineering social, economic and political processes in order to enable societies to manage change without resorting to violence[7]—the focus of this research barely provides an insight into critical junctures, pathways, interests or motivation. The question is, what sort of knowledge is needed to engage in conflict *prevention*?[8] What sort of questions should be asked to produce the information needed to target *potential* violent conflict early enough to be effective?

Secondly, the prevailing academic debate is dominated by cause and effect. This is true for both the predominant 'grievance' and 'greed' schools of thought. Since the mid-1990s research into Africa's conflicts has been heavily biased towards the question of what has brought about certain violent conflicts. Obviously the genocide in Rwanda and the apparent failure of many actors to translate early information on imminent violence into any meaningful political strategy or action has fuelled this tendency. Early debates among practitioners have concentrated on early warning systems. At the same time a broad consensus has emerged according to which violence in Africa is caused by a mixture of insecurity, inequality, private incentives and perceptions (Gardner 2002: 15 f.; see also Porto 2002). In addition, it is widely felt that the reasons for violence interact over time and space, that there are structural factors at play (or 'root causes') and mobilizing factors (Gardner 2002: 16).

Currently more sophisticated conflict prevention approaches are investing heavily in enhanced research into questions of causation. Thus, practitioners have begun addressing more complex scenarios which include conflict mapping (the reconstruction of popular dominant narratives), structure (root causes, including political culture,

---

[7] This follows the definition of the EU Commission (1996, 2001).

[8] Defined by the EU as, respectively, 'activities undertaken over the short term to reduce manifest tensions and/or to prevent the outbreak or recurrence of violent conflict' and 'activities undertaken over the medium and longer term to address root causes of violent conflict in a targeted manner'.

inadequate governance, unequal opportunity, inequality), actors (interests, relations, capacity and resources, strategies, dynamics, peace
agendas, incentives) and dynamics (aggravating factors, inhibiting
factors, exit options, voice options, existing mechanisms, government
policies, donor policies, triggering factors).[9]

Against this background von Trotha (1997) has denounced as deficient the state of research and theory building on violent conflict
(although he was not looking at Africa specifically, his general statement applies nevertheless). The current scholarship that von Trotha
criticized was not, however, a sociology of violence after all but a
sociology of the *causes* of violence. Indeed, the debate on Africa is
characterized by a lopsided concentration on certain obvious questions
of causation, neglecting the nature and dynamics of violence as such.
Mainstream research on African conflicts seems to be fascinated by
violent conflict itself rather than by the question of how societal principles of regulation have changed towards the use of violence. There
is a preoccupation with the 'quantity' rather than the 'quality' of conflict. The advanced decline of the state's monopoly on the legitimate
used of violence generates more attention than the early stages leading up to this process. Groups seem to be more important than individuals and their decision to participate in or instigate violence. There
is much analysis after the event as to what went wrong, but little
evaluation before of the actual pathways leading to violent conflict.

Thirdly, apart from the 'greed vs. grievance' dichotomy little effort
has been made to build theory when it comes to conflict in Africa.[10]
Thus the relative mix of the 'root cause' of conflict, its systematic
correlation and work within specific contexts is far from being understood. Jackson (2003: 7) rightly argues that although this research is
important it usually 'fail[s] to explain why very similar societies that
share the same structural features most commonly associated with
conflict—poverty, salient ethnic or social divisions, minority grievances, failing government institutions, lack of national identity, low
levels of state legitimacy—produce radically different conflict histories. And why internal wars erupt when they do, and not earlier or
later.' While some observers suggest that the fragmentation, interconnectedness and, at times, mutual exclusivity of current attempts
to understand conflict in Africa are the key problems (cf. Porto 2002: 1),

---

[9] See DfID 2001 and GTZ 2001.
[10] For exceptions to the German debate see von Trotha 2000 and Elwert 1997.

I would like to take this argument a step further. What is missing is an ontological debate linking 'root causes' and other structuring determinants impinging on agency to the individuals who perpetrate violence or experience it.

What Do we Know about Conflict Prevention in Africa?

Conflict prevention is dominated by reactive policies, as van Walraven explains in detail in chapter 4. In real life politicians, bureaucrats, aid workers and the military are predominantly concerned with peace enforcement, (increasingly armed) humanitarian interventions, pragmatic power-sharing arrangements, the demobilization of ex-combatants, proliferation of small arms, post-war reconstruction, etc. Very few interventions are designed and implemented with a prophylactic, precautionary or protective purpose. Administrative and political routines are constrained by limited resources and the need for immediate answers to often rather unpredictable—and in the end open-ended—questions. Thus, time, funds and manpower are prioritized for the benefit of what is perceived as the world's, and sometimes also Africa's, most pressing problems. And these are obviously related to the volatile and precarious nature of the post-Cold War international system and, on occasion, the nature of the African state.

The image of 'new wars' is closely related to another popular representation—that of Africa's 'failed states' (like 'new wars', 'failed states' also preceded the end of the Cold War).[11] In many countries neo-patrimonial rule has reached the limit of sustainability. Subsequently elites have had to reconfigure their states (Villalón and Huxtable 1998). This has worked fairly well in some cases; in others decline has accelerated and the state has had to give up any claim to the legitimate monopoly of the means of violence.[12] Large geographical

---

[11] An outline of this discourse appears in Engel 2002.

[12] This process has been described in terms of 'juridical statehood' (Jackson and Rosberg 1986), 'state collapse' (Zartman 1995), 'degrees of statehood' (Clapham 1998), 'triumph of the shadow state' (Reno 1996), the 'instrumentalization of disorder' (Chabal and Daloz 1999) and 'criminalization of the state' (Bayart et al. 1999). Africa's new social spaces have been conceptualized either in terms of 'para-stateness' (von Trotha 2000), 'violence-open space' (Elwert 1997—denoting spaces used and created by warlords, where the state monopoly of the means of violence is absent), 'state-free space' (Stroux 2003) or 'state-distant social space' (Baberowski et al. 2003) where the state has not penetrated society, either deeply or permanently, and dominant perceptions of power are not rooted in the state but in societal forms of organization.

areas have become war zones where the state has ceased to 'function' and any useful social structure barely exists. New frontiers have emerged where states have no authority. Instead self-sufficient and self-imposed forms of violence dominate (cf. Nobles 1997). New transnationalisms and translocalisms have arisen (cf. Callaghy et al. 2001). And new actors have emerged—although some, if not all, may have been there already but failed to achieve either political or academic recognition.

The extent to which current efforts at conflict prevention, management and resolution in these new social spaces depend on the existence of at least a modicum of state control is crucial from the point of view of policy (cf. Duffield 2001; Maull 2002, Mehler 2003). This applies in two ways. Firstly, many policies which were meant to address the practical problems relating to state disintegration were devised under the Westphalian order of territorial and sovereign nation-states with a view to address state structures. Their operation is overwhelmingly dependent on the existence of structures of a similar nature. They are therefore difficult to implement where these structures are absent. And, secondly, the implicit purpose of all these interventions is the re-establishment of the state itself.[13]

Here conflict prevention, management and resolution face a difficult situation:[14] how can institutions be reinvented *and* sustained when they have failed because of institutional weakness? How does one reinforce 'pockets of rationality' in neo-patrimonial settings, that is, rational bureaucratic order as opposed to patrimonial rule? How can crumbling state monopolies of violence be protected?[15] How can conflict be reduced in powerful constituencies and peace strengthened in weaker ones? How can the current policy instruments be applied, developed or improved to increase a state's legitimacy and efficiency? How can economic performance and the capacity to deliver be improved? Why should one assume that 'the international community' is interested in devoting financial and human resources to achieve

---

[13] I am not discussing the normative desirability of the state as an organization nor the question of whether the state in many parts of Africa is the standard or the exception.

[14] From an academic point of view these problems may reflect different methodological questions. Yet from a practitioner's point of view, this debate really seems fairly academic.

[15] Or are there ways to establish sustainable and legitimate oligopolies of the means of violence, Mehler (2003) asks.

any of this—provided that there was a deeper understanding of the problem—given the narrow self-interest of the OECD. And why would one expect international organizations such as the UN or the World Bank to be able effectively to ease the burden of violence affecting African societies, knowing that their culture of bureaucracy often favours 'dysfunctional, or even pathological, behaviour' which undermines their own objectives?[16] It seems to me that the information available on violent conflict and conflict prevention in Africa cannot provide satisfying answers to most of these questions. Although many, but certainly not all, participants would profess that their research has immediate practical relevance, I doubt that this is really the case. Careful scrutiny of current developments indicates that from a problem-solving perspective other questions should be asked.

The major challenge conflict prevention is facing today is, however, related to defining intervention points *before* 'state failure' becomes an issue. Irrespective of limited funding, few commitments, lack of interest from the media, etc. the development of a culture of prevention rather than the continuation of the orthodoxy of post-conflict policy response is the only way of having a chance of tackling these problems more effectively, more cheaply and with a greater prospect of success.

Conventional wisdom suggests it is plausible, and recent research confirms that there are important points to address regarding external intervention prior to 'state failure'. Clearly, the loss of state monopoly on the instruments of violence is not automatic. The very reason for the disintegration of the African state is the result of low levels of institutionalization, the neo-patrimonial nature of post-colonial politics (cf. Erdmann and Engel, forthcoming), and the combined effects of permanent economic crisis, structural adjustment and globalization (van de Walle 2001). The process of state disintegration usually develops along four trajectories (Engel 2003):[17] through deliberate transfer (weak state monopolies have led to the outsourcing of key functions, resulting in delegated legitimacy), abandonment because of under performance (i.e. inability to fulfil core functions such as

---

[16] As discussed by Barnett and Finnemore 1999 who illustrate their theoretical argument, *inter alia*, with examples from UN peace-keeping.
[17] For a slightly different set of pathways cf. Clapham 1998 who is looking at the displacement of the state, the emergence of insurgencies and 'the privatization of state power'.

the provision of public goods or security); erosion caused by illegit-
imate state action (such as despotism); or violent contestation (see
Allen 1999 on 'politics as violence'). Detailed knowledge of the dynamics of these trajectories will prove essential to a new assessment of
the conflict prevention debate.

What Should we Know? An Alternative Research Agenda

This short overview of the history of the discourse on violent conflict and conflict prevention in Africa has pinpointed a number of
shortcomings. This discourse is characterized by fragmentation of
disciplines and, occasionally, mutually exclusive theoretical assumptions. It is preoccupied with cause and effect. The relative mix of
causes, their correlation and their function within specific contexts
is not at all clear. The literature concentrates on conflicts that have
already escalated into violence and on violent conflict involving large
numbers of victims, rather than on potentially violent conflict before
the outbreak of hostilities has actually begun, or on small-scale violence with few casualties. Despite the abundance of literature on the
subject, a sociology of violence in Africa has not yet been developed.
In short, the focus is on conflict, not on violence.

In addition, even superficial scrutiny of current efforts at conflict
prevention, management and resolution reveals that a culture of prevention *sui generis* does not yet exist. Policy is concerned with real,
but rarely with potential, 'trouble spots'. Despite advances in systematic approaches, administrative routines are rarely informed by
conflict prevention. Public attention is still centred on conflicts that
have already broken out rather than those likely to erupt in the distant future. In short, the 'mainstreaming' of conflict prevention—
another buzzword from the technocratic global governance world—has
only begun (Lund 2002; Engel 2001). There is instead a preoccupation
with situations where the state monopoly of the means of violence
has already have disintegrated.

It would seem there is too little academic information available for
practitioners to develop in this respect. In order to be able to produce information with practical relevance to conflict *prevention*, different questions need to be asked and another method has to be
devised. There are at least two possible avenues for the study of vio-

lent conflict in Africa, for which the potential has not yet been fully developed: 'cultural studies' and 'post-modern sociology'. Neither represents a consistent theory or a distinct body of thought, but they provide a certain scientific perspective. And important insights into the dynamics of violent conflict have already been produced by research informed by these ideas, though rarely relating to African Studies. Among the most interesting contributions on Africa are Mbembe's treatises on the post-colony (1992a), the banality of power and the aesthetics of vulgarity (1992b), and some studies on street culture and youth violence (Biaya 2000; Glaser 1998; Gore and Pratton 2003). These share a perspective on violence that goes beyond effect/cause debates because they address the dynamics of violence (rather than conflict) and ask how and why actors act in the way they do. Although by no means informed by a common approach or methodology, these works help in understanding certain mechanisms operating outside bounded rationality that make people change from non-violent to violent behaviour.

The developing body of literature on the close relationship between witchcraft and violence (Geschiere and Fisiy 1994; Mavhungu 2000), to give another example, provides an additional facet to understanding the emergence of violence between local and national arenas in the processes of 'modernization'. Another crucial aspect—the context of violence and the meaning and relevance of 'local' and 'cultural' in respect to this—is highlighted in the controversy that has developed between Ellis (2003b) and Mkandawire (2002, 2003). The latter rightly stresses that the context of violence is not only cultural, but also 'economic, political, epistemological, and so on' (2003: 480); 'it is also layered and situated between the local, translocal, . . . and global' (cf. Latham 2001).[18]

However, more research is necessary not only to analyse violence as a cultural resource (e.g. the legitimacy of violence, ideologies of violence, the role of religion and other belief systems), but also to make a serious attempt at establishing a more systematic approach. There is a great need for information on the actors involved in violent action, their rationale and the dynamics between the actors and

---

[18] Mkandawire also argues against a culturalist, almost essentializing perspective allegedly employed by Ellis.

their actions. This includes the interplay between the fantasies of violence of intellectuals on the one hand, and the interests of the poor, urban under-classes and/or peasants on the other.[19]

Whilst these questions should certainly produce some of the information now lacking, one needs to be careful about the method of approach to avoid some of the pitfalls of shifting from social history to cultural history, as experienced by, for example, Latin America Studies (resulting in a concentration on discourses, hidden transcripts of social action, rituals of power and symbolism, to the neglect of the political dimension of violence; cf. Baberowski et al. 2003).[20] The innovative concerns of cultural studies have to be recontextualized from a perspective of discursive analysis (Abrahamsen 2003) with a view to dissecting structures of signification and legitimation (Jabri 1996: 82 f.). The sociology of violence (von Trotha) that is called for in research on Africa's violent conflicts should find the 'place of discursive practices as well as structural systems of domination' (Jabri 1996: 23). Jabri, with help from Giddens's structuration theory, has been looking into violent conflict as a product of society. Accordingly, war is seen as the result of discursive formations and institutional continuities which are manipulated by political elites. War is conceptualized as a social continuity.[21] Jabri offers a fascinating attempt at understanding 'the discursive and institutional processes which reproduce war and violent conflict' (ibid.: vii). With the help of structuration theory, she develops an ontological argument on the place of war in the constitutive relationship between self and society. Her focus is on how individual and exclusionist identities are shaped by social discourse and institutional formations: 'The argument is that violent conflict is itself structurated through the actions of agents situated in relation to discursive and institutional continuities which both enable war's occurrence and legitimate it as a form of human behaviour' (ibid.: 4).

---

[19] Though not specifically geared towards African Studies, Nedelmann (1997) *inter alia* has called for the integration of the (cultural, political, ideological, etc.) meaning given by persons involved in violent interaction and the development of a theory of the bodily constitution of social subjectivity. See, for instance, reflections on masculinity in Natal (Campbell 1992; Waetjen and Maré 1999).

[20] These trends have been criticized as 'decorative sociology' (Rojek and Turner 2000); the alternative is a restoration of cultural sociology.

[21] One conclusion of Jabri's approach is that agency, in principle, has the capacity to address war discourses by counter-hegemonial peace discourses. In practice, this idea still calls for an operationalization.

'One of the insights that post-colonialism borrows and develops from post-structural and postmodernist perspectives', Abrahamsen (2003: 198) maintains, 'is a view of power as productive of identities and subjectivities'. From this perspective 'power is no longer perceived as only repressive, nor is it understood in purely material or institutional terms. Instead, power is productive, and creative of subjects' (ibid.). From the point of view of social science in general this perspective is not new. With a similar interest in mind Fearon and Laitin (2000: 846 f.) have called for the rigorous testing of different constructivist approaches (based on discursive logic, the strategic actions of either elites or masses). To them one of the major puzzles still to be solved is 'why ethnic publics follow leaders down paths that seem to serve elite power interests most of all' (ibid.: 846). On this very point Jackson (2002b: 3) argues that non-violent discourses are replaced 'with socially constructed war discourses'.

In his—and Jabris's—perspective, 'it is the rise and domination of certain minds of conflict discourses (and not simply the presence of certain structural features or processes of political conflict) that turn weak states into societies at war' (ibid.: 7). Discourses on war are understood, according to Foucault's notion of discourse formation, as 'large power-knowledge regimes' that go beyond language and text, and are constituted in social and institutional practices (ibid.: 8). In short, what needs to be scrutinized is the mutual construction of violent agency and violent action through discursive formation. The analysis of physical violence, cultural taboos and power needs to be integrated with a focus on both discursive and institutional continuities and disruptions.

Finally, and looking beyond the perspective of mere problem-solving, the debate on conflict prevention must also critically address the mutual constitution of endogenous and exogenous agency: how do external interventions and the reasons for them taking place contribute to violence and how are they affected by discourses on violence? There are at least two interrelated aspects that call for closer scrutiny: the 'commodification' of conflict prevention, and the use of violence as a means of interaction. Conflict prevention has increasingly been a part of international politics. It is an area with clear budget lines and protocols for intervention in, among other places, Africa. The mere existence of these resources, one could argue, could become a conflict-prolonging factor. Humanitarian assistance, track-two mediation, post-war recovery and reconstruction money, etc. have increasingly become part of the rationale of parties in conflict.

On the other hand, becoming a party to conflict in the first place is often seen as the only chance to air grievances or to voice concern.[22] Here, the interventions of the donor, the representations of the causes of conflict can be as crucial as the nature of the parties to conflict themselves. Jabri (1996: 180) rightly warns that hegemonic discourses on violence are also 'reproduced through the representations of observers, conflict researchers and third parties attempting mediation'. This relationship is more complicated than the debate on the simple causation of 'harm' in terms of the 'unintended consequences of aid'. The 'annexation of social science' by politics (Bilgin and Morton 2002) may be one of the unintended consequences of the discourse on violent conflict and conflict prevention in Africa. So is the effect of the analysis of representation and identity formation which are believed to fuel violent conflict.

Bibliography

Abrahamsen, R. (2003), 'African Studies and the postcolonial challenge', *African Affairs*, vol. 102, no. 407, pp. 189–210.

Allen, C. (1999), 'Warfare, Endemic Violence & State Collapse in Africa', *Review of African Political Economy*, vol. 26, no. 81, pp. 367–384.

Anderson, M.B. (1999), *Do No Harm. How Aid can Support Peace—or War*, London, Boulder CO, Lynne Rienner.

Baberowski, J., U. Engel and M. Riekenberg (2003), 'Intellektuelle und Unterschichtengewalt in staatsfernen Gesellschaften—Rußland/Sowjetunion, Südafrika und Mexiko 1870–1940', Berlin, Leipzig (mimeo).

Barnett, M.N. and M. Finnemore (1999), 'The Politics, Power, and Pathologies of International Organizations', *International Organization*, vol. 53, no. 4, pp. 699–732.

Bayart, J.-F. (1989), *L'État En Afrique. La politique du ventre*, Paris, Fayard.

Berdal, M. and D.M. Malone (eds.) (2000), *Greed and Grievance: Economic Agendas in Civil Wars*, Boulder CO, Lynne Rienner.

Biaya, T.K. (2000), 'Jeunes et culture de la rue en Afrique urbaine (Addis-Abeba, Dakar et Kinshasa)', *Politique africaine*, no. 80, pp. 12–31.

Callaghy, T. et al. (eds.) (2001), *Intervention and Transnationalism in Africa. Global Local Networks of Power*, Cambridge, Cambridge University Press.

Campbell, C. (1992), 'Learning to Kill? Masculinity, the Family and Violence in Natal', *Journal of Southern African Studies*, vol. 18, no. 3, pp. 614–628.

Chabal, P. (1991), 'Pouvoir et violence en Afrique postcolonial', *Politique Africaine*, no. 42, pp. 51–64.

——— and Daloz, J.-P. (1999), *Africa Works. Disorder as Political Instrument*, Oxford, Bloomington IN, James Currey.

---

[22] The dynamics in Nigeria's Niger Delta are a striking example (cf. Gore & Pratton 2003).

Cilliers, J. and P. Mason (eds.) (1999), *Peace, Profit or Plunder? The Privatization of Security in War-torn African Societies*, Halfway House, Institute for Security Studies.

Clapham, C. (1998), 'Degrees of Statehood', *Review of International Studies*, vol. 24, no. 2, pp. 143–157.

Collier, P. and A. Hoeffler (2002), 'On the Incidence of Civil War in Africa', *Journal of Conflict Resolution*, vol. 46, no. 1, pp. 13–28.

—— and N. Sambanis (2002), 'Understanding Civil War: A New Agenda', *Journal of Conflict Resolution*, vol. 46, no. 1, pp. 3–12.

Debiel, T. and V. Matthies (2000), 'Krisenprävention: Was wurde erreicht? Eine Bestandsaufnahme zur deutschen Entwicklungs-, Außen- und Sicherheitspolitik', Bonn, *Arbeitsstelle Friedensforschung*.

DfID (Department for International Development) (2001), *Conflict Assessment*, London, DFID.

Duffield, M. (2001), *Global Governance and the New Wars. The Merging of Development and Security*, London, New York, Zed Books.

Eberwein, W.-D. and S. Chojnacki (2001), 'Scientific Necessity and Political Utility. A Comparison of Data on Violent Conflicts' (= WVB. P01–303), Berlin, *Wissenschaftszentrum Berlin*.

Ellis, S. (2003a), 'The Old Roots of Africa's "New Wars"', Internationale Politik und Gesellschaft, no. 2, pp. 29–43.

——. (2003b), 'Violence and history: a response to Thandika Mkandawire', *Journal of Modern African Studies*, vol. 41, no. 3, pp. 457–475.

Elwert, G. (1997), 'Gewaltmärkte. Beobachtungen zur Zweckrationalität von Gewalt', *Kölner Zeitschrift für Soziologie und Sozialpsychologie*, special issue no. 37, pp. 86–101.

Engel, U. (2003), 'Governance beyond the African state: Donor policies in new social space', paper presented at an international workshop at the Stellenbosch Institute for Advanced Studies (STIAS), Stellenbosch, 5 July (*mimeo*).

——. (2001), 'Conflict prevention in Africa: International norm diffusion and the German debate', Leipzig, *University of Leipzig Papers on Africa. Politics & Economics Series*; 50.

—— and A. Mehler (eds.) (1998), *Gewaltsame Konflikte und ihre Prävention in Afrika. Hintergründe, Analysen und Strategien für die entwicklungspolitische Praxis*, Hamburg, Institut für Afrika-Kunde.

Erdmann, G. and U. Engel (forthcoming), 'Neo-patrimonialism reconsidered—Critical review and elaboration of an elusive concept', *Journal of Comparative and Commonwealth Studies*.

EU Commission (2001), 'Communication from the Commission on Conflict Prevention', COM(2001)211, 11 April, Brussels, *EU Commission*.

——. (1996), 'The European Union And The Issues Of Conflicts In Africa: Peace-Building, Conflict Prevention And Beyond', Communication from the Commission to the Council, SEC(1996)332, 16 March, Brussels, *EU Commission* (<http://www.europa.eu.int/comm/external_relations/cfsp/news/com2001_211_en.pdf>).

Fearon, J.D. and D.D. Laitin (2003), 'Ethnicity, Insurgency and Civil War', *American Political Science Review*, vol. 97, no. 1, pp. 75–90.

—— and ——. (2000), 'Violence and the Social Construction of Ethnic Identity', *International Organization*, vol. 54, no. 4, pp. 845–877.

Finnemore, M. and K. Sikkink (1998), 'International Norm Dynamics and Political Change', *International Organization*, vol. 52, no. 4, pp. 887–917.

Gardner, A.-M. (2002), 'Diagnosing Conflict: What Do We Know?', in F.O. Hampson and D.M. Malone (eds.), *From Reaction to Conflict Prevention. Opportunities for the UN System*, Boulder CO, London, Lynne Rienner, pp. 15–40.

Geschiere, P. and C.F. Fisiy (1994), 'Domesticating personal violence. Witchcraft, courts and confessions in Cameroon', *Africa*, vol. 64, no. 3, pp. 323–341.

Glaser, C. (1998), 'Swines, hazels, and the Dirty Dozen. Masculinity, territoriality and the youths gangs of Soweto, 1960–1976', *Journal of Southern African Studies*, vol. 24, no. 4, pp. 718–736.

Goodhand, J. (2001), 'Conflict assessments. A snythesis report: Kyrgystan, Moldova, Nepal and Sri Lanka', *The Conflict, Security and Development Group*, <www.dfid.gov.uk/Pubs/files/Book%201_Synthesis.pdf>.

Gore, C. and D. Pratten (2003), 'The politics of plunder: The rhetorics of order and disorder in Southern Nigeria', *African Affairs*, vol. 102, no. 407, pp. 211–240.

Govea, R.M. and J.D. Holm (1998), 'Crisis, violence and political succession in Africa', *Third World Quarterly*, vol. 19, no. 1, pp. 129–148.

GTZ (Deutsche Gesellschaft für technische Zusammenarbeit, Manuela Leonhardt) (2001), 'Konfliktanalyse für die Projektplanung und -steuerung. Eine praktische Handreichung', draft, Eschborn, *GTZ Abt. 43 Sektorvorhaben Krisenprävention und Konfliktberarbeitung* (<http://www.gtz.de/crisisprevention/download/impactassessment.pdf>).

Gurr, T.R. (1995), *Minorities at Risk: A Global View of Ethno-political Conflicts*, Washington DC, US Institute for Peace.

Hulme, D. and J. Goodhand (2000), 'NGOs and peace building in complex political emergencies: Final report to the Department for International Development', Manchester, *Institute for Development Policy and Management*.

Jabri, V. (1996), *Discourses on violence: conflict analysis reconsidered*, Manchester, Manchester University Press.

Jackson, R. (2002), 'The Social Construction of Internal War: Towards a Framework of Understanding', paper presented at 'Cultures of Violence', 3rd Global Conference: Diversity within Unity, 12–16 August, Prague (<http://www.inter-disciplinary.net/jackson%20paper.pdf>).

Jackson, R.H. and C.G. Rosberg (1986), 'Sovereignty and Underdevelopment: Juridical Statehood in the African Crisis', *Journal of Modern African Studies*, vol. 24, no. 1, pp. 1–31.

Joint Evaluation of Emergency Assistance to Rwanda (eds.) (1996), *The International Response to Conflict and Genocide: Lessons from the Rwanda Experience*, vol. 1–5, Copenhagen.

Kaldor, M. (1999), *New and old wars: organized violence in a global era*, Stanford CA, Stanford University Press.

Klingebiel, S. (1999), 'Wirkungen der Entwicklungszusammenarbeit in Konfliktsituationen. Querschnittsbericht zu Evaluierungen der deutschen Entwicklungszusammenarbeit in sechs Ländern', Berlin, *Deutsches Institut für Entwicklungspolitik*.

Landgraf, M. (1998), 'Peace-building and conflict prevention in Africa: A view from the European Commission', in U. Engel and A. Mehler (eds.), *Gewaltsame Konflikte und ihre Prävention in Afrika. Hintergründe, Analysen und Strategien für die entwicklungspolitische Praxis*, Hamburg, Institut für Afrika-Kunde, pp. 103–117.

Latham, R. (2001), 'Identifying the contours of transboundary political life', in Th. Callaghy et al. (eds.), *Intervention and Transnationalism in Africa. Global-Local Networks of Power*, Cambridge, Cambridge University Press, pp. 69–92.

Lederach, J.P. (1997), *Building Peace. Sustainable Reconciliation in Diveded Societies*, Washington DC, US Institute of Peace Press.

Lund, M.S. (2000), 'Creeping institutionalization of the culture of prevention?', in SIPRI, *Preventing Violent Conflict. The Search for Political Will, Strategies and Effective Tools. Report of the Krusenberg Seminar*, organized by the Swedish Ministry for Foreign Affairs, SIPRI and the Swedish Institute for International Affairs, (<http://editors.sipri.se/pubs/Krusenberg.html>).

———. (1997), *Preventing and Mitigating Violent Conflicts: A Guide for Practitioners*, Washington DC, Creative Associates International.

——— and A. Mehler (principal contributors) (1999), 'Peace-Building & Conflict Prevention in Developing Countries: A Practical Guide', Brussels, Ebenhausen, *Conflict Prevention Network* (draft).

March, J.G. and J.P. Olsen (1998), 'The Institutional Dynamics of International Political Orders', *International Organization*, vol. 52, no. 4, pp. 943–969.

——. (1989), *Rediscovering Institutions: The Organizational Basis of Politics*, New York, Free Press.

Marchal, R. and C. Messiant (2002), 'De l'avidité des rebelles. L'analyse économique de la guerre civile selon Paul Collier', Critique Internationale, no. 16, pp. 58–69.

Maull, H.W. (2002), 'Containing Entropy. Rebuilding the State: Challenges to International Order in the Age of Globalization', *Internationale Politik und Gesellschaft*, no. 2, pp. 9–28.

Mavhungu, K.N. (2000), 'Heroes, villains and the state in South Africa's witchcraft zone', *The African Anthropologitst*, vol. 7, no. 1, pp. 114–129.

Mbembe, A. (1992a), 'Provisional Notes on the Postcolony', *Africa*, vol. 62, no. 1, pp. 3–37.

——. (1992b), 'The Banality of Power and the Aesthetics of Vulgarity in the Postcolony', *Public Culture*, vol. 4, no. 2, pp. 1–30.

Mehler, A. (2003), 'Legitime Gewaltoligopole—eine Antwort auf strukturelle Instabilität in Westafrika?', Fokus Afrika. IAK-Diskussionsbeiträge, no. 22, Hamburg, *Institut für Afrika-Kunde*.

—— C. Ribaux (2000), *Krisenprävention und Konfliktbearbeitung in der Technischen Zusammenarbeit*, Wiesbaden, Universum Verlagsanstalt.

Miall, H., O. Ramsbotham and T. Woodhouse (1999), *Contemporary Conflict Resolution: The Prevention, Management and Transformations of Deadly Conflict*, Oxford, Polity.

Mkandawire, T. (2003), 'Rejoinder to Stephen Ellis', *Journal of Modern African Studies*, vol. 41, no. 3, pp. 477–483.

——. (2002), 'The terrible toll of post-colonial ‚rebel movements‘ in Africa: towards an explanation of the violence against the peasantry', *Journal of Modern African Studies*, vol. 40, no. 2, pp. 181–215.

Nedelmann, B. (1997), 'Gewaltsoziologie am Scheideweg. Die Auseinandersetzung in der gegenwärtigen und Wege der künftigen Gewaltsoziologie', Kölner Zeitschrift für Soziologie und Sozialpsychologie, special issue no. 37, pp. 59–85.

Nobles, G.H. (1997), *American Frontiers: Cultural Encounters and Continental Conquest*, New York, Hill and Wang.

Porto, J.G. (2002), 'Contemporary Conflict Analysis in Perspective', in J. Lind and K. Sturman (eds.), *Scarcity and Surfeit. The ecology of Africa's conflicts*, Pretoria, Institute for Security Studies, pp. 1–49.

Reno, W. (1996), 'Business Conflict and the Shadow State: The Case of West Africa', in R. Cox (ed.), *Business and the State in International Relations*, Boulder CO, Westview Press, pp. 149–164.

Rojek, C. and B. Tuner (2000), 'Decorative sociology: towards a critique of the cultural turn', *Sociological Review*, vol. 48, no. 4, pp. 845–877.

Rotberg, R.I. (2002), 'Failed States in a World of Terror', *Foreign Affairs*, vol. 81, no. 4, pp. 127–140.

Stroux, D. (2003), 'Rohstoffe, Ressentiments und staatsfreie Räume. Die Strukturen des Krieges in Afrikas Mitte', International Politics and Society, no. 2 (http://fesportal.fes.de/pls/portal30/docs/FOLDER/IPG/IPG2_2003/ARTSTROUX.HTM).

UNSG (UN Secretary-General) (1992), *Agenda for Peace: Preventive Diplomacy, Peacemaking and Peace-Keeping. A report of the secretary-general pursuant to the statement adopted by the summit meeting of the Security Council on 31 January 1992*, New York A/47/277—S/24111, 17 June 1992 (<http://www.un.org/Docs/SG/agpeace.htm>).

Uvin, P. (1999), 'The Influence of Aid in Situations of Violent Conflict', DAC Informal Task Force on Conflict, Peace and Development Co-operation, Paris, OECD.

van de Walle, N. (2001), *African Economies and the Politics of Permanent Crisis, 1979–1999*, Cambridge etc., Cambridge University Press.

Villalón, L.A. and P.A. Huxtable (eds.) (1998), *The African State at a Critical Juncture. Between Disintegration and Reconfiguration*, Boulder CO, London: Lynne Rienner.

von Trotha, T. (2000), 'Die Zukunft liegt in Afrika. Vom Zerfall des Staates, von der Vorherrschaft der konzentrischen Ordnung und vom Aufstieg der Parastaatlichkeit', *Leviathan*, vol. 28, no. 2, pp. 253–279.

—— (1997), 'Zur Soziologie der Gewalt', *Kölner Zeitschrift für Soziologie und Sozialpsychologie*, special issue no. 37, pp. 9–56.

Waetjen, Th. and G. Maré (1999), 'Workers and Warriors: Inkatha's Politics of Masculinity in the 1980s', *Journal of Contemporary African Studies*, vol. 17, no. 1, pp. 197–213.

Waldmann, P. (2002), *Der anomische Staat. Über Recht, öffentliche Sicherheit und Alltag in Lateinamerika*, Opladen, Leske and Budrich.

Wallensteen, P. and M. Sollenberg (2001), 'Armed Conflict, 1989–2000', *Journal of Peace Research*, vol. 38, no. 5, pp. 629–644.

World Bank (2003), 'A Selected Bibliography of Studies of Civil War and Rebellion', Appendix 2 to Breaking the Conflict Trap: Civil War and Development Policy, Washington DC: *The World Bank* (<http://econ.worldbank.org/prr/CivilWarPRR/text_26671/>).

Zartman, W.I. (1995), 'Introduction: Posing the Problem of State Collapse', in W.I. Zartman (ed.), Collapsed States. The Disintegration and Restoration of Legitimate Authority, Boulder CO, London, Westview Press, pp. 1–11.

Mɪʀᴊᴀᴍ ᴅᴇ Bʀᴜɪᴊɴ, is an anthropologist with the African Studies Centre in Leiden whose work has a clear interdisciplinary character. She has done fieldwork in Chad and Mali and an important theme throughout her work is how people manage risk (drought, war, etc.), both in rural and urban areas. Her fields of interest are: nomadism, social (in)security, poverty, marginality/social and economic exclusion, violence, slavery, and human rights. In Mali she worked in the Mopti area with the Fulbe (Peul) and in Menaka with Tamacheck (Tuareg), while in Chad she has worked in N'djamena (the capital) and in Central Chad with Hadjerai and Arab groups. In the coming years she plans to work on a programme concerning 'human rights and economic exclusion (or failed inclusion)'. Major publications include *Mobile Africa: Changing Patterns of Movement in Africa and Beyond* (Leiden 2001, with R.A. van Dijk and D.W.J. Foeken); and *Arid Ways, Cultural Understandings of Insecurity in Fulbe Society, Central Mali* (Amsterdam, 1995, with J.W.M. van Dijk).

Pᴀᴛʀɪᴄᴋ Cʜᴀʙᴀʟ, a political scientist, is a professor at the University of London (King's College). He has taught and carried out research in a number of African countries as well as in the USA, France, Italy, Portugal and the UK. He has published widely on the history, politics, and culture of African countries. His main book publications are *A History of Postcolonial Lusophone Africa* (London, 2002, with others); *Africa Works: disorder as political instrument* (Oxford, 1999, with J.-P. Daloz); *The Postcolonial Literature of Lusophone Africa* (London, 1996, with others); *Power in Africa: an essay in political interpretation* (Basingstoke, 1992 and 1994); *Political Domination in Africa: reflections on the limits of power* (Cambridge, 1986, editor); and *Amílcar Cabral: Revolutionary Leadership and People's War* (Cambridge, 1983).

Cʜʀɪsᴛᴏᴘʜᴇʀ Cʀᴀᴍᴇʀ, a political economist, is a senior lecturer at the School of Oriental and African Studies (SOAS), London. He teaches on the political economy of Africa and runs the MSc in 'Violence, Conflict and Development'. He has worked in a number of African countries, including Mozambique, South Africa, Tanzania and Ethiopia: working on poverty reduction, aid policy, commodity processing policy, privatisation, and labour markets. *Wars of the Poor, Wars of the Rich: Making Sense of Violence and War in Developing Countries* will be published in 2006 by Hurst and Co. Other publications include 'Homo Economicus Goes to War: methodological individualism, rational choice, and the political economy of war' in *World Development*, 2002, vol. 30, no. 11; 'Try Again, Fail Again, Fail Better? War, the State, and the 'Post-conflict' Challenge in Afghanistan', in *Development and Change*, (November 2002, with Jonathan Goodhand); and 'Women Working for Wages: Putting Flesh on the Bones of a Rural Labour Market Survey in Mozambique', forthcoming in the *Journal of Southern African Studies* (co-authored with J. Sender and C. Oya).

HAN VAN DIJK, is an anthropologist with the African Studies Centre in Leiden and studied forestry. His research focuses around a number of topics such as political decentralization, land tenure, natural resource management and farmer-herder strategies in response to climate variability and development policy. These topics all centre around the interaction between society and the environment and the social and political struggles arising out of this interaction. In 2004 he has also been appointed Professor of Law and Governance in Africa in the Department of Social Sciences at Wageningen University. He will remain attached to the African Studies Centre as an anthropologist specializing in forestry and environmental issues. Major publications include 'Insecurity and Pastoral Development in the Sahel', *Development and Change*, 1999, vol. 30, no. 1 (with M.E. de Bruijn and H. van Dijk); *Pastoralists under Pressure? Fulbe Societies Confronting Change in West Africa* (Leiden, 1999, co-edited); and *Arid Ways, Cultural Understandings of Insecurity in Fulbe Society, Central Mali* (Amsterdam, 1995, with M.E. de Bruijn).

ULF ENGEL, a political scientist, is associate professor 'Politics in Africa' at the Institute of African Studies, University of Leipzig. He has published widely on German Africa policy, crisis prevention and conflict management, and politics in particular in Southern and Eastern Africa. He published *Die Afrikapolitik der Bundesrepublik Deutschland 1949-1999: Rollen und Identitäten* (Hamburg, 2002); *Die beiden deutschen Staaten in Afrika: Zwischen Konkurrenz und Koexistenz 1949–1990* (Hamburg, 1998, with H.G. Schleicher); and *The Foreign Policy of Zimbabwe* (Hamburg,

1994). Among others, he co-edited *Africa and the North: Between Marginalisation and Globalisation* (London, New York 2005, with G.R. Olsen); *The African Exception* (Aldershot, Burlington 2005, with G.R. Olsen); *Germany's Africa Policy Revisited. Interests, images and incrementalism* (Hamburg, 2002, with R. Kappel); and *Tanzania Revisited: Political Stability, Aid Dependency and Development Constraints* (Hamburg, 2000, with G. Erdmann and A. Mehler).

ANNA MARIA GENTILI is full professor of History and Institutions of Afro-Asian countries at the Faculty of Political Science of the University of Bologna where she is chairperson of an interdisciplinary course on Development Cooperation. She has been working since the 1970s at the University of Bologna and in various African Universities, notably in Dar es Salaam and at the Centro de Estudos Africanos of the Eduardo Mondlane University in Maputo, Mozambique. She is the director of the Amilcar Cabral Library on Africa, Asia, and Latin America of the city of Bologna. The main research focus is on politics, political parties, development issues with special reference to land and decentralization reforms in sub-Saharan Africa. Main publications include: *Elites e Regimi politici in Africa Occidentale* (Bologna, 1974); *Ruth First: alle radici dell'apartheid* (Milano, 1984); *Il Leone e il cacciatore. Storia dell'Africa subsahariana* (Rome, 1995); and *O leao e o caçador. Uma historia da Africa da Africa sub-saariana*, Arquivo Historico de Moçambique, Estudos 14, Maputo 1999. With M. Zamboni she also published *Stato, Democrazia e legittimità. Transizioni politiche in Africa, America Latina, Balcani, Medio Oriente* (Rome, 2005).

GERTI HESSELING, is a researcher in legal anthropology and former director of the Africa Studies Centre in Leiden. She was appointed by the Minister for Development Cooperation as Chair of the Netherlands Development Assistance Research Council (RAWOO) in 2003. The Council advises the Dutch government on policy for development-related research. Her publications include *Election Observation and Democratization in Africa* (Basingstoke, New York, 1999, co-edited with J. Abbink); 'Legal and Institutional Incentives for Local Environmental Management', in H.S. Marcussen (ed.), *Improved Natural Resource Management—The Role of Formal Organisations and Informal Networks and Institutions* (Roskilde, 1996); and *Histoire Politique du Sénégal. Institutions, Droit et Société* (Paris, 1985).

SHAMIL IDRISS is Director of Search for Common Ground's (SFCG) Partners in Humanity Program and Senior Advisor to the World Economic Forum for programmes of Islamic-Western reconciliation. In this dual capacity, he manages a broad range of Islamic-Western reconciliation programmes which the two organizations are advancing jointly. He served as SFCG's Chief Operating Officer from 2000–04, managing the organization's global operations and its headquarters in Washington, DC. From 1999–2000 he served as Director of SFCG's Burundi Programme, managing projects of Hutu-Tutsi ethnic cooperation, including the first independent multi-ethnic radio outlet in Burundi, Studio *Ijambo*. He serves on the Boards of the Alliance for International Conflict Prevention and Resolution (AICPR) and *Soliya*, a youth leadership development organization. He has published articles on international conflict resolution, media and social change, and Islamic-Western relations in German, South African, Arab and American journals and newspapers, including 'Siblings Under the Skin: Human Rights & Conflict Resolution', ACResolution Quarterly (Summer 2003).

ANDREAS MEHLER, a political scientist, is Director of the Institute of African Affairs (Hamburg). Previously he was senior researcher at the EU Conflict Prevention Network (managed by the Stiftung Wissenschaft und Politik, Berlin). He has published extensively on causes of violent conflict, conflict prevention, state and statehood in Africa, democratisation processes and elections in Francophone Africa. Among his most recent publications are 'Structural Stability in an African Context' (Uppsala, 2003, with R. Kappel and H. Melber); 'Legitime Gewaltoligopole—eine Antwort auf strukturelle Instabilität in Westafrika?' (Hamburg, *Diskussionsbeiträge des IAK*, 2003); *Die Vielfalt von Gewaltkonflikten. Analysen aus regional-wissenschaftlicher Perspektive* (Hamburg, 2002, edited with S. Kurtenbach); 'Structural Stability: Meaning, scope and use in an African context', *Afrika Spectrum*, 2002, vol. 37, no. 1; *CPN Practical Guide*, electronic version (Berlin, 2001, with L. van de Goor and C. Moyroud); and *Crisis Prevention and Conflict Management in Technical Cooperation. An Overview of the National and International Debate* (Wiesbaden, 2000, with C. Ribaux).

DONALD ROTHCHILD, professor of Political Science at the University of California, Davis (USA). His recent books include *Managing Ethnic Conflict in Africa: Pressures and Incentives for Cooperation* (Washington DC, 1997); and *Sovereignty as responsibility: Conflict management in Africa* (co-author, Washington DC, 1996). He also co-edited *International Spread of Ethnic Conflict: Fear, Diffusion, and Escalation* (Princeton NJ, 1988); and Ending Civil Wars: The Implementation of Peace Agreements (Boulder CO, 2002). *Sustainable Peace: Democracy and Power-Deviding Institutions After Civil Wars*, co-edited with P.G. Roeder, will be published in 2005.

THEODORE TREFON does political science and anthropology research on central Africa at the University of Brussels and is currently visiting professor at the Katholieke Universiteit Leuven. A DR Congo area specialist, his research interests focus on state-society relations, forest-city links, urban anthropology and environmental governance. After completing his Ph.D. in Political Science at Boston University, he has worked on European Union-funded projects and was an advisor to the USAID *Central African Program for the Environment*. He has served as a consultant to CIFOR, UNESCO, CARE and the World Bank. He is also visiting professor at ERAIFT (University of Kinshasa). In addition to numerous journal articles and book chapters, he has edited *Reinventing Order in the Congo: How people respond to State failure in Kinshasa* (London, 2004) and *Ordre et désordre à Kinshasa: Réponses populaires à la faillite de l'Etat* (Tervuren, Paris, 2004), co-edited 'State Failure in the Congo: Perceptions and Realities', *Review of African Political Economy*, 2002, no. 93/94, and a thematic issue on social science research methods in DRC for the Belgian journal *Civilisations* (forthcoming, 2005) and authored *French Policy Toward Zaïre During the Giscard d'Estaing Presidency* (Brussels, 1989).

KLAAS VAN WALRAVEN, a political scientist, is senior researcher at the African Studies Centre in Leiden, The Netherlands. He has published on international politics, democratisation, conflicts and resistance in sub-Saharan Africa, with special emphasis on the West African region. He published *Dreams of Power: The Role of the Organization of African Unity in the Politics of Africa, 1963-1993* (Aldershot, 1999); *The Pretence of Peacekeeping: ECOMOG, West Africa and Liberia (1990-1998)* (The Hague, 1999) and, more recently in the field of international relations, 'From "Union of Tyrants" to "Power to the People"? The Significance of the Pan-African Parliament for the African Union', *Afrika Spectrum*, 2004, vol. 39, no. 2. He also edited *Early Warning and Conflict Prevention: Limitations and Possibilities* (The Hague, London & Boston, 1998). In the field of democratization he published 'The End of an Era: The Ghanaian Elections of December 2000', *Journal of Contemporary African Studies*, 2002, vol. 20, no. 2. Recently, he has turned his attention to a historical study of the Sawaba rebellion in Niger.

INDEX